A Picture
of Health

How to use guided imagery for self-healing and personal growth

Helen Graham

PIATKUS

Also by Helen Graham

The Magic Shop: An Imaginative Guide to Self Healing
Time, Energy and the Psychology of Healing
The Human Face of Psychology
Mental Imagery in Health Care: An Introduction to
Therapeutic Practice

First published in 1995 by
Judy Piatkus (Publishers) Ltd
5 Windmill Street, London W1P 1HF

The moral right of the author has been asserted

A catalogue record for this book is
available from the British Library

ISBN 0-7499-1425-4

Edited by Carol Franklin
Designed by Sue Ryall

Set in 10.5/12.5 Sabon by
Datix International Limited, Bungay, Suffolk
Printed & bound in Great Britain by
Bookcraft Ltd, Midsomer Norton, Avon

Contents

Introduction   1

Chapter 1   Becoming a Picture of Health   13
Chapter 2   Acting Well   34
Chapter 3   Steps to Health   66
Chapter 4   Understanding Dis-ease   93
Chapter 5   Combating Dis-ease   117
Chapter 6   Raising One's Spirit   152
Chapter 7   Inspiring Health   181
Chapter 8   Healthy Priorities   213
Chapter 9   Healing Forces   235
Chapter 10   Energetic Treatment   257
Chapter 11   Healthy Solutions   277

Appendix I   Progressive Relaxation Augmented
                by Imagery   301
Appendix II Gold-prospecting   308

             Bibliography   309
             Index   315

Introduction

A few years ago I was invited to contribute to a short residential course on psychological approaches in healing to National Health Service (NHS) personnel. This course, which attracted participants from all over the UK, proved successful, and as a result I was asked to offer an extended course in a large regional hospital and to contribute to staff training in a psychiatric hospital. Before agreeing to do so I decided to 'test' the material on a wider audience, and offered courses on psychological healing to the general public via the Adult and Continuing Education programme at Keele University, where I am a full-time lecturer in psychology.

The response was overwhelming, so much so that the initial 11-week course had to run several evenings a week to cope with the numbers attracted. I went on to run two or three evening courses a week and weekend workshops in different venues in three counties for a number of years. I also presented workshops to various professional groups in different parts of the country.

Those people who attended ranged in age from 18 to 88, and included men and women, although women generally outnumbered men by three to one. Some were ill, often seriously or terminally. Many suffered persistent pain. Others had dependants who were sick, terminally ill or disabled, while others had health problems that were not serious but moderately disabling or irritating. A number had been told by their doctors that conventional medicine could do nothing more for them or that they must learn to live with their conditions.

Others had a history of emotional or psychological problems: chronic anxieties, phobias, depression or eating disorders. Some had experienced 'nervous breakdown', others more serious psychiatric disorder. A number had been in or out-patients in psychiatric hospitals. Many had received psychotherapy or counselling.

Many, disillusioned with conventional medical approaches, especially medication, wished to explore alternatives. Some, dismayed by the shortcomings of the NHS or the prospects of its dissolution, were determined to minimise their dependence on it or private medicine through self-help and preventive strategies. Others wished to gain greater understanding of the psychological factors they recognised or suspected as a component of their illnesses, or those of others. A number had been introduced to psychological approaches in the course of treatment for illnesses such as cancer, in stress management programmes or through reading, and wished to sustain or develop them.

Many had no health or health-related problems as such, but suffered from what might be regarded as problems in living, including occupational stress and various life crises; marital, family, personal, interpersonal and professional difficulties, or were coming to terms with loss, bereavement, divorce, loneliness or other trauma. Nevertheless, people with identifiable problems comprised a relatively small proportion of those who attended. Some had no particular problem, only a feeling that they could be getting more out of life.

A significant proportion had a professional interest in the subject. These included doctors, nurses, social workers, and students of psychology, psychiatry and medicine. Many were practitioners of complementary medicine, hypnotherapists, art therapists, spiritual or clairvoyant healers and an appreciable number were professional or voluntary counsellors and psychotherapists. Stress management consultants, organisers and members of self-help and support groups, and those wishing to establish such groups were also represented. In addition there were many people who attended simply out of interest or curiosity, for a change of routine, a chance to relax, meet others and enjoy themselves.

Often people attended the course two or three times and as a result the initial course evolved. Its content shifted from informal lectures on and discussion of different psychological approaches to healing illustrated with practical exercises, to a linked series of exercises employing imagery as a means of addressing and exploring issues relevant to health and illness, each introduced by relevant theory, research and practice, and followed by discussion.

Even though the courses developed, many people at the end of a workshop would express the desire to explore themselves further and in greater depth, having recognised that many of their physical problems were symptomatic of underlying and unresolved psychological issues. As one young woman observed, 'Every time I focus on my physical pains, I realise it's my feelings that are hurt'. In response to this demand I developed a further series of 'imaginative' exercises directed to previously untapped psychological factors relevant to health and illness, including self-concept, self-esteem, personal powers and potentials, and inner dialogue. Each of these exercises used imagery as a means of addressing and exploring a specific issue or complex of issues in progressive sequence so that it built on the one before it. Nevertheless, each exercise could stand alone as complete in itself. I presented the exercises to the general public in a series of workshop-based courses over a two-year period, and subsequently to members of professional groups and students. Over time they were modified and refined accordingly. The resulting exercises, presented in *A Picture of Health*, are a potent and reliable tool for self-healing and transformation.

THERAPEUTIC USES OF IMAGERY

You may be wondering how imaginative exercises of this kind can bring about such effects. Throughout history healers have brought about healing by actively provoking the imagination, which they recognised as providing access to features of the self that are normally hidden, and of which we are unaware, thereby yielding important clues to unconscious processes relevant to health and illness. More recently these methods have been employed effectively within the field of psychotherapy, and most recently within the field of orthodox physical medicine, notably in support of therapy in the treatment of cancers and other serious conditions. The processes of the imagination have also been intensively investigated by psychologists and as a result of these studies it is now known that imagery serves important psychological functions, both cognitive and emotional.

Imagery provides us with a different way of thinking about issues by enabling them to be represented non-verbally as opposed to verbally. In so doing it provides, quite literally, a new perspective on, or different way of looking at, them. Imagery therefore increases the range and flexibility of mental functioning, enabling problem solving, decision making and creative thinking. Moreover, it is particularly suited to dealing with issues that are non-verbal, that is, physical and emotional processes; health, illness and the whole complex of the self.

In so doing it often gives rise to feelings that might otherwise not gain expression and thus serves an important emotional function. Imagery is therefore potentially very effective in promoting greater self-awareness or insight, and also provides some indication of our outlook or attitude, which is now recognised as an important determinant of health. As this becomes more widely acknowledged, imaginative methods are increasingly being explored within the fields of both physical and psychological medicine, more especially since it is now understood that imagery tends to promote absorption, which is now recognised as fundamental to relaxation. Working with imagery is therefore very relaxing and therapeutic. Moreover, extensive research has demonstrated that imagery can influence physiological processes both directly and indirectly, and can be employed effectively to this end in treatment. The effects of imagery can therefore be not only life-changing, but life-enhancing.

GUIDED IMAGERY

While most therapists prefer to work with the imagery spontaneously produced by individuals it is widely recognised that in many instances their representational style or habitual way of thinking about issues may be too limited or inflexible to enable coping in a given area. In order to provide us with a means of representing issues that has previously been lacking or inadequate, or one that challenges the existing representational mode, guided imagery is often used to good effect. It can be thought of as a situation where a storyboard is provided for a series of pictures or 'movie' in the mind which we cast, enact, direct, produce and review; and likened to a waking dream in which guided by another, we create in our imagination a new experience that enables us to confront the contents of our personal unconscious and relate these directly, and often dramatically, to our life circumstances and problems.

From the novel perspective afforded by imagery you may find that you are able to confront and overcome your fears and anxieties, discover or rediscover suppressed or dissociated aspects of yourself, and reassess yourself and your life. You may be able to identify what you want from life or, equally importantly, what you don't want; the moral and other codes by which you live, and the ways in which these govern your thoughts, feelings and behaviour. You may be able to recognise the ways in which you obstruct your personal growth and development, and the realisation of your goals and potentials. Imagery also frequently highlights our failure to seize or make the best of the opportunities presented to us, tendencies to be inhibited by doubts, self-destructiveness, negativity, scepticism, anxiety and guilt, and enables us to realise the unhealthy consequences of self-denial.

Guided imagery is therefore particularly suited to exploration of personal needs and potentials that are often unconscious, unacknowledged or confused. By exploring these personal images and the symbols inherent in them it is possible to establish contact with the generally unrecognised or dissociated aspects of the self, and thus effect an integration or healing.

WORKING WITH IMAGERY

Every feature of the imagery you produce is your own creation and as such is potentially very meaningful. Most of us are aware that these images are significant, although we may not be able to discern their meaning. There is a tendency to believe that 'solutions' to puzzling imagery reside outside rather than within ourselves. Such a view is encouraged by a plethora of books on the interpretation of dreams, which perpetuate the misleading notion established by Sigmund Freud that only 'experts' and 'authorities' such as he and his followers can divine the meanings of images produced in dreams, daydreams and fantasies. This is simply not the case. As Hermann Hesse has observed, 'we can understand each other; but each person is able to interpret himself to himself alone' (*Demian*). You are, therefore, the ultimate authority on your own imagery and need to be encouraged to realise this.

Although your imagery may have certain universal features, it represents a unique symbolic language, which you must learn to translate and understand. The 'interpretation' of your imagery by another, however 'expert', will reveal only the features of the symbolic language of that person and as such may be highly misleading. It is essential in working with imagery that you explore your own symbolic vocabulary, its meanings and usage. This is achieved in much the same way as you might discern the meaning of an unusual word or code, that is, by examining its context, other available clues, similar words or symbols, and their patterns of usage; the associations it evokes and such like. In this way you can become expert in your own symbology. Image explication, the attempt to characterise as clearly and as systematically as possible the nature of our imagery, therefore 'draws on our experiences of ourselves, rather than upon any observations that we might make, as outsiders of others' (Shotter, 1975, p. 42) . In my workshops participants are discouraged from seeking explanations of their imagery in the many publications that claim to provide them and from allowing others to impose their meanings upon them. However, they are encouraged to discover the meaning of their images by working with others, in pairs or small groups.

Others may be able to assist you in understanding your imagery in a number of ways. It may be by helping you to explore the feelings that attach to it, the responses it evokes and the associations it conjures for you. It may require some form of externalisation like drawing, painting, sculpting, dance, storytelling or acting.

It can also be amplified in other ways, such as other people expressing the responses and associations the image elicits in them or pointing to the significance of similar symbols in mythology and elsewhere.

A good deal of understanding can be achieved by working on the imagery yourself. This can be achieved primarily by identifying the association or links between the various components of elements of the images you produce. Simple word association may be effective, but the tendency to generate lists of words should be avoided. It is preferable to 'brainstorm' by writing or drawing the image or its component features in the centre of a large piece of paper or blackboard and then generating associations – both verbal and pictorial – to each of the associated ideas and images you produce. Each associated item can then be 'mapped' by placing each one, as it emerges, close to the word or picture that triggered it, until no further associations can be made, or the available space is used up. In this way thousands of associations may be generated to the 'target' image. The connections between these can then be made by joining them. This invariably results in a huge circular plan not unlike a mandala or web. As such it represents a mental 'map' of multiple, simultaneous and multisensory associations very different to the results you get from simply listing verbal or memory associations to any given image. You should also take note of verbal and visual puns generated by imagery. These are often highly significant and repay careful examination.

Drawing, painting, various kinds of artwork and colour can be incorporated into this mental map, which may be used not only for the explication of images but also for generating ideas, planning essays, and projects, and stimulating creative thinking of all kinds. However, as most of us have been educated and trained to organise our thoughts with lists and flow diagrams, it may require a good deal of practice before you feel comfortable with this unusual procedure and can use it effectively.

Images can be worked on in many other ways. One of the most striking illustrations is presented in Steven Spielberg's film *Close Encounters of the Third Kind*, where the hero attempts to clarify a vague mental impression he has formed of a landscape by drawing, modelling in clay and mashed potato, earthworking and various other constructions. In this way he refines his image sufficiently to be able to recognise its real-life counterpart when this is shown fleetingly on television – a classic example of the way in which coincidence often serves to amplify, illuminate and resolve puzzling imagery. Imaginary scenes may be dramatised, using cartoon figures, puppets, dolls, toys, other persons, or by the individual acting out or talking through each of the 'parts' of the imagery in turn. Role-play games can be elaborated around the themes or characters of imagery and board games developed for this purpose.

KEEPING RECORDS

However, if you are to make significant progress in understanding your imagery then you must keep a record of it and your responses to the exercises each time they are attempted. Repetition of exercises is desirable because the insights they afford will alter as your life situation changes. Often it is assumed quite wrongly that an exercise will produce the same images and insights however many times it is repeated. This is rarely the case and, where it is, the possibility that this represents resistance to the emergence of new insights and experiences should be considered. When similar imagery is evoked on successive trials novel and/or additional insights also usually emerge. For this reason, and because imagery, whether that of dreams or deliberate fantasy, however intense or significant, is only fleeting and quickly forgotten in the manner of dream imagery, it is desirable that you make some record of your responses to any particular exercise. The record may be in the form of an audio recording or written 'log' book. The former has the advantages of greater immediacy and speed, and considerable detail, but it restricts the record to verbal content, whereas ideally imagework aims to integrate verbal and non-verbal modes of consciousness, and enhance communication between them. A written commentary produces the best results.

A verbal and visual record of experiences, in both words and pictures, incorporating sketches and paintings, is most appropriate to the task. It may also be useful to add a 'pictionary' in which you record your interpretations of specific images so that you

begin to build up a symbolic vocabulary and recognise the significance of a particular symbol when it is encountered subsequently
in dreams or elsewhere.

Certain features of imagery tend to recur in different contexts
and detail in the course of working with them, and what might
initially appear obscure, meaningless or trivial becomes progressively more clear, intelligible, relevant and significant. The record
should therefore include details of incidental and coincidental
material; that is, experiences and insights which occur *as a result*
of the exercises rather than during them, such as when a feature
or theme of an exercise recurs or is amplified in a subsequent
dream, reverie or actual life experience. 'Coincidences' like these
are invariably highly significant but are often overlooked or
dismissed. A record helps jog the memory and clarify thoughts
about imagery.

Images may produce 'side-effects' in that they tend to stimulate
a good deal of thought long after an exercise is over and also
other unconscious processes such as dreaming. It is therefore not
unusual to encounter the same symbols or motifs in subsequent
dreams, daydreams or fantasies, so that a dream may yield
further clarification or understanding of a previously unfathomed
image, just as waking imagery may clarify the content of a dream.
Indeed it seems that once communication with formerly unconscious aspects of the self has been established it becomes more
frequent. Dreaming typically becomes more frequent and more
vivid, and impresses itself more powerfully, so those who have
not previously dreamed in colour may find that they begin to.
Indeed, the entire imaginal system seems to develop and become
elaborated.

The meaning of certain images may be discerned as a result of
other activities, in sudden flashbacks or flashes of insight, which
in some cases may be dramatic. However, while this 'Eureka'
effect often brings about a sudden transformation of consciousness, understanding and awareness, images may recur without
any increased insight or understanding. These should not be
dismissed or ignored, but carefully noted. Usually resolution will
occur quite spontaneously, but you may need to seek help if
troubling images persist for too long.

A record helps you to identify various patterns in your life and experience by highlighting significant issues or themes, and encourages greater self-awareness. Importantly it also helps cultivate a disciplined approach to self-examination. It is essentially, however, an *aide-mémoire*, and valuable because the effects of imagery are progressive and cumulative. It enables you to refer back to earlier images, and to keep track of both process and progress. Most importantly, however, it helps you to understand what is happening in the present.

For this reason it is a good idea to record your imagery and responses to it in the first person present tense. The personalisation which results from the description of imagery in this way not only locates the experience in the immediate present, but also helps to reverse any tendency to projection whereby responsibility for personal creations or products, whether imaginings, thoughts, feelings, pains, actions or illnesses, is attributed to external causes. It helps you to acknowledge personal responsibility and locus of control; that is, the sense of being effective in the world rather than a passive victim of circumstance, and awareness of the ways in which you contribute to your problems and illnesses.

This verbal ploy also helps to highlight the possible significance of imagery. There is sometimes a tendency for people to deny that there is any and to argue that the image they produce corresponds to some feature of the 'real' world. However, while your imagery may match a feature of the external world, it is nevertheless a product of your imagination and its potential significance lies in why, of all the features of the world you could have brought to mind or invented, you chose to represent this one. Describing imagery in the first person present tense helps you to recognise it as a specific personal product or creation for which you are responsible and which, for this very reason, is almost certainly meaningful when scrutinised more closely.

' If you cannot readily see the relevance of an image when viewed objectively it may be that you feel differently when you personalise it in this way. For example, thus translated, 'I imagine a cool, unmoving pool with murky depths' becomes 'I am a cool, unmoving pool with murky depths', which gives food for thought at the very least.

HOW TO USE THIS BOOK

The exercises in this book are set out in progressive sequence so that each builds upon those before it, but they all stand alone as complete in themselves. The directions for some of the exercises are rather long, so it is recommended that, initially at least, someone reads them to you or you record them on audiotape, leaving pauses for responses where necessary, until you have memorised them and are able to go without external aids. The directions have been written explicitly for this purpose.

Imagery exercises tend to be absorbing and to promote relaxation. Initially, however, you may find it difficult to generate imagery because of intrusive or persistent thoughts, concerns and preoccupations, and the physical tensions and pains these often give rise to. Should you find this a problem, a progressive relaxation exercise is provided in Appendix I. Although it may seem long, this should take little more than 20 minutes to complete and can be employed before any of the exercises as an alternative to the methods recommended. You should allow 20–30 minutes for each exercise.

You may find that you have difficulty generating visual images or pictures in your mind's eye. This is quite common, and with practice you should find that your images become clearer and more vivid. However, some people are very much more visual in their imagery than others and it may be that you are one of those people for whom sounds, smells and other sensations are stronger. If so, you should work with the form of imagery that is easiest for you, and be aware that impressions and sensations of all kinds are equally important and valuable.

Every exercise is introduced with an explanation of its aims, purpose and relevance to health in the broadest sense, and references and suggestions for further reading are provided at the end of the book. Each exercise is followed by a commentary on the issues it typically highlights, illustrated with comments drawn from 'real life' experience of working with groups and individuals. If you feel that knowledge of other people's responses will affect your experience you are advised not to read the commentary sections until after completing and recording the details of each exercise.

It will be clear from these commentaries that many of the responses of workshop participants are examined and discussed, and that some participants generously allowed me to examine their personal records and to quote from them. Others have provided me with details of their experiences by way of various personal communications, and many people quite spontaneously provided illustrations of various kinds, some of which are included in the text by the kind permission of the artist. I would like to record here my gratitude to the many hundreds of people who, by their participation in these workshops, have provided the rich and fascinating material upon which this present book is based.

☙ CHAPTER ONE ☙

Becoming a Picture of Health

I felt like a jigsaw puzzle being put back together and
when the last bit was in place, my mind shifted, and saw
the whole perfect picture.

EVY MCDONALD (*cited Siegel, 1990*)

How often have you heard it said of someone that their world has
fallen apart? This may be because of some trauma – disaster,
death, divorce, disappointment, disillusionment, disease or disability. When examined more closely these can all be found to
involve a loss of some kind. It may be the loss of a family
member, friend, pet animal, other love object; relationship; home,
possessions; job, dream, personal ambition; faith, ideals; youth,
vitality, some aspect of normal physical functioning; or loss of
face, identity, dignity, confidence, respect, status or prestige.

When, as a result of losses such as these, a person's world falls
apart, it is not uncommon for them to fall apart also. We say that
they have gone to pieces, cracked up or broken down. In many
instances this reaction is immediate and obvious, while in others
it is delayed and is not immediately apparent, sometimes occurring
months or even years later. The ways in which it manifests may
also be quite different, appearing in some people as physical
illness and in others as emotional or psychological disorder.
Irrespective of the kind of illness that occurs it represents a
breakdown in the normal harmonious flow or pattern of functioning which constitutes health in its true sense.

Abundant research evidence supports the age-old observation
that trauma invariably precedes serious illness. Loss has long been

recognised as an antecedent condition in the development of cancer and in recent years research has confirmed that people with cancer have often suffered some kind of serious loss 18 months to 2 years before the onset of their illness.

Loss has also been identified as a highly significant feature of depression. Indeed it is perhaps in the area of emotional or psychological illness that we are most aware of breakdown. We say people have suffered 'nervous breakdown' – which is a misnomer because the nerves are not affected. However, 'Nervous breakdown is often preferred as a description because it suggests an almost physical illness rather than a mental weakness' (Coward, 1992, p. 56). What has actually broken down is the normal social functioning of the person – that is, the ability to perform social roles, responsibilities and duties adequately. However, despite the degree to which they are incapacitated, and this may be considerable, we tend to be less sympathetic to people whose breakdown manifests at the psychological level than those who suffer physical illness. Sometimes we tell them (and not necessarily politely) to get their act together, implying, in so doing, that it is their social performance that is impaired rather than any other aspect of their functioning. Frequently we advise them to get a grip on things and pull themselves together, the popular view being that by so doing their world will also be put to right. This wisdom is expressed in the adage that when all is well with the self all is well with the world, and in the following anecdote:

> A businessman was entertaining a client at home on a wet
> Sunday, and was constantly pestered by his bored five year old
> son who could not go outside to play. After the child had
> played with everything on his father's desk, the father found a
> map of the world and tore it up into a hundred pieces, telling
> his son not to come back until he had stuck the world back
> together again. To his astonishment the child returned after
> five minutes with the world complete. When his father asked
> him how he had managed in so short a time he replied, 'on the
> back of the picture of the world I had already drawn a big
> picture of myself, and when I put myself together the world
> came together also'.
>
> CADUCEUS, 1990, 10, p. 6

This delightful story embodies an understanding that can be traced back to ancient times and which underpins all traditional healing practices throughout the world. In these systems of healing one encounters the idea that humanity is a microcosm of the macrocosm, its fundamental nature being identical with that of the world or cosmos. Thus in healing ourselves we heal the world and vice versa. Therefore you can put your world back together, just as the little boy did, by putting yourself together, and this act of making oneself whole constitutes healing. Indeed the terms health and healing derive from words meaning whole, and in the modern world this ancient concept of health as wholeness is reflected in the World Health Organisation's definition of health as a state of complete physical, mental and social well-being, not merely the absence of disease or infirmity.

The admonition to pull yourself together is therefore sound advice. Unfortunately it is virtually impossible to act upon for the simple reason that most people are insufficiently in touch with the various parts of themselves to be able to do it. This is hardly surprising, for, while there is a tendency to speak of the self as if it is a unitary entity, as the poet Walt Whitman observed, 'it contains multitudes'.

Nevertheless, just because there are many rooms to the mansion of the self it doesn't make it any less of a house, and if we are to live in it comfortably we must be able to take account of both its composite nature and its component features. This involves recognising or identifying individual elements and how they fit together with others to form a unified whole. In this respect it is much like a jigsaw, a picture assembled from a number of irregularly shaped, interlocking pieces, and needs to be tackled in the same way.

THE PUZZLING PRINCIPLES OF HEALING

Competent jigsaw puzzlers generally attempt to start building a complete picture by identifying and interlocking those pieces of the puzzle with a regular contour, whether straight or curved, aligning these so as to establish the boundaries of the whole picture and, in the case of rectilinear puzzles, framing it by positioning the corner pieces first. Having done so they then begin to work inwards towards the centre, fitting together the more complex, irregular pieces that have more connections than the pieces on the perimeter, continuing to do so until all the links are established and the picture complete. Where puzzles comprise constellations of component pictures, these may be dealt with individually and then combined together.

The same principles are central to the psychology of health and healing in that if you are to become or remain whole or healthy you need to establish and retain some fairly clear and coherent picture of yourself. However, this is rather more difficult than working on a wooden puzzle because the self that is being pictured is not static, but dynamic, changing its contours and components in response to everchanging life events. A fairly 'together' person is therefore engaged in an ongoing and continuous process, attempting to fill the gaps in their knowledge of themselves, working to resolve areas of difficulty, and responding to changes in their life pattern as and when they occur.

In the case of those people who have cracked up or broken down, or who are about to, this picture is usually in bits, often because the pieces they are trying to fit together no longer constitute the picture they are trying to assemble, or simply because they have given up in the attempt. At best it is complete or nearly complete only at the edges where the self comes into contact with others and the environment. Such people, who are 'living on the edge', 'up against it', 'at the end of their tether' who have 'reached their limits' or have been 'brought up sharp', are in danger of losing their grip on themselves totally and, understandably, tend to be 'edgy'. They are out of touch with their centre, alienated from the core of themselves; cut off from who and what they really are. They are unfulfilled, in the sense that the picture which should be complete is substantially lacking and the person empty. In order to prevent total breakdown such a person must begin to work towards redefining themselves, addressing the puzzle of who and what they are by re-establishing connections with their inner self, thereby enabling a new picture to emerge.

PATTERNS OF HEALTH

These principles are embodied in various approaches to psychological medicine, most notably gestalt therapy, the brainchild of Frederick (Fritz) Perls, a German psychiatrist. *Gestalt* is a German word which has no exact equivalent in the English language, its closest approximation being configuration or pattern. More precisely, a gestalt is a whole which cannot be described merely as the sum of its parts. It is irreducible and destroyed if divided into components. The term was applied to various principles of perception discovered by experiments conducted in the early twentieth century by the Gestalt School – a group of German psychologists who showed that we do not perceive things as unrelated isolates, but organise them in the perceptual process into meaningful wholes. It is thus the organisation of phenomena and not the individual items of which they are composed that defines them, and gives them their specific meaning. Accordingly we see any situation as a unified pattern which constitutes a meaningful gestalt. On entering a room full of people, for example, we do not see only blobs of colour and movement, faces, bodies and objects. We perceive the room, the people and objects within it as a unit or whole, which in its totality may have meaning as 'a wedding reception', for example. However, by focusing attention on certain aspects of the room we may impose meaningful patterns which emerge as unified elements from the diffuse background, while the others recede.

Gestalt therapy

The basic premise of gestalt therapy is that human nature is also organised into patterns or wholes; that it is experienced by the individual in these terms and can only be understood as a function of the patterns or wholes of which it is comprised. Moreover the individual can exist only in an environmental field. Inevitably at every moment the individual is a part of some field, and his behaviour is a function of the total field which includes both him and his environment. However, the boundary between the two is all important, because this defines the individual and it is at this

17

contact boundary that psychological events take place. 'Our thoughts, our actions and our emotions are our way of experiencing and meeting these boundary events' (Perls, 1976a, p. 17). Thus the nature of the relationship between a person and his environment is of key importance because it determines his 'being' in the world. It differentiates between the self and otherness. Accordingly, in attempting to understand yourself it is necessary first to examine how you function at this boundary.

Perls saw the becoming of 'what one is' as an inborn goal of all human beings, plants and animals, and as such a fundamental need of all living things. He said this can only occur through the integration of the various parts of the self because 'the true nature of man, like the true nature of any other animal, is integrity' (1976, p. 49) and it is through integration that the self emerges as a unified figure against its environmental field. When the self is clearly defined and located in relation to others and the world, the individual can distinguish his or her needs from the demands of the environment. Only then does it become possible for the individual to act effectively, because this integrated self, like any unified field, is more able to utilise its potential. Such a process requires constant monitoring of the self because the patterns or gestalten of the environmental field are dynamic and ever-changing, as the demands of self, others and the external world alter. The satisfaction of various needs, equivalent to health, is something of a balancing act, maintained by a kind of homoeostasis or self-regulation, the fundamental requirement of which is awareness of the immediate situation. So the aware individual can perceive changes in existing gestalten and act accordingly to create new patterns, restoring the equilibrium between the self and its surroundings.

Without such awareness we can have difficulty in establishing boundaries between self and others, and the external world, becoming confused as to where we end and others begin, and unable to satisfy our needs because we are not aware of what they are. Such self-denial may ultimately lead to complete disintegration, or breakdown of a physical or psychological nature, or both. Perls viewed much psychological illness as the inability to perceive boundaries clearly, with the result that we characteristically respond by fear, anxiety, avoidance tendencies and elaborate defences all aimed at avoiding an encroaching world. Moreover, being unable to define personal boundaries such a person typically manipulates the environment for support in various ways rather than utilising his personal potential. The individual is thus unable to satisfy his needs and remains in a state of disequilibrium that might justifiably be thought of as 'unbalanced'.

Physical illness is frequently one of the ways in which people attempt to manipulate others and the world for support, albeit not necessarily consciously. For many people illness is the only way in which they can meet important needs, define themselves or prevent others and the outside world encroaching upon them. It may enable them to say 'no' to unwanted responsibilities, and to avoid unpleasant and stressful activities or situations; or permit them to do things they have always wanted to do such as paint, write or study. It may be the only way they have of asking for love, care and attention; or it may serve as an excuse for failure. When ill a person can excuse themselves without guilt, anxiety or the need to explain and justify. For some people permanent disability may be more attractive than health, but the benefits or 'secondary gains' of illness may not be consciously recognised by the sufferer, so its meaning is all too often overlooked. However, close scrutiny invariably reveals that illness of whatever kind is the outer manifestation of some inner turmoil or disintegration.

The aim of gestalt therapy is integration, or synthesis, rather than analysis. The ultimate goal of treatment is 'to achieve that amount of integration which facilitates its own development. . . . A small hole cut into an accumulation of snow sometimes suffices to drain off the water. Once the draining has begun the trickle broadens its bed by itself; it facilitates its own development' (Perls, 1977, p. 52). This is because the disintegrated or dissociated person is inhibited or even degenerating in his development, and it is therefore necessary to restore self-regulation or homoeostasis, which is crucial to self-actualisation.

Person-centred therapy

The aims of gestalt therapy share much in common with the person-centred therapy of American psychologist Carl Rogers, who is widely regarded as the founding father of the counselling movement. Rogers considered there to be an actualising tendency inherent in all life forms such that they move towards growth and the fulfilment of their true nature or being. However, he also recognised that this tendency is easily frustrated, suppressed and overwhelmed, giving rise to both physical and psychological illness; can be stunted or even stopped; and is sometimes only able to exert itself in 'warped, bizarre or abnormal manifestations' (Rogers & Sanford, 1989, p. 1492). He noted that during therapy many people voice profound dissatisfaction with themselves or their ability to express themselves, and often make remarks such as 'I feel I can't be myself'; 'I don't know who I really am'; or 'If others really knew me they wouldn't like me'.

Rogers observed that the person's view of himself also fluctuates, often dramatically and suddenly. One minute the person might experience himself as confident, assured and successful, and the next as insecure, inadequate and a failure. Moreover, this may result from only a brief remark or encounter. Like Perls, Rogers concluded that these changes indicate a self which is not a fixed entity but a fluid changing gestalt; the product of the person's responses to experience. It is composed of perceptions about 'I' or 'me', perceptions of how these features relate to others and to various aspects of life, together with the values attached to these perceptions. For Rogers the degree of agreement between a person's self-concept and experience on the one hand, and his interpretations of environmental stimuli on the other determine the extent to which he is capable of self-actualisation or health. If the two are relatively harmonious, then the individual remains unified, self-actualising and healthy, but if they are discordant then the self-actualising tendency is thwarted and the integrity or health of the person breaks down. The individual's concept of himself and his world is thus dependent on innumerable experiences and past learning, but also on unpredictable events and interactions which can occur from moment to moment. Obstacles to self-actualisation may also come from sub-parts of the self which have been adversely affected by a whole range of environmental circumstances, both physical and psychological. Given the complexity of human life and experience it is therefore unsurprising that for many people the process of self-actualisation is fraught with difficulty, and often breaks down. However,

Rogers believed that the individual has the capacity to reorganise his perceptual field, changing his view of himself and his world so as to bring about a concordance between them, thereby effecting an integration or healing.

Becoming healthy

The psychiatrist Carl Gustav Jung indicated that there are aspects of the self of which a person is unaware or unconscious, facets that have been neglected, dissociated or never recognised. He considered that these have to be addressed simultaneously with conscious aspects of the self so they can be rediscovered and reintegrated. Moreover, he recognised that as the self has a dual aspect and can be oriented either inwardly or outwardly, the reality of *both* these inside and outside worlds also have to be reconciled. He termed the process whereby all aspects, conscious and unconscious, inner and outer, are integrated resulting in the experience of a new centre of personality or self, individuation.

> Individuation means becoming a single, homogeneous being, and, in so far as 'individuality' embraces our innermost, last, and incomparable uniqueness, it also implies becoming one's own self. We could therefore translate individuation as 'coming to selfhood' or 'self-realization'.
>
> 1953, para. 405

He considered this to be synonymous with perfect health and, as such, an unattainable ideal. The individuation process thus results in 'an integration or *completeness* of the individual, who in this way approaches *wholeness*, but not *perfection* (1955, para. 616). Implicitly, therefore, he drew attention to a principle of the greatest importance, which is that health should be conceived not as a state but as the process of healing or becoming healthy.

This process is similar to that involved in the completion of jigsaw puzzles. Visual perception – seeing – is fundamental to the latter in that a person has to be able to see both the individual pieces and the picture they constitute. It would be extremely difficult to complete a jigsaw if one had to rely on someone else's vision and only had their verbal descriptions as a guide. Yet, as the psychiatrist R.D. Laing (1976) has observed, this is precisely the way human beings tend to live their lives:

> We live within, or can easily come to live within, a skein of words, such that we see, as it were, other people's descriptions of the world, instead of describing what we see. Other people are not 'seeing' the world either, very often. The map is not the territory, the menu is not the meal.

Nevertheless, we surrender to this influence, and as a consequence tend to lose sight of ourselves and our purpose.

Psychological healing is essentially a process of revision which helps us realise ourselves by reminding us who we are and what we are about. This fundamental awareness is achieved primarily by facilitating perception of our inner and outer worlds; i.e what is occurring *here* and *now* both within and outside yourself. The following exercise addresses these issues. It is recommended that having attempted it, you repeat the exercise, preceding it with the progressive relaxation provided in Appendix I.

EXERCISE 1

Find somewhere quiet and make yourself comfortable, either sitting or lying (preferably the former as the latter is likely to promote sleep).

Close your eyes, or focus with open eyes on a fixed point or object. Now imagine somewhere you can be really yourself, to the extent that this is possible. Imagine being there. Be aware of all the sights, sounds, smells and sensations you experience, noting them in as much detail as you can. Notice how you feel, and any features of the 'real' you that seem particularly significant or strange. Allow yourself to enjoy this experience as fully as possible.

Also be aware of any difficulty you have in imagining yourself in such a place; and of any intrusive or distracting thoughts, feelings, memories or sensations which arise. Don't dwell on these and do not try to suppress them. Merely make a mental note of them and allow them to disappear.

Ask yourself what it is about this situation that enables you to be real; and what it is about everyday life that prevents you being real. When you have answered these questions gradually allow yourself to return to normal consciousness. Then make a verbal or written report of your experience, in the first person present tense, noting all the features of the imagery and your answers to the questions in as much detail as possible.

Commentary

I-dentifying with imagery

Few people actually report their experience in the first person present tense as requested. Initially most find it difficult, or strange, when urged to do so. However, there are several reasons why it is a good idea. One is that in so doing the verbal representational mode is re-engaged and can be brought to bear on the visually represented issues, thereby maximising mental flexibility, and effective functioning which involves the whole person, rather than any specific part or parts. Using the first person present tense also personalises experience, and locates it in the here and now. Many people lack 'presence': the ability to be here, now, and adopting this verbal style enables people to I-dentify with their experience in the here and now of the present. There is also a tendency in people to deny personal responsibility for their own creations or products, whether their imaginings, thoughts, feelings, pains, actions or illnesses, attributing them to external rather than internal causes. Frequently people will deny the personal significance of the imagery they produce, arguing that what they imagined has a 'real' existence outside of their imagination. However, while it may correspond with a feature of the external world it is nevertheless a product of their imagination, and its potential significance lies in why, of all the images they could have brought to mind or invented, they chose to imagine what they did. These features are not simply random, but quite specific personal productions or creations for which they are responsible, and which, for this very reason, are almost certainly meaningful when scrutinised more closely. People who cannot readily see the personal relevance of an image when viewed objectively may feel quite differently when they personalise it or 'try it on'.

The projection of features of the self on to others and the outside world gives rise to the idea that these external forces are responsible for or cause them. Typically therefore people say 'It made me anxious', rather than 'I make myself anxious', or angry or sick, in response to who or whatever it might be. This attribution of personal features to external agencies necessarily leads to confusion between the inner and outer worlds of the person and a failure to establish clear-cut boundaries between them. The personalisation and immediacy of experience brought about by the use of the first person and present tense reverses this tendency, helping to promote acknowledgement of personal responsibility and locus of control: that is, the sense of being effective in the world rather than a passive victim of circumstance; and awareness of one's personal agency. As Perls explains:

> The 'I' is the foreground figure experience. It is the sum of all emerging needs, the clearing house for their satisfaction. It is the constancy factor within the relativity of inner and outer demands. It is the responsibility agent for whatever it identifies with: Response-able, capable of responding to the situation – not 'responsible' in the moralistic sense of taking on obligations dictated by duty.

> 1972, p. 115

Guided imagework is therefore concerned with the images produced by people, and their responses as and when they identify with them.

Freedom to be

Most people report imagining themselves outdoors, on beaches, in mountains or woods, by the sea, rivers or lakes, or in gardens. Being in touch with nature is clearly a very important condition of their sense of realness or authenticity. The feeling of freedom is paramount, and seems to depend upon the removal of man-made conditions and constraints; release from the demands and pressures of modern society and civilisation, notably noise, and the necessity of making money; buildings, greyness – and people.

This sense of freedom is often accentuated by running, dancing, riding, swimming; and, in some instances, hang-gliding. One young woman indicated that when hang-gliding she 'has only herself as a measure', whereas normally she is aware of and worried about other people's view of her. Many people specify the feeling of wind on their face or in their hair as representing this sense of freedom. One woman's description of realness as feeling warm inside, despite a cold wind on her face, highlights the sense of being in touch with both inner and outer aspects of the self.

The vast majority of people describe being alone, or with a cat, dog or horse. When asked to account for the animal's presence they invariably indicate that it provides companionship without the problems and demands of human communication, and an accepting relationship free of evaluation. The therapeutic benefit of companion animals is now widely recognised and is being made use of in a wide variety of institutional contexts (Scarlett, 1987; Whyte, 1989). It is therefore ironic, given the importance of animals and the natural environment to his sense of himself, that both are under growing and relentless threat from man.

Only rarely do people describe feeling real in the presence of children. Those who do are invariably women, and the children they describe are usually babies or toddlers, who appear to offer a limited challenge to authenticity before they can fully articulate their demands and impress them on others. Irrespective of their age, children clearly compromise the sense of self and realness of some people. One woman recalled to the last detail, including the record playing and the perfume she was wearing, her 'one moment of being real – the last moment of peace in my life – sitting with the dog, in front of the fire, before the kids, before my life speeded up'. However, one unmarried and childless young woman who imagined herself with a child she knew to be her own recognised it as symbolic of the need to break free from her feminist principles in order to realise her authentic self.

In fact only a very small minority of people report feeling real in the presence of others. Where they do so the other people are usually somewhat distant, and are always non-evaluative and non-intrusive. They can be described as 'doing their own thing and allowing others to do the same'. Sometimes people describe being in the company of one other person, with whom they are intimate and whom they can trust to accept them 'for themself'. They may be physically close or more distant. One young woman, for example, described feeling real in a room without windows where no one could see her, and her mother, the only person she feels herself with and can trust, in an adjoining room.

Most people feel real only when alone. They describe the conditions of realness variously, as 'leaving behind everything and everybody'; 'getting away from serving others and meeting their needs'; or from 'constantly having to monitor behaviour to suit others'. One man described needing to 'get away from trivial, superficial, shallow, disapproving people'. One woman, who described the feeling of realness as being in control, realised that she couldn't be in control in the presence of others.

Some people are overwhelmed by the demands of others and have difficulty asserting themselves when in their presence. An extreme example of this challenge to the self is provided by a man who described taking other people's feelings of disapproval into himself, claiming that 'it is as though they leap or jump into me'. Reporting an incident where he had complained to some neighbours about the noise they were making, he described feeling 'far worse afterwards, because it was as though I had brought their anger back into the room with me'. This man is clearly very confused as to the boundaries between himself and others, because he projects on to them his feelings of disapproval and anger, which he then experiences as having come from them rather than himself. He has no ownership over his feelings, believing they emanate from outside him and, not recognising them as his own, he is incapable of taking responsibility for them.

Some people describe being real in situations where other people are present and in reasonably close proximity – when dancing in a disco or playing an instrument in a band, for instance, but to all intents and purposes these people are in a world of their own, unaware of and unaffected by the presence of others, rather than in a truly social situation.

People are frequently surprised by the appearance of their 'real' selves. Many women describe themselves wearing light, cotton dresses which appear to represent for them youth, freedom, simplicity, lack of regulation, formality, style and pretence. One woman, who described herself as real when climbing a mountain in 'a totally unsuitable cotton dress', recognised in this her desire not to be sensible, to go against convention and to revert to childhood. For others childhood seems to be represented by going barefoot. Indeed both men and women frequently imagine themselves as children. For some childhood represents a time, perhaps the only time, when they were happy. This feeling of happiness or contentment generally characterises the experience of being real, together with feelings of power or potentiality. One woman described herself as real when aged four, which was the only time in her life she remembered being accepted as herself. For others this return to childhood represents their desire to retreat from adult life and its responsibilities – relationships, family and domestic circumstances, 'bread-winning', cooking and domestic chores. Few people experience themselves as 'real' at work. Regrettably the only man to do so admitted that this was not in his current job, which he desperately wanted to get away from.

Many people therefore wish to escape from the responsibilities they have acquired with age or the passage of time. Indeed, time itself is experienced by many people as a pressure. As one man put it, 'time acts against realness rather than for it'. Some people feel that they are always 'up against it' and 'in a rush', and never have time for themselves. One woman explained that 'in everyday life I am always very aware of what I have to do next, and I often feel very pressured by this'. So for many people the experience of realness involves a loss of the sense of time, a timelessness described by one woman as a 'stepping out of time' and by another as 'a golden moment out of time'.

Both men and women often report being naked, and their relief at not having to dress up or down, or for the occasion, whatever that might be. One young man was astonished to imagine himself naked because of his prudishness, which he attributed to having been reared in a home with an absolute taboo on nudity, where everyone always had to be covered up. Women are often surprised by their nakedness because of their customary displeasure or dissatisfaction with their bodies. One reported relief at not having to suck in her stomach or adjust her hair. Several describe being naked in a place with no mirrors and thus where they are free

27

from self-evaluation. Only in these circumstances do they feel able to get in touch with and accept their bodies.

My experience highlights many of these features. Finding myself in an Austrian hotel which boasted numerous facilities, I used a solarium for the first time. I found the experience strangely uplifting and repeated it several times throughout my stay in the hotel. I gave little or no thought to the matter, it being just one feature of a very pleasant holiday. I was therefore very surprised when later engaged in the above exercise to discover my 'real' self in this solarium. On closer examination of the situation I realised that it represented a total retreat from ordinary reality: a silent, dark, wood-panelled room, locked from within and away from all the demands of the world. I could not be disturbed by the other people or the telephone and I had no audience to consider, not even me, as there were no mirrors. I could please myself and I did, by being myself.

I am not the only person to be surprised by the situations in which they experience themselves as real. One woman imagined herself in her garden 'staring at my own muck heap and feeling OK about it'. In so doing she recognised that being real involved her acceptance of the 'muckier' aspects of herself. Another woman who found herself watching trains full of people passing out of a coalyard was able to acknowledge that she could really be objective about and accepting of the grimness of her past.

In some instances the situation in which the person perceives their real self is almost surreal and quite unrelated to their present or past experiences. One young woman described 'homing' in on a puzzling scene in which she sat embroidering in front of a fire, surrounded by her husband, children and cat. There is nothing exceptional about this 'homely' scene other than the fact that not only has she no husband or children, but she has never had a home as such, having been placed in a series of boarding schools after losing her parents in early childhood. Until she engaged in this exercise, 'home' only had meaning for her as being with friends. Subsequently, however, she found that being able to summon this image proved very useful in enabling her to relax and alleviate stress. As she explained, 'I now have no need to run away from things, to run home, because home is me'.

Some people find that they cannot imagine a situation in which they can be real and this awareness may give rise to powerful emotions. One young woman tried in several places and with various people including her sister, who she believes knows her better than anyone else, but was unable to feel real. She thus realised how many faces she puts on for others and that even with friends she acts not as she wants but as they expect her to. An older woman reported being unable to find anywhere she could escape the demands of being female and a daughter; while another described herself on a beach, surrounded by the black silhouettes of people whose needs she feels she has to meet. Several other women have reported being unable to find any situation in which they didn't feel the need to please other people. An extreme example was provided by a woman who claimed that she could only escape the demands of others when asleep. For some women anxiety about what is expected of them, or that other people might be watching them during the exercise, prevents them relaxing sufficiently to complete it. As one young woman explained, she had 'the awful thought' that she was the only person doing the exercise with her eyes closed and that other people were laughing at her.

There may be other reasons given as to why a person cannot experience herself as real. A woman who found her visual field divided into two halves each showing contradictory scenes, indicated that she didn't know which was really her. Another blamed her inability to find a place where she could be real on to a headcold. When asked how often she used colds and illness as an excuse for not doing things she replied 'Oh. All the time'.

Men appear to be less compromised by the expectations and demands of others but frequently have quite powerful emotional reactions when they recognise the constraints on their realness. One man felt grief upon realising that the one time he could be real and the one person he could be real with were both lost to him. Another man became anxious as he began to question his ability to be real and the genuineness of his feelings and thoughts, and worried that he might portray an untrue image of himself to others because he didn't know himself as a person.

Being 'really' relaxed

Prior relaxation may be necessary if anxiety prevents a person engaging in or completing the exercise. Irrespective of whether or not it is necessary, the experience of deep relaxation produces important insights. When asked to describe somewhere they can be fully relaxed people always describe the place where they can be real. This is because relaxation is fundamentally a letting go of, and a freedom from, habitual physical and psychological tensions, which, when examined closely, are invariably generated by the demands imposed on the person by others. Relaxation can be thought of as the cultivation of muscle sense or bodily awareness, but it is much more than this. Studies have shown that complete physical relaxation is possible only when all mental processes are suspended. This is because bodily tensions are generated in response to mental attitudes, preoccupations and concerns, and the resulting emotional tensions, conflicts, fears and anxieties. If these psychological tensions are not relaxed then it follows that physical relaxation will prove difficult and, at best, will be limited. Relaxation procedures should therefore be directed to the whole person rather than focused solely on the body and as such they constitute an important feature of self-awareness training. The progressive relaxation exercise detailed in Appendix I has been developed with this aim and often yields valuable insights into the self. These may be general or more specific, as the following examples illustrate.

Frequently people are unaware of how tense they are normally, even when the degree of tension is extreme. One hypertense man was horrified to realise how little he had to do to achieve maximum tension in all his muscles. When asked, while focusing on her back, if anything 'gets her back up', one young woman realised she is *really* quite aggressive, with hostile feelings towards several people which only find expression in lower back tension and pain. Another woman responded in much the same way, recognising that although annoyed by other people's selfish demands she normally 'allows them to walk all over her' without protest. As a result she decided to assert her real self and subsequently found that her chronic back pain was alleviated.

Another woman who found herself unable to comply with the

instruction to throw away an imaginary gold coin in her grip simply pretended to. Afterwards she realised that she was scared of losing something precious to her, as she had done in early childhood when her father left home, and that fear of losing her boyfriend prevented her showing her real feelings towards him and was jeopardising their relationship. This insight prompted her to risk letting go of her fear and become more real towards him, acting as she wanted to towards him rather than how she thought she should.

When focusing on his shoulders and the question of whether or not there might be a 'chip' there, a man remembered his anger when his brother had made such a claim. He realised he had not been concerned whether he had or not, only that others might think he did. In each of these instances the person was able to identify tensions within themselves generated by difficulties in being real with others of which formerly they had been unaware.

The butterfly image used in the relaxation exercise emerges as a very potent symbol of the real, true or authentic self. This is intriguing because the Greek term for butterfly, *psyche*, also means self or soul, and universally the butterfly represents spiritual qualities, transformation, metamorphosis, change and freedom. Attention to this aspect of a person's imagery invariably reveals important issues. One woman was very alarmed by her butterfly, which spread very wide across her chest. However, every time it attempted to fly off she tried to catch it, until finally it crumpled totally. Subsequently she acknowledged always having had difficulty holding on to anything in life and losing what she wanted to hold on to by trying too hard. So, by trying too hard to relax she had been generating tension and anxiety. She also recognised that the colour of her butterfly – pale mauve edged with black – was significant, as was the fact that she was dressed in a suit of the same colour. She associated purple with mourning and with the sadness of being a 'loser'; and realised that mauve, a dilute purple, represented her attempt to conceal this sadness from others so as to be acceptable to them. Only the black edges of the butterfly's wings revealed her true feelings. However, within the imaginary exercise she finally relaxed, enabling her butterfly to take wing and she followed it, becoming real when she 'got away from everyman'.

Many other people find that they quite spontaneously follow their butterfly and in so doing discover themselves. One woman described following a butterfly whose wings were formed of coral shells of a kind found in her native West Indies, which led her back to her roots and her real self. A man who wanted to get away from the demands of modern life followed his butterfly to a Kibbutz where he had been happy some years ago. A woman whose butterfly retained its cocoon could only find her real self in childhood. In another instance the butterfly spread its wings and fell from the woman's breast to her feet, where she was frightened of trampling on it. She discovered the significance of this later, when she found her real self in the garden of her own home after failing to be real in any of the exotic holiday locations she imagined herself in, and in so doing became aware that she didn't have to move or travel anywhere to find herself. Her awareness is reminiscent of the teaching of the Chinese sage Lao Tsu:

> There is no need to run outside for better seeing.
> Nor to peer from a window;
> Rather, abide at the centre of your being;
> For the more you leave it the less you learn.
>
> THE WAY OF LIFE

Difficulties in experiencing a sense of realness are also often reflected in the butterfly image. Numerous people describe being unable to breathe life into the butterfly, which remains two-dimensional – a tattoo, silhouette, template, appliqué decoration or cardboard cut-out. Many butterflies are extremely delicate and fragile. Some butterflies flutter their wings but are unable to stretch them fully or fly. Some – usually large butterflies – crumple horribly at the first attempt; while others remain with outstretched wings but still unable to fly. Smaller butterflies appear to be more agile, although these often merely flutter their wings and make gestures towards flying without actually doing so. These images are suggestive of people who want to be free but who are in some way restrained or restricted, and who crumple in the face of their own authenticity. This seems to give rise to sadness in those who describe large butterflies, which is suggestive perhaps of their reaction to this loss of considerable potential.

One woman felt envious of her large yellow butterfly, and wanted to be like it, indicating thereby that she couldn't identify with the image she had produced herself.

A number of people restrain the butterfly because they fear they will lose it and some flatten it in the attempt. Others find that despite their efforts it will not fly. One woman observed that her butterfly had part of its cocoon attached to its wings, which she took as a sign that she needs to shed something before she can actualise herself.

The colour of the butterfly is often highly significant; perhaps an indication of the person's 'true colours' (see Chapters 9 and 10). One man described holding his butterfly close to his chest, thus being aware of his 'true colours' but not showing them to others. Dark colours appear to be associated with negativity and diluted colours with potentials that are not adequately utilised or expressed. One woman, for example, felt that her very pale butterfly reflected the fact that she did not express her true self at all.

Surprisingly few people feel really happy about their butterfly. Most seem to feel that it 'isn't doing what it should do', that is, stretching itself, drying out, preparing itself for flight and then flying. Their reactions prompt a similar conclusion to that expressed by John Collee (1991, p. 58):

> Some children, exposed to too many stimuli, lose the ability to concentrate on things that really matter. It strikes me that many adults suffer from a similar disorder.

⊱ CHAPTER TWO ⊰

Acting Well

And one might therefore say of me that . . . I have only
made up a bunch of other people's flowers, and that of
my own I have only provided the string that ties them
together.

MONTAIGNE

The previous exercise highlights a very intriguing paradox, which
is that man, a social animal, needs to dissociate from his fellow
man in order to be real or authentic. Indeed his identity depends
upon it. The idea of oneself – or self-concept – as separate and
distinct from others implies an ability to perceive the boundaries
between them and yourself. It emerges out of various experiences
during the first few years of life and is therefore the 'result of a
gradual and progressive dissociation and not a primitive intuition'
(Piaget, 1930, p. 128).

BECOMING SOMEBODY

Very young children are probably not aware of a clear boundary
between themselves and their environment, but by touching and
the coordination of voluntary body movements they develop
awareness of a body boundary, and of themselves as the initiators
of actions and intentions. Self-identity also develops as language
is acquired, with the use of names and the personal pronouns, I,
me and mine. With the knowledge of their own name and other
personal properties a sense of I-ness, or individuality, begins to
emerge as children begin to understand more of their independ-

ence as separate entities, and gain an idea of who and what they are. What was little more than a loose collection of labels applied by others then comes to encompass the sum total of all that they know about themselves. As such the self-concept is not a unitary entity but a collection of cognitive representations, not all of which are alike, and some of which are more peripheral than others. These elements, whether positive, negative, actual or ideal, are not static, but change with time and circumstance.

A universal feature of human social interaction is a difference in response to males and females. This is activated by the assignment of a child to one or other gender category on the basis of the appearance of its genitals at birth. The subsequent process has been likened to a recipe (Adams & Laurikietis, 1976) which goes as follows: take any newly born baby, of any race or colour, assign it to a gender, then dress it in pink, give it a doll, encourage its passivity, don't expect too much of it, protect it, teach it about 'femininity', encourage its incompetence, discourage its independence, instruct it in domesticity and subservience. This, it is claimed, will produce a 'real' woman. If a 'real' man is required, dress the baby in blue, give it a toy gun, encourage its activity and independence, expect a hell of a lot from it, make it protect itself, encourage its confidence and assertiveness, and train it to earn a living. This recipe works, not because it is natural, innate and inviolable as is often thought, but because it is known to all and passed on from generation to generation, ensuring that everyone learns the limits of appropriate and permissible behaviours for individuals categorised as members of a given sex.

However, given that these limits or boundaries define what are generally referred to as gender 'roles', it is perhaps more appropriate to think of the process whereby gender identity is learned in theatrical terms.

CASTING THE PRODUCTION

Roles in the theatre are most usually allocated or 'cast' on the basis of the physical attributes of the actors and the performance demanded of those cast in the roles scripted in advance rather than improvised. The casting of roles gives rise to certain responses in the production team and other members of the cast, who have expectations as to how any given part should be played. Similarly at birth when an individual is assigned his or her gender role this sets in motion responses in parents and others. Indeed the assignment of gender provides the first real cue as to how others are to behave in relation to the child. Thus, despite minimal differences between them at birth, babies are treated quite differently according to their gender (Seavey, 1975; Meyer & Sobieszek, 1972; Will et al., 1976). Mothers look at and talk more to their baby daughters than to their sons (Lewis, 1972). However, during the first three months of life, but not thereafter, boys are touched, kissed and cuddled more than girls, and after the age of six months girls are encouraged to remain closer to their mothers than boys, who are encouraged to play at a distance, and to be more active and curious in their play.

Play-acting

There is also a clear difference in the toys offered to boys and girls, boys being given significantly more vehicles such as cars and aeroplanes, and girls significantly more female dolls. Boys are also provided with objects that encourage activities away from home, while girls are given objects that encourage activities within the home. The decoration of children's nurseries, play and bedrooms also frequently reflects these differences (Rheingold & Cook, 1975). The choices made by parents do not necessarily reflect the preferences of the child. Studies of children in play groups have shown that when offered a selection of toys traditionally identified as for 'girls' or 'boys', most children choose the boys' toys because they are more interesting and versatile. There are, when all is said and done, relatively few things that you can do with a miniature ironing board.

Reading between the lines

On being allocated a role, actors are provided with a written copy of the play or script. Children are also provided with a script in that everyday language is permeated with gender stereotypes or standardised images of and assumptions about, males and females. The psychologist Geoffrey Beattie (1979, 1980) has highlighted this strong gender bias and pointed to its enormous psychological and social significance, arguing that its power arises from its pervasiveness. He illustrates his argument with reference to the terms 'men', 'women', 'boy' and 'girl'. As he observes the term 'men' is by far the most common for males, while the term 'boy' which is used almost exclusively for the male child, signifying immaturity and lack of status, has derogatory connotations. The term 'girl', however, is frequently substituted for 'woman' in contexts where boy would not appear for man. Teenage males are invariably described in the media as men, whereas females of the same age and older are usually described as girls.

However, these linguistic conventions may have rather more serious implications. It has been shown that in virtually every language throughout the world the word 'girl' is perceived as being more positively evaluated than 'woman', but is much less potent, being highly stereotyped predominantly in respect of physical attributes such as smallness, prettiness, beauty and loveliness, but also traits like weakness and dependence. In contrast, the term woman elicits responses of maturity and unattractiveness. So, whereas a boy greatly increases his status when he becomes a man, a girl loses status on becoming a woman. To describe a female as a woman may therefore offer a challenge to her self-concept. The term 'gentleman' is rarely used except on lavatory doors, but the term 'lady' is very commonly applied to women. It has been suggested (Lakoff, 1975) that this is because the concept 'woman' lacks inherent dignity and requires ennobling. Certainly it has been demonstrated that the less status and dignity a woman has, the more her status is likely to be enhanced by recourse to the term 'lady', hence 'cleaning', 'char' and 'serving ladies' (Hancock, 1963). Even more pervasive than these terms is the use of male pronouns to represent all humankind, and the suffix 'man' to denote occupancy of occupational and other worthwhile roles in society. Moreover, little has changed with the move towards so-called gender equality and political correctness. We no longer speak of 'firemen' but of 'firefighters', thus replacing a male suffix with a term suggestive of a stereotypically male quality.

Learning the part

Children are thus presented with a script which is explicitly and implicitly sexist, and this is learned in much the same manner as in the theatre. The script, as the actor Jonathan Pryce has observed, tends to be 'absorbed' rather than studied. Individuals are acutely sensitive to information regarding their roles and appropriate behaviours, and they pick up cues in both conscious and unconscious ways. Usually they are unaware of learning the script and others are not necessarily aware of teaching it or prompting, so they believe the ensuing performances are natural rather than studied. Yet these ways of acting are learned from parents, teachers and society as a whole, and from children's books, textbooks, comics, magazine features, television programmes, films and advertising.

Not only can the existence of these stereotypes be demonstrated but also the fact that children are influenced by them (Deutsch, 1975; Jennings, 1975). Indeed there is much evidence that pre-school children learn about their roles in society from the media and from television in particular (DeFleur, 1964). Many studies of children's television confirm the power of gender role stereotyping on children's behaviour and attitudes, having shown that children accept and imitate what they see. Analyses of gender role portrayals in a variety of programmes suggest that by emphasising the domesticity of women and the independence of men, television provides role models that reinforce stereotypical definitions of femininity in passive – dependent terms and masculinity in active – masterful terms, which serve to enhance the male image and diminish that of the female. Relatively little has changed in the 20 years since these observations were first made. Females are still predominantly depicted in domestic situations, as dependent on men, as sex objects or household functionaries. Males are significantly more likely to be shown outdoors or in work settings and men over 50 outnumber women of that age by a factor of 2. Similarly, the majority of adverts, documentaries, sports and current affairs programmes employ 'authoritative' male 'voice-overs' or commentators. One thing which is known to have altered, however, is the age at which children develop their sense of identity. It is now recognised that the media is so successful in shaping the identity of children that this emerges between the ages of 2 and 3, considerably earlier than 20 years ago (BBC, 1991).

While there are many ways an actor might interpret any role, even within the theatre there are constraints that restrict the individual to certain kinds of performance. Performances that have received wide critical acclaim, such as Olivier's Hamlet or Sher's Richard III, tend to be held up as 'classics' or standards against which all others are judged. Young and not-so-young actors tend to imitate these models. Similarly, children first learn how to play their gender roles through imitation, performance of which is maintained by their being rewarded for manifesting appropriate gender traits and behaviour, and punished for those perceived as inappropriate. Imitation of gender role is generally held to involve two processes – identification with members of the same gender and complementation with members of the opposite gender. So in theory the traditional family unit provides the two models necessary for normal gender role development. Anomalies in gender development are thus often attributed to inadequate modelling afforded by the breakdown of the nuclear family or to inappropriate learning.

Dressing the part

If a child is to identify with members of the same gender and complement those of the opposite gender it is essential for it to be able to discriminate them. One of the first ways it learns to do so is through costume or style of dress. Indeed this discrimination is regarded as so fundamental to cognitive and social development that discrimination items of this kind invariably feature in standard intelligence tests.

Costume or dress has a dual function, as any actor knows. It helps the theatre audience to identify the role of the wearer and can be extremely precise. Similarly, everyday dress helps to identify social roles and determines to a great extent the way others respond to a person. The other aspect of dress is that it confers on the wearer a sense of identity. Many actors claim that they can only learn their part 'from the outside in', gaining the 'feel' of their role from the costume. Dress thus has important social and psychological significance. Where gender roles are defined such that very different patterns of behaviour are expected of them this is reflected in different forms of dress. Female clothes traditionally have tended to emphasise the wearer's uselessness, dependence and vulnerability, whereas male clothes emphasise the wearer's strength, industry and dynamism. These characteristics are often reflected in the names given to items of clothing by manufacturers. Thus, while one cannot too easily change a tyre in an evening dress and high-heeled 'court' shoes, so when functionally attired in 'Tuf' boots, 'Wrangler' jeans, sweat shirt and bomber jacket, it is difficult for the male to express the aesthetic side of his nature.

Styles of dress not only convey value but also status. This has less to do with the materials from which garments are made but their style, which is often synonymous with the stylist's label or trademark. It is thus possible to dress 'up' or 'down', by adopting a style and displaying conspicuously various labels and motifs. The appropriate 'look' is essential if a person is to 'dress the part' and this has to be sought. As American fashion designer Shawn Stussy (1992) observes, 'Everybody's out looking for an identity'. This is not merely a self-justification created by the fashion world but a psychological fact. 'Identification is the counteraction to alienation. Alienation means "that's not me, that's something else, something strange, something not belonging to me"' (Perls, 1976a). I-dentification is crucial to the development of gender and social identity. The fashion industry simply exploits this need for identity by providing it, for the most part, ready-made, off-the-peg and in bulk.

Equipped, therefore, with a detailed script, role models, costume and prompters in the wings, the child learns to perform its primary role in society, upon which virtually all other roles depend.

Acting the part

The hallmark of good acting is versatility or flexibility, the ability to adapt to many roles and be convincing in them. This requires the ability to interpret roles and to find new meaning in the accompanying scripts. An ability to improvise or extemporise is therefore highly desirable. For capable individuals there are many rewards. In the short or long term they may provide a good deal of satisfaction and security, opportunities for self-development and discovery, the realisation of numerous potentials, success and acclaim, social mobility and much else. These roles are demanding, however. They require time, energy and application in their execution, and a considerable degree of single-mindedness; together with sensitivity and intelligence in their interpretation. These demands are challenging for the talented actor, but for the less able they may become crippling.

Some actors lack these desired traits. They 'get by' simply rote-learning their scripts, adhering to the prescribed performances and bringing little in the way of creativity or originality to their roles. In some instances, however, it is their ability to play a role, rather than their inability, that creates problems. They may be so successful in the enactment of a role that they become 'typecast' as particular characters, only being offered very similar roles, which give very little scope for them to explore the full range of their talent or finding that audiences refuse to accept them in unaccustomed roles when they are attempted. Successful characterisation may thus become a trap. Sometimes the roles actors are required to play provide no scope for them to express or explore their potentials; and so it is in life.

Character training

It is through playing various roles that an individual's personality emerges. The term personality is theatrical in origin, deriving from the *personae* or masks used in Ancient Greek theatre to depict certain character traits. It describes the sum total of all the characteristics by means of which an individual is recognised as being unique. Like some actors, certain people express themselves distinctively, individualistically and spontaneously. They have a quality of uniqueness and are described as 'having personality'. Other people are described as lacking personality or insipid; devoid of any distinctive or interesting characteristics. Such people fail to express themselves. They lack spontaneity, are conformist and dull.

However, in many cases, as in the theatre, a person's distinguishing features become set and he develops a 'character'.

Once you have a character, you have developed a rigid system. Your behaviour becomes petrified, predictable, and you lose your ability to cope freely with the world with all your resources. You are predetermined just to cope with events in one way, namely as your character prescribes it to be. So it seems a paradox when I say that the richest person, the most productive, creative person is a person who has *no* character.

PERLS, 1976, p. 7

However, as Perls points out, in our society we *demand* a person to have a character, especially a *good* character, 'because then you're predictable, and you can be pigeon-holed' (1976, p. 7).

Irrespective of the nationality, race or creed a child is born into – all of which impose their own performance demands – and so-called 'equality of opportunity', different patterns of life tend to be prescribed for men and women. Marriage is still the primary universal standard by which women are evaluated, with work or career the standard for men. Males are told from childhood onwards that they need to work in order to be fulfilled, and females that they need marriage and a family. Accordingly males are expected to be 'breadwinners', and to strive and achieve in the world outside the home. They are encouraged in the belief that in order to do so they need to be competitive and assertive, aggressive and strong, and that they must suppress emotion, vulnerability and all signs of weakness. These expression/suppression tendencies are encouraged from early infancy onwards and reinforced throughout subsequent development, so boys quickly learn to be self-reliant and controlled. Their aptitudes and interests are channelled into scientific and technological endeavours, into 'hard' and manly activities, and away from artistic, aesthetic and domestic pursuits.

By contrast the 'soft option' is obligatory for girls. Females are still expected not to achieve outside the home but to confine themselves to the domestic sphere and depend on or care for others. As babies and children their interpersonal sensitivity, emotional expressiveness and nurturant qualities are encouraged more than physical activity, exploratory behaviour and curiosity. They are not expected to display intellect, initiative, independence, drive and ambition; and schooling generally reinforces these expectations by encouraging girls in domestic 'science', home 'economics', languages and the creative arts.

Tragic roles

The implications of these gender stereotypes for health and illness are now widely recognised: 'Modern man lives in a state of low grade vitality. Though generally he doesn't suffer deeply, he knows little of true creative living' (Perls, 1976, p. xi). Many do suffer, however. They have taken great pains, quite literally, to build their self-concept to fit their social roles. They live only for their image. Perls observed that many people dedicate their lives to actualising a concept of what they should be like rather than actualising themselves. This difference between *self*-actualising and self-*image* actualising is very important. At best the conflict between the two creates tension and stress. At worst it manifests in breakdown, as physical or psychological illness. Jung took a similar view to Perls, claiming that if the natural self is suppressed rather than expressed it erupts as symptoms of physical or mental disease.

Men are prone to certain types of physical illness such as coronary heart disease, gastric ulcers and lung cancer; and the cultural expectation that men are self-reliant, independent and strong often results in those who are most at risk from stress dismissing it and failing to seek help. Not uncommonly men seek relief in alcohol, which is one of the few socially acceptable ways in which they can express emotions such as sadness, guilt, anxiety and fear. Drinking often leads to aggression and violence, thus reinforcing socially expected patterns of male or macho behaviour, and physical and psychological illness.

Females are encouraged to express emotions and weakness, to be helpless and dependent on others, and these characteristics are frequently reflected in the illnesses to which they succumb (Greer & Morris, 1975; Derogatis, 1979; Meares, 1977; Simonton et al., 1975; Moos, 1964; Moos & Solomon, 1965), and the tranquillising drugs from which they seek relief, which further induce passivity and dependence (Hewitt, 1986).

Traditionally, mental health has been seen as largely dependent on the successful adoption of the personality traits and behaviours appropriate to the individual's gender. This view owes much to Sigmund Freud, who claimed that passivity, dependence and nurturance are healthy female attributes, and that assertiveness in women is a sign of neuroticism. Despite evidence that rigidly sex-typed individuals are more reactive to stressful life events and less well-balanced than individuals who are more flexible (Roos & Cohen, 1987; Bancom & Danker-Brown, 1979; Shaw, 1982), it still prevails within the health professions, with the inevitable consequence that standards of mental health differ for men and women (Llewelyn, 1981). Whereas it is relatively healthy for a man to adopt the traits associated with his gender, an inverse relationship holds for women because the normal feminine traits of dependence, passivity and irrationality are not positive corre-lates of mental health (Broverman et al., 1970). Femininity is found to be highly related to unhealthy traits such as anxiety and negativity, and to show a very low relationship with positive indices of health such as adjustment, autonomy and assertiveness. Not surprisingly, therefore, women are twice as likely to seek help or treatment for mental disorder as men and are twice as likely to be treated in psychiatric outpatient clinics or hospital wards. Moreover the conditions males and females suffer show consistent differences. Males tend towards conditions character-ised by destructive hostility, self-indulgence, impulsiveness and violence, whereas females tend to show higher levels of nervous-ness, anxiety, confusion and depression.

The types of treatment offered also tend to reflect assumptions about males and females held by the culture as a whole. Women in general, and 'housewives' in particular, tend to be prescribed psycho-active drugs such as tranquillisers, whereas men are more likely to be told to take it easy or to take up a leisure activity. This tendency is clearly reflected in drug advertising, where psycho-active drugs are invariably associated with women. This implies that women experience emotional or mental illnesses, whereas men suffer 'real' or physical illnesses. Male disorders tend to be attributed to 'real' causes such as work and female disorders, even if ostensibly physical, to neuroses. A female complaint is therefore more likely to be regarded as neurotic than that of a male, as is highlighted in recent studies of the fatigue syndrome known as T.A.T. (Tired All the Time). Striking gender differences are found (Popay, 1992) in the occurrence of this condition, which preponderates among women, and reactions towards it. Men's experience of tiredness are given more legitimacy by their partners than is the case for women. Male tiredness is seen as work-related, whereas in women it is regarded as 'unreal', despite the fact that most of them continue working unless or until the symptoms become totally debilitating. Men are also reluctant to take time off work, but typically they show no such reluctance at home, where their partners are expected to care for them.

Physicians may also reflect cultural expectations about the sexes in other ways, by suggesting that a woman 'cheer herself up' with a new hair-do, for example – a very unlikely prescription for a male. Many male therapists take the place of husbands or male partners in controlling and advising women patients (Chesler, 1974), and much therapy is based on the notion that it is important for a man to regain control over his wife and family (Levine et al., 1974).

It is therefore easy to presume that the roles men and women play in society predispose them to certain types of illness or disturbance. Marriage has been identified as particularly 'unhealthy' for women. Freud observed that women have to be very healthy in order to tolerate marriage. Indeed, there is fairly consistent evidence that there are higher rates of mental and physical illness in married women than in those who are single, and higher rates of mental illness in married women than in married men. So in health terms marriage is considerably more advantageous to men than women, while being single is slightly disadvantageous to men (Brown & Harris, 1978; Gove & Tudor, 1972). More generally, there is evidence to suggest that conformity and compliance are characteristic of those who succumb to serious physical and psychological illnesses (Greer & Watson, 1985; Schmale & Iker, 1966, 1971; Bahnson & Bahnson, 1966).

Expressiveness

Arguably, however, there is nothing inherent in these roles that necessarily predisposes a person to illness of any kind. It is much more likely to be that which is left out that gives rise to difficulty in that aspects of the self perceived as inconsistent with these roles are not expressed, but suppressed and disowned. Furthermore, needs appropriate to these disowned features are not acknowledged so cannot be satisfied, resulting in illness. Abundant research supports this premise, suggesting that people who succumb to serious physical or mental illness characteristically lack awareness of themselves and their needs, are rigid in their thinking, attitudes, beliefs and behaviours; authoritarian, socially conformist and resistant to change (Le Shan, 1966; Solomon, 1969; Achterberg et al., 1977). They also tend toward self-sacrifice, blame and self-denial (Abse et al., 1974). Moreover, the connection between serious illness and repressed emotions is very well established. Cancer patients have been found to be repressed in their expression of anxiety (Temoshok, 1985), negative emotions (Temoshok & Heller, 1981) and in their reaction to life events that would normally produce strong emotional reactions, whether anger or fear (Eysenck, 1988). They deny and repress emotions to a far greater degree than other people, and this leads to a kind of self-alienation. This disconnection from important parts of their inner self creates a veneer of personality, which while generally pleasant and likeable, is unable to mobilise itself defensively and thus becomes vulnerable. Characteristically, cancer patients shun quarrels and try to bring about harmony (Grossarth-Maticek et al., 1985). The self-concept of individuals with such 'an inordinately pleasant personality' (Greer, 1975) is perhaps most succinctly expressed in the comment of my niece, aged seven: 'If I wasn't so nice I'd hit her in the face'. Such 'nice' people can be sickening – quite literally, it seems. Hence they have been described as suffering from the pathological niceness syndrome (Renneker et al., 1983).

The discovery of these factors has given rise to the idea of a cancer-prone, type 'C' personality who suppresses emotion and complies with external authorities (Temoshok, 1985). Certainly it would appear that tumour growth is strongly associated with this behavioural pattern, whereas tumour regression is positively associated with greater emotional expression. Expressiveness, particularly of sadness and anger, thus emerges as an adaptive coping response that has implications for the immune system (Levy, 1984). However, perhaps the most significant characteristics common to people who succumb to serious illness are lack of awareness and 'rigidity'.

By comparison healthy people; survivors, whether long-term hostages or prisoners of war; and exceptional patients who considerably outlive medical prognoses for serious illnesses such as cancers and AIDS, or reverse their HIV status from positive to negative, characteristically demonstrate both awareness of situations and their needs within them, and flexibility in responding so as to meet those needs (Siegel, 1990; Newton, 1980; Achterberg, 1975). All the indications are, therefore, that it is the way people behave, that is, the way they enact their social roles rather than the roles *per se* that predispose them to health or illness.

Clearly much illness is attributable to the self-denial that results from *rigid* conformity to enduring social roles. This conformity necessitates repression: the banishment from conscious awareness of all aspects of the self that conflict with conventional standards of conduct. Many people would admit that conformity to these roles is 'second nature' to them. The difficulty for them is to become aware of, in touch with and responsive to their *first nature*. Perls was committed to the idea that all external controls, including internalised external controls – the shoulds and should nots dictated by convention – interfere with the healthy working of the organism and that it is only by being self-controlled that the authentic self can be realised. Contrary to popular belief, this means *expressing* rather than repressing oneself, and amounts to following one's own intuitions, feelings and interests; becoming one's own authority rather than submitting to the authority of others. He encouraged the exploration and expression of these features of the self through active use of the imagination in fantasy and role-playing. Jung also advocated active or creative imagination as a means of allowing people to experiment with their own nature instead of remaining in a fixed state.

Improvisation

The desire to be free of the definitions, controls and constraints imposed by others is clearly evident in the previous exercise. In attempting to find situations in which to be themselves people distance themselves from their fellows. They strive to get away from features of human interaction such as noise, communication, evaluation, assessment, conformity, restraint, peer pressure, and conventions of dress, appearance, manners and behaviour.

Yet, distancing oneself physically from society does not guarantee freedom from its preoccupations or dictates, most of which have been internalised mentally. Creating a situation or space in which to be oneself is therefore not a question of physically removing oneself from others, but of becoming psychologically detached from them. Traditionally, in both Eastern and Western societies, detachment of this kind has been cultivated through meditation.

Essentially meditation involves a complete relaxation or letting go of all notions about the self and the world, all beliefs and ideals, social expectations, demands, definitions and the tensions they generate. What emerges in this 'empty' space or void is a quality of being that is extremely difficult to comprehend because it is difficult to conceive of oneself independent of other people's expectations, demands and definitions. Although often referred to as a state of pure being, it is beyond verbal description and can only be experienced. The exercise that follows combines guided imagery with a relaxation procedure derived from traditional meditational practice.

EXERCISE 2

Find somewhere quiet and make yourself comfortable, either sitting or lying (preferably the former as the latter is likely to promote sleep).

Close your eyes, or focus with open eyes on a fixed point or object. Become aware of your breathing by inhaling through your nose and exhaling through your mouth.

With each out-breath silently say 'One' and continue to

repeat this formula, breathing in and out to the count of one.
Don't worry about achieving relaxation, simply allow this to
occur at its own pace.

Don't dwell on distracting thoughts, memories or concerns
which may arise, and do not try and suppress them. Merely
make a mental note of them and allow them to disappear.
Then return your attention to your breathing and the repetition
of the word 'one' and continue to do so for 10–20 minutes.

Now imagine that an eminent sculptor has completed a
sculpture of you and you have been given the key to the
sculptor's studio so that you can view it in private before it
goes on public show.

You find yourself standing outside the door of the studio,
key in hand. Imagine looking down at the key, noting its
features and your feelings. How eager or reluctant are you to
enter the studio? What are your thoughts?

When you have fully identified these open the door and
enter the studio, where you find the sculpture, entirely covered
by a dust sheet. As you approach it, examine your feelings and
thoughts, and remove the dust sheet. How do you feel as you
are doing so? Remove the dust sheet completely and stand
back to look at the sculpture. What is your first impression?
What do you feel about what you see? What are the most
salient or significant features of the sculpture? Note its size,
colour and the material from which it is made. Touch it and
note how it feels.

View the sculpture from every angle possible and make an
assessment of the person it represents. If you were asked to
make one observation about it what would it be? How do you
feel about the public seeing it? What, if any, aspects would you
like changed? How could these be achieved?

Before giving you the key the sculptor asked you to provide
a name for the piece. What name seems appropriate?

Having named it, decide whether or not to cover the
sculpture, and leave the room.

Now ask yourself what this experience may tell you about
you and what you can learn from it. When you have answered
these questions gradually allow your awareness to return to
your surroundings and open your eyes. Then make a verbal or

written report of your answers, together with a first person account of your experience in the present tense.

Commentary

> In oneself lies the whole world and if you know how to look and learn, then the door is there, and the key is in your hand. Nobody on earth can give you either the key, or the door to open, except yourself.
>
> KRISHNAMURTI, 1972

Although the present exercise focuses on an essentially static image, that of a sculpture, the self that is being represented thus is dynamic and changing. It therefore reveals what might be thought of as a freeze-frame of the individual as you appear to yourself at a given point in time. To the extent that you change over time, it will also change and thus repays fairly regular repetition.

Contextual features

The sculpture exercise is very rich in the imagery it evokes and the emotions thus elicited. The latter often betray an individual's attitudes towards self-awareness and exploration; and his feelings about himself. Many people describe excitement, anticipation, curiosity and impatience, which sometimes get the better of them so that they enter the studio before being directed to. Some individuals describe a mixture of anxiety and excitement or apprehension, while others simply feel anxious. Occasionally they will describe feeling 'horror' at the prospect of seeing a sculpture of themselves. One young woman expected the sculpture to be horrible because she considered herself to be unphotogenic. Indeed, many people expect that they will not like the sculpture. The comments of one woman possibly express a common fear: 'I know I'm going to hate it and be really embarrassed to think people will be looking at it and passing judgement'. Another woman, who anticipated the worst possible view of herself in the hope that she would be pleasantly surprised, found, to her horror, that the sculpture was far worse.

Anxiety about the appearance of the body is reflected in various preoccupations, such as that of the woman whose first thought about the sculpture was 'I hope the nose will be OK'. Some anticipate its appearance before they enter the studio. They claim that they know what it will be like and are frequently surprised to find that it is quite different. Such people reveal a fixed view of themselves or a certainty about themselves which is belied by the ensuing experience. Invariably their view of themselves is negative. Many who express anxiety at the prospect of confronting the sculpture do so because they fear that they will be disappointed by it, again reflecting a poor self-image. Very occasionally a person will feel anger or resentment towards the sculptor for 'invading their privacy' or 'using them' as a model. This reaction, which I have only encountered in women, is curious given that in this exercise the sculptor, the sculpture and the sculpted are all one and the same person. It is suggestive of some anger or resentment towards the self. One woman attributed her resentment to the fact that she had 'no artistic ability', suggesting that she expected the sculptor's efforts would leave something to be desired.

Intriguingly, almost everyone presumes their sculptor is male. Only one person has ever specified that the sculpture was created by a woman, which may serve to highlight the extent to which our self-images are shaped by male expectations and requirements. A minority of people describe themselves as having been sculpted by well-known figures. In some cases this is a known sculptor such as Henry Moore or Jacob Epstein, thereby suggesting that the sculpture is valuable, individualistic and worthy of attention, although it might be someone from a quite different field. One person identified the sculptor as the psychotherapist Carl Rogers, suggesting that his self-image had been shaped by Rogers's influence.

These 'incidental' features may prove to be as or more significant than the image of the sculpture itself. Context may be significant. Often it is a situation known to a person, although it may not have been thought of consciously for many years, such as a nursery or schoolroom. One woman imagined that her sculpture, which was standing on the standard plastic-topped table of a middle-school classroom would be much better situated in an open air setting such as a park. She considered this to be more significant than the sculpture itself, indicating her need to leave the artificiality of an academic environment and move into the 'big, wide world'. Another woman imagined her sculpture in a very drab situation where it would 'shine' in contrast with its dull, bleak surroundings. She recognised in this her low self-esteem and particularly her concern that, as a mature student, she may not be 'bright' enough to cope with the demands of her university degree course. Another younger student, who reported having difficulty seeing the sculpture because the lights in the studio were so dazzling and brilliant, considered this to be an indication of her difficulty in picturing herself at university. Most people describe the situation in which they imagine the sculpture to be 'ordinary', but there are exceptions. One woman who had to struggle through a beach of deep pebbles, buffeted by high winds, in order to reach hers, was puzzled as to why she had made such 'heavy weather' seeing it. Another woman, whose sculpture was housed in a pyramidal glass structure, reminiscent of the gallery at the Louvre in France, considered herself something of a 'work of art'.

For many people the door to the studio appears significant. Doors appear in every shape, size and colour, frequently as solid and very old or, just as commonly, as new and lacking substance. One man, who imagined himself standing in front of the huge heavy doors of the British Museum, realised he was dwarfed by authority and formality. One young woman considered that the black door she imagined was a sign of her sense of foreboding. Another woman described a glass door, which she considered to be an indication of her 'transparence'. Many people recognise the door as representing the point of access to their inner self and they acknowledge that its features reflect something of their attitude towards themselves. One young woman described it as the protection which stopped others destroying her. One man highlighted this function of the door by imagining that on entering the studio he turned and locked it behind himself so that no one else could gain entry. Heavily fortified doors such as those found in prisons, cold stores and ships are thus possibly indicative of defensiveness. Many clearly reflect the nature of the contents within; those described as 'safe' doors or like those in bank vaults or deposit boxes suggesting something of value, or to be treasured, whereas those described as 'cheap', flimsy or insubstantial convey a sense of there not being much of value beyond them. Prison doors suggest that perhaps less desirable, and possibly dangerous, features are 'locked away', while ship doors suggest submerged features and, in contrast to fire doors, cold store doors suggest a certain frigidity or coolness within. One woman described a padded door, thereby suggesting sound-proofed, insulated and possibly repressed contents, padded cells normally being associated with those whose behaviour is unacceptable to others. The door may be some other form of entrance or means of access, such as a wicket gate leading into a field or landscape, suggestive of openness.

There is very frequently an obvious disparity between the kind of door, the lock and the key that opens it. Medieval castle doors yield to small Yale keys and huge, ornate 'dungeon' keys often open flimsy modern panels. In some cases the door opens easily, in others with difficulty. Not uncommonly the person is anxious to find that the key does not fit the lock, and may revert to kicking or battering the door only to discover that the door is not locked and opens at a touch. It many not even require contact. One man described the door swinging open as he approached it. The means by which the door opens may also be significant as in the case of the woman who described a hydraulic door, 'which only opens under pressure'. In contrast those people whose doors push open or open easily see this as an indication of their 'openness'.

If the door is the way in to oneself, then the key 'unlocks' its hidden features. Many people attach significance to it. The woman who described a transparent glass door to the studio saw her key as a combination of numbers written on her hand which opened a circular lock in the manner of a safe. She recognised in this something of a paradox, because although she believes others 'can see through her' she also acknowledged that they do not have access to what is within and that she alone has the combination 'on hand' to do so. Hence her apparent transparency is a defence that enables others to know something of her while keeping them at a distance.

Some regard the nature of the material from which the key is made as an indication of the value they place upon it. Thus some keys are described as made from precious metals, gold, silver; or as 'jewelled'. Others find that their keys are large and heavy. Some rusty keys give the impression of not having been used frequently or recently. Many people describe difficulty inserting the key in the lock, sometimes because the two appear not to fit together. One woman saw the smallness of her key in relation to the size of the door lock as a sign of her inadequacy. Another woman described having great difficulty in turning a tiny key in a huge lock, whereas a man found his key difficult to handle, quite literally, because it constantly changed shape as he tried to use it.

Some people identify their key with certain childhood experiences or features of their life they have hidden or locked away. One woman saw her key as that to a wardrobe belonging to her grandparents and was reminded of a dress she had worn when aged six. She described feeling that some aspect of her childhood relating to her grandparents, whom by choice she rarely sees and about which she feels guilty, remains locked in the studio. Similarly, a man who found himself opening his door with a corkscrew of a kind made to open pressure-sealed bottles interpreted this as an indication that his inner self is highly pressured and could easily explode 'if shaken up'. He also remembered that his father, whom he had not seen since the age of eight, following his parent's separation when he was five, had owned this corkscrew-key. Pondering the significance of this long-forgotten key, he concluded that his view of himself was influenced by events relating to his father and that these were the key to him discovering his true self.

Having been given the key to themselves most people appear to retain it, with the exception of one woman, who reported wanting to return the key to the sculptor and, finding that she could not locate him, left it by the door on leaving.

The sculpture

Another incidental feature which may prove to be highly significant is the sheet with which the sculpture is covered. Not uncommonly this is described as a 'shroud', which suggests that whatever it covers is dead. One man described a multi-coloured modern art sculpture under a shroud that he didn't recognise as himself and 'didn't care for'. Subsequently he acknowledged that this accurately reflects his lack of self-knowledge, dislike of and lack of care for himself, claiming: 'I am screwed up like it because I don't know myself'. Others may describe the sheet as a veil, which is more or less transparent. For some people the colour of the covering is important. Black and other dark colours appear to be associated with generally negative attitudes, and white with fairly positive views. Women sometimes specify that the cover is pink, which they associate with security and protection. Indeed the colour pink is known to have subduing effects and is used for this purpose in US prisons and reformatories, which raises questions as to its traditional association with women, female babies and children.

The way the sculpture is revealed may also be significant. Some describe themselves 'exposing' it, as though bringing a scandal or crime to public notice; others reveal it more gradually, even gingerly. Some lift a corner or fold and only display the whole sculpture when they are satisfied that it is not as dreadful as they feared. Some simply refuse to remove the sheet from the sculpture, preferring to keep it and themselves 'in the dark'.

First impressions of the sculpture may be revealing in more senses than one. They are invariably of bodily characteristics and many people see themselves naked. A number of women who do so report blushing upon first seeing themselves thus. Many of those whose expectancies are quite negative at the outset are surprised, and often delighted, to discover positive physical features emphasised in the sculpture. Some are surprised and even embarrassed to discover it is much more attractive and beautiful than they perceive themselves to be in real life. This is not necessarily an idealised view but one which results from a more objective perspective. Preoccupation with features such as fat hips, lack of height, 'dumpiness', bulging stomachs and thighs, which many women admit to, become relatively insignificant when seen in the context of the whole, although this is not always the case. Obsessional tendencies may be highlighted. One young woman reported that she would only look at the face of the lifelike sculpture of herself because she knows this to be pretty and that in so doing she was unable to see her bottom, about which she has such a complex that she tries to prevent others 'scrutinising' it by always facing them. A woman who was shocked and embarrassed by the Rubens-like nude of generous proportions totally at odds with her ordinary slim appearance, subsequently revealed that dislike of her natural body shape had led her into the disordered eating pattern of bingeing and purging known as bulimia nervosa. Female dissatisfaction with their form is often very evident in their initial descriptions of the sculpture, but perhaps more surprising is the degree of acceptance and liking which emerges as these superficial features are put in greater perspective.

Only rarely are male sculptures naked and men usually report shock or surprise at seeing them thus. This may reflect social convention regarding male nudity, but it may well reveal other factors, such as their lack of confidence in and dislike of their bodies. Certainly men are as surprised as women to find themselves without physical defects. One man decided that a sculpture of a Roman emperor could not be him because it was not wearing spectacles! Another realised that his focus on the head of his sculpture represented his unhappiness with his body. Several men have been concerned by the thinness of their sculptures and one was appalled by what he described as his 'limp-wristed appearance'. As such these reactions reflect stereotypical concerns about male appearance.

Some first impressions are very significant. One woman, seeing a rear view of herself running, asked ' What am I running away from?' and subsequently was able to provide herself with answers. Another woman whose sculpture was depicted running and holding a baton as though in a relay race, realised that 'even at her stage in life' – middle age – she was always on the go, and getting nowhere. One woman, when asked what it might mean that she could see no sculpture upon removing the cover, replied 'Chicken', adding that she wanted to see herself, but was frightened to. Sometimes, however, the person is aware that the superficial features betray a far deeper reality, as in the case of the woman who saw herself as a 'dreadful mess' and wanted to lock the studio so that no one could see her.

Sometimes the sculpture represents a view of the self which the person identifies as idealistic. One young woman who was initially delighted with her sculpture realised it was 'too perfect', a superficial and hollow statue that revealed nothing of her real self. Another very pretty young woman described the sculpture as representing the ideal state she would like to attain and never will. She then admitted to worrying '24 hours a day' about her looks and also being plagued by awareness of her 'shallowness'. Her obsession with her appearance led her to repeat the exercise several times. Each time she found herself changing more and more of the sculpture, rubbing bits and pieces off it, until she finally realised that she was both figuratively and literally 'wearing herself down' with her constant concern about her appearance and her attempts to be perfect.

For some people the first impression of the sculpture gives them an insight into the way they present themselves which acts as an impetus for change, as in the case of the man who recognised that his smiling face looked false and insincere, and the woman who saw herself looking miserable and dejected, although she did not feel herself to be so.

The sculptures are as different as the people they represent. Their height is often a salient feature, with many people describing them as 'larger than life'. One man, who initially denied that an awesome and impressive steel figure was him, admitted that he did so because he found the potential it appeared to represent daunting. Some people are astonished to discover that they have to look up to themselves, which, on examination, invariably reveals that ordinarily they tend to 'put themselves down' or have a low opinion of themselves.

Some sculptures are small and this may be a reflection of the way a person 'belittles' him or herself. An example of this came from a former ballerina, whose sculpture was a miniature replica of herself in full ballet costume. She admitted that she had always longed to perform the lead in *Swan Lake*, but never had and that this tiny sculpture represented her view of herself as a failure. She believed that if she had fulfilled her potential the sculpture would have been life-size. Many women describe sculptures which are small or half-sized, or which shrink in size when the cover is removed from them. This suggests that they may perceive themselves as having failed to actualise their potential, which may be a reflection on the traditional female roles they occupy. For some small stature indicates their low self-esteem. One woman had been unaware of just how low this was until she saw a statue of herself only 18 in high.

Certainly many people equate height with a positive view of themselves. One woman who found that her sculpture was so large that she could only see its base, which depicted the hem of a skirt, imagined herself rooted to the spot staring upwards with an aching neck as she tried to see more. She interpreted this as an indication that there might be a good deal more to herself than meets the eye and identified her frustration at not being able to see it. However, although she recognised the sculpture as herself she named it 'Mother'. In doing so she realised that her neckache – a long-standing disability – lessens at times when she achieves independence from her mother, which are also the times she feels most happy with herself as a woman. She concluded that 'The sculpture fantasy indicates that this may not be coincidental'. Thus it would appear that identification with her mother prevents her from being fully aware of and at ease with herself, her femaleness and her potentials. Another woman's sculpture was a huge slab of concrete with a chipped, jagged corner. She interpreted this as showing not only her enormous potential – which she only reluctantly acknowledged – but also the enormous amount of work she needs to do 'to make anything' of herself. She claimed that because the sculptor was unable to shift or work on her material, it represented failure on a monumental scale. When it was suggested to her that this sounded like an excuse for not trying she retorted, 'No. It's just too hard'; and then revealed that she never finished anything she embarked on because she was terrified of failure. For her to try and fail was worse than not trying at all.

Another woman interpreted the elevation of her sculpture on a pedestal as indicating her desire always to catch the attention of others, while a young man saw this feature of his sculpture as an indication of his elevated status. However, one man who saw a figure of himself standing tall on three steps in the centre of a room saw this as a reflection of the 'stand-offishness' that has led to his isolation and alienation from others. Curiously one way in which people attempt to alter the standing of the sculpture they perceive is not to change its dimensions or basic structure but to change its style of dress. Hence one man who felt that the powerful Roman emperor he imagined could not be him, changed its toga, ceremonial robes and sandals into jeans and training shoes.

For some people only part of the sculpture is visible. This may be an indication that they don't see themselves very clearly, or completely. One sculpture depicting a woman's limbs without any centre was interpreted by her as indicating that she is not in touch with the core of herself; and a woman who imagined the sculpture to be without arms like the Venus de Milo, recognised this as being out of touch with her native Italy, for which she yearns. Some people who only see a head or bust of themselves consider that this may reflect their tendency to be too cerebral or intellectual, and cut off from their feelings. Some are unable to 'put a face' on the sculpture or find that the face keeps changing. This may be an indication that they have difficulty facing themselves or others, or of a tendency to 'put on a face to meet the faces that they meet', in the manner described by T.S. Eliot. Others find that the face is blank, impassive, expressionless, featureless. Others comment on the sculpture's rigidity and the way this restricts expression. For some the fact that the sculpture is unfinished suggests their unworked potential.

Not all sculptures are realistic in the depiction of their subject. One woman was delighted with a sculpture composed of cogs, springs and part of a grandfather clock, not only because it was novel and interesting, but also because it could stand in a public place and not be recognised as her. She concluded from this that she didn't want other people to know her real self and also that her grandfather was more influential in her present 'make-up' than she had realised previously. Another woman was less pleased with her futuristic non-human sculpture which she described as 'cold, hard and closed-off, just like myself'. As this suggests, there is often a profound realism in many of these apparently unrealistic images. A woman who imagined her sculpture as a modern abstract form, headless and without limbs or trunk felt that this was an important reflection of her belief that everything of importance is within her, and her greater emphasis on her heart than her head. To her this limbless form felt complete. The surreal sculpture of a naked male, standing upside down on his hands, with a chair resting on his feet, was for one man a very accurate reflection of his private self, indicating that he had regained his ability to laugh in a healthy way at the absurdity of himself and the world. Another man saw the depiction of himself as 'old' in the manner of Rodin's *Burghers of Calais* as an accurate reflection of the way he appears older and more mature than his years. By comparison a middle-aged woman who had expected to see a rounded 'Rubenesque' figure was pleased to see herself portrayed as a Henry Moore abstract with a hole through her stomach and a classical style head depicting her as she was 20 years before. She interpreted this as reflecting her concerns about being overweight and over 40. Another woman liked the amorphous shape of her sculpture because she could see it in different ways depending on her points of view, and she took this as an indication that she is largely independent of other people's perceptions of her, and that she is able to be who and what she wants, rather than shaped and moulded by others.

For some people the posture of the sculpture is revealing. They perceive resignation in their slumped shoulders; defensiveness and lack of trust in their folded or twisted arms and legs. Several describe themselves 'as all screwed up'. One young woman described her sculpture as being 'all wrapped up in itself', which she found pleasing because no one would recognise it as her. However, she shocked herself by her admission that it had been done in this way because she was too repulsive to model upright. Until then she had not fully appreciated how poor her self-image was. She revealed that she had been raped six years earlier, and had subsequently lost all confidence and self-esteem. The imagery had shown her that she still had not recovered from the experience. It also enabled her to realise how important other people's views of her appearance were to her. Another woman who saw herself reclining on a couch felt that this showed her feet are not on the ground and that she needed the couch for support, whereas a woman who saw the sculpture as free-standing, took this as an indication that she is self-supporting. Some are delighted by their open relaxed postures and expression; by the fact that they appear natural and not posed. Many realise that the impression they give is off-putting and may not represent how they know themselves to be or want to be.

The materials from which the sculpture is formed are clearly important. Many people see their sculpture as crafted in marble, alabaster, jade; valuable or semi-precious stone such as quartz, or less valuable stone. White marble is very commonly described and its ambivalent features are noted by many people, for while it suggests value, quality and substance, it is also cold, hard, somewhat severe and often featureless. Therefore some people who initially admire it later realise that it represents a coolness, aloofness or hardness they don't really like. Similarly some people appreciate that the character of these sculptures is 'set in stone' and fixed, and they dislike the rigidity and restriction implied. Some wish to be more physically expressive than this 'stoniness' allows and especially less 'stonefaced'. One man was dismayed by the featureless expression of his sculpture. He wanted it to smile, although he realised this is something he finds difficult to do. Certainly, as the writer Judith Guest has observed, 'People with stiff upper lips find it damn hard to smile'.

Others perceive the sculpture as formed from concrete or cement, which may be hard or soft, rough 'like breeze blocks' or smooth, and as considerably less valuable than marble or stone. Some are made of metals of variable hardness and density. Steel, like marble, has qualities of hardness and strength, but also shines and may be brilliant or flashy. Nevertheless 'steely looks' may not be regarded as particularly attractive or desirable. Very occasionally the material is gold. Some metals are described as hollow, and thus lacking in substance despite appearances, and others as solid. Thus bronze, which is very frequently described, differs qualitatively depending on whether it is 'cold cast' or not. Sculptures may be made of wood, which is natural rather than manufactured, forged, cast, moulded or pressed, but may be rough rather than smooth. Occasionally artificial materials such as plastic are specified. Many sculptures are formed from soft substances such as chalk, which are fragile and easily damaged. One man described a sculpture made of egg shell. Some people are aware that they, like their sculptures, are fragile, easily rubbed the wrong way or become worn down by contact with others and the environment; or as in the case of the woman referred to previously, by pressures they create themselves, such as the obsession with being perfect. Some sculptures are prone to crumble, suggesting brittleness, or leave a powdery deposit when touched, so that they 'rub off on to others'.

Clay is a very commonly described medium, which suggests pliability when wet and possibilities for change. Indeed some people, such as the man whose head was 'drying out', describe their sculptures as not 'set' or finished. One woman observed that clay takes a long time to harden and thus is preferable to terracotta, which she said 'can be shattered by one upheaval'. Thus softer, more flexible substances are less likely to suffer irreparable damage than those that are hard and rigid. A few people describe their sculpture as made of wax, which suggests pliability but also sensitivity to heat or warmth. Some people have described fleshlike substances; one young woman indicating that her apparently lifelike flesh was 'stuffed', although she did not know with what. In some cases the sculpture is composed of several different substances, so a stone figure may have real hair. One man could only see bits and pieces of himself, some of which were made of marble, and these he did not like because they were cold, hard and sharp. He felt more reassured by the wooden parts, which had a warmer feel to them.

The materials from which the sculpture is made not only determine its appearance but also its feel and to a great extent the person's feelings towards it. This may be consistent or it may not. Appearances can therefore be deceptive. Occasionally people describe touching marble and discovering that it feels like flesh. One woman who perceived a statue apparently made of cool stone described being pleasantly surprised to discover it felt like marshmallow. Moreover, she said that it felt like pink marshmallow. This synaesthesia, sensing colour by touch, is by no means uncommon, and in her case pink was associated with sensitivity and feelings. She was therefore somewhat disconcerted by the awareness that her soft, sensitive nature may be belied by a somewhat cool, hard exterior.

Similarly, some people are discomfited to realise that although their sculpture looks smooth it is sharp or prickly to the touch. Many people, especially men, feel that the hard exterior suggested by their sculpture accurately reflects the way they present themselves, although this is often not how they experience themselves 'from within', and indeed their sculptures are often soft and warm to the touch. For many the awareness that others may have to come quite close to them to appreciate these qualities is rather alarming. By comparison one woman described a gold statue which gave off a bright light so warm that it could be felt some

12 in away. Others perceive the coldness of the materials, their sharpness or rough edges as accurate reflections of themselves. One young man reported that he 'could not make out' the identity of the white statue he imagined. Upon approaching it he discovered that it was bronze overlaid with alabaster, which he likened to the pyramids of Giza whose smooth appearances belie their rough steps and edges. He interpreted these features as possibly signifying that he is cold and insensitive, as others have claimed, and he had previously denied. One woman who did not like the discovery that only the shoulders felt warm on an otherwise cold statue, recognised this as indicating that in personal relationships she is cool and remote. A woman who described her sculpture as an alabaster flame, considered it to be symbolic of the contrasting features of herself, being at once cold and warm, hard and soft, rigid and mobile.

For most people the emotional 'feelings' that their sculptures give rise to are the most important feature of the exercise. Some of the 'feelings' expressed are in fact intellectual assessments of their reactions, which serve to highlight the confusion people often experience in discriminating their thoughts from their emotions. Some people indicate that the exercise reveals their confusion about themselves. For others their feelings betray their poor self-image. One woman simply could not accept that a sculptor would use her as a model. Her belief that she is not important enough to merit such attention, and that she would be the only person who would want to look at it, reveal her lack of self-esteem and self-worth. Another woman felt dissatisfied with the sculpture of herself, wanting to straighten it so as to widen its outlook on the world and remedy its narrow, restricted vision. The sculpture usually represents the person as they perceive themselves at the present time. However, in some cases the sculpture represents an image of how the person has been in the past, but which has relevance to the present. One woman saw her sculpture as a very accurate picture of herself as she had been eight years previously when she had consciously made an important change of direction in her life. She saw this sculpture as a reminder of what she had been and what she did not want to become again.

Reactions to the sculpture vary enormously. Most people identify with it and accept it as themselves, whether or not they like it. Some do not identify with or accept it. Others realise that even though they cannot readily identify with the sculpture it is their creation and therefore says something about them. However they may initially reject certain features of it, as in the case of a woman who described her sculpture as accurate in every detail, except for the eyes, which, she claimed, belonged to someone else. She wanted to avoid looking at these alien eyes but was unable to because the sculpture rotated on a plinth so that the eyes came to rest at the same level as her own as she looked upon it. She was therefore transfixed by these eyes and felt compelled to close them. Examining this subsequently she concluded that the staring eyes reflect her 'desperation' to know what other people think of her and whether they like her or not, which often leads her to 'act out of character'. She interpreted this concern with the opinions and views of others as her failure to trust herself and to look inwards for answers. She considered that closing the eyes of the sculpture represented a step towards trusting herself more.

Reactions to and assessments of the sculptures are often reflected in the names given to them. Epithets such as 'screwed up', 'confused', 'shrinking violet', 'doormat', 'macho man', 'man of steel', 'earth mother', 'joy', 'ecstasy' are descriptive. Some are clearly negative and are generally consistent with those people who do not like what they see and want to change it, while others are very positive. A number sum up the fluctuating characteristics of the self; 'hot/cold', 'hello, goodbye', 'come-day/go-day'; and others, such as 'running scared' or 'just idling', convey characteristic reactions. The meaning of some epithets, such as 'a lie', are not clear, even to those who have applied them and they have to be explored in much the same way as the imagery they are applied to. Initially the label 'Pisces' given to the chair-balancing figure by its creator had no meaning until someone suggested to him that it is a symbol of something swimming against the tide, which summed up his unconventionality. Those people who feel quite satisfied with the sculpture and are happy to identify with it usually give it their own name or a pronoun such as 'me'.

The decision whether or not to leave the sculpture covered is also of interest. It never occurs to some people that others will look at the sculpture; they simply don't regard themselves as significant, interesting, important or worthy enough. When asked to consider their reaction to it being publicly displayed they usually don't like the idea. As has been noted, some people want to cover the sculpture and lock the door to the studio so others cannot see it. Others do not want it to be seen by others and cover it, but don't lock the studio on leaving. Some are ambivalent about this, not particularly wanting others to see it, but realising that the features portrayed are valid and significant. One man felt that the sculpture's qualities of strength and richness were undermined by its bowed stance and restricted outlook. While he felt he didn't want other people to see these features, he felt none the less that it was important for him to be reminded of them. The man who described his sculpture upside down balancing a chair on its feet felt that this reflected his own private joke; part of his inner self that he wanted to keep private and so he decided to cover it. This impulse to cover or veil the statue may suggest a reluctance to disclose the self to others, or subject it to scrutiny.

There may, however, be quite different reasons for covering the sculpture. The woman identified above who found the statue cold except for the shoulders, which were warm to the touch, left a transparent veil around the shoulders so that they could retain their warmth. One young man, who subsequently described himself as boring, covered the statue because, as he explained, 'You should always leave things as you find them', which seems laudable, except that it suggests a somewhat rigid and rule-bound attitude to life that doesn't allow for changing the status quo.

The insights into the self yielded by this exercise are frequently quite startling and revelatory. The new perspectives it affords invariably challenge existing views and definitions of the self, and often provide an impetus for change, as individuals begin to grapple with some of the issues embodied in T.S Eliot's conundrum: 'Must I be after all what you would make me?'

❧ CHAPTER THREE ❧

Steps to Health

A man is like two doves sitting in a cherry tree. One bird is eating the fruit, while the other silently looks on.

INDIAN UPANISHADS

Although we may feel the need to distance ourselves from our fellows in order to be authentic or real, contact with other human beings is as necessary to us as food and water. Indeed identification with the group is probably *the* primary human psychological survival impulse. Quite simply, human beings need each other in order to survive. Left entirely to ourselves our chances of physical survival are slim, and our chances of psychological and emotional survival even slimmer. Individually, therefore, we are not self-sufficient. We are, however, self-organising.

The gestalt approach to psychology, which considers the individual as a function of the total organism/environment field, and his behaviour as reflecting his relatedness within that field, embodies the view of man as both an individual and a social creature. Perls (1976a) observed that the individual is at every moment a part of some field which includes him and his environment, and his behaviour is a function of that whole. It is thus the nature of the relationship between the individual and the environment that determines his behaviour. If the relationship is mutually satisfactory the individual's behaviour is considered 'normal', but if the relationship is one of conflict it is considered 'abnormal'. However, 'the environment does not create the individual, nor does the individual create the environment. Each is what it is, each has

66

its own particular character because of its relationship to the other and the whole' (pp. 16–17). The individual organism and the environment are thus mutually interdependent, and 'neither is the victim of the other' (Perls, 1976a, p. 18,). The relationship between the individual and others is like that between an actor and an audience. Both need the other, each becoming meaningless in isolation. So we will return to a theatrical analogy when considering the processes that influence the development of self-concept.

AUDIENCE EFFECTS

Rehearsals during childhood prepare the individual for the parts he will play in life's drama, providing feedback on the acceptability or otherwise of his performance. Subsequently the audience adds its praise or reproof, declaring as 'queer', 'odd' or 'peculiar' those who fail to play their parts acceptably and applauding those who meet with their approval. Through these experiences the individual develops an identity or ego, which may either be fairly prestigious, leading to a positive view of himself and his worth, or quite the opposite. In many instances, where praise and reproof have been received in equal measure, the individual's view of himself is likely to be confused. Thus a person's self-esteem, the affective component of his self-concept, or how he feels about himself, is influenced by audience reaction and his assessment of how others feel towards him. If the assessment is generally favourable a person will tend to feel good about himself and will develop confidence in his performance, strengthening it, and rendering it more distinctive and authoritative. But where he perceives his performance as being poorly received he is likely to feel bad and will tend to adjust his performance to the requirements of others, suppressing those aspects which generally don't find favour and expressing those that do. While this may not attract hostility it is likely to result in a bland, undistinguished and superficial performance. Moreover, attempts to gain the approval of many different audiences are likely to give rise to conflict and confusion. Thus while the person with positive feelings as to his worth is likely to experience a sense of being in control of his performance and of well-being in it, the opposite is true for the person with a poor sense of his own worth, who has, in effect, abdicated control of his performance to the audience.

PLAYING TO THE AUDIENCE

Because people tend to value themselves as they are valued by others, social support or approval normally serves to increase self-esteem and as such is quite healthy. Indeed, social support has been found to enhance health by reducing or preventing the negative psychological consequences of stress, which can lead to lowered self-esteem, a well-recognised symptom of depressive illness, that in turn may lead to susceptibility to physical disease. Social support may therefore act as a buffer against stress. It has been shown, for example, that a close confiding relationship with a partner significantly reduces women's risk of developing depression following a major loss or disappointment (Brown & Harris, 1978). Conversely, lack of social support tends to be associated with low self-esteem and related to negative health outcomes, including mental illness, morbidity, mortality, suicide, clinical depression, anxiety and adverse stress reactions (Ganster & Victor, 1988).

However, reliance on social support in order to maintain self-esteem is potentially unhealthy. Storr (1990) indicates that most people can tolerate disappointment in one sphere of their existence without becoming deeply depressed provided the other spheres remain undamaged. Therefore, although people may mourn or experience disappointment, where they have an inner source of self-esteem they do not normally become or remain severely depressed for long. By comparison, those who rely on external sources for self-esteem are much more vulnerable, being more prone to despair and depression if anything goes wrong. 'If, at a deep internal level, a person feels himself to be predominantly bad or unlovable, an actual rejection in the external world will bring this depressive belief to the surface, and no amount of reassurance from well-wishers will, for a long time, persuade him of his real worth' (p. 19). Nevertheless, negative feedback, which appears to be more consistent with what such a person already feels about himself, is likely to be believed. Indeed, as Hamachek (1982) observes, reliance on external sources for self-esteem is ultimately self-defeating:

> We can believe what others say about us – particularly if it is positive – only when we believe that others see us as we really are. Ironically, the more successful we are at achieving indirect self-acceptance, the more difficult it is to take credit for any favourable feedback we may get. Inside we realize that the applause is simply the consequence of a successful performance: the friendly attitude we convey, but only act; the helping hand we offer but without caring; the smile we flash, but without sincerity; the agreements we offer, but without conviction.
>
> p. 7

Inevitably over-reliance on the approval of others produces an exaggerated concern for outward appearances and inauthenticity. 'It leads to anxious conformity and a tense struggle for recognition ... It leads to the fake, a mode of existence that, like a Hollywood set, is only an elaborate front with nothing but a few props to shore it up' (Putney and Putney, 1974, p. 74).

Those people who suppress rather then express themselves authentically tend to perceive the locus of control for their actions and specific events as lying outside in the situation rather than within themselves. Such people are much more likely to be concerned with establishing what others want them to do than with what they themselves want to do and to lack a sense of being in control. Indeed, as Coopersmith (1967) observes there is every reason to conclude that persons with high and low self-esteem live in markedly different worlds. People with low self-esteem are likely to be less capable than people with high self-esteem of resisting pressure to conform; less capable of independence; less creative; less likely to perform well on tasks when they know they are being observed; more likely to work harder for a person they perceive as relatively undemanding and uncritical; more inclined to feel threatened when interacting with people in authority positions or whom they regard as in some way superior; and more likely to be influenced by persuasive communication such as strong arguments, fear-arousing appeals, prestigious endorsements. They are less likely to influence others and more likely to be concerned about personal adequacy; to think negatively about themselves; to be generally less confident and happy. Those with low self-esteem, although otherwise less likely to express emotion than those with high self-esteem, are more likely to exhibit higher levels of anxiety, and to exhibit psychosomatic symptoms and feelings of depression more frequently (Coopersmith, 1967; Hamachek, 1982).

Indeed, there is evidence that perceptions of one's ability to control events are critical to mental health. Those who lack a sense of personal control generally respond less favourably to stress (Watson et al., 1990). Indeed stressful events pose a direct challenge to both self-esteem and personal control. Feelings of personal effectiveness and mastery are significant factors in successful adjustment (Bandura, 1977; Calhoun et al., 1974; Wallston & Wallston, 1982), influencing the tendency of people to adopt positive or desirable health-related behaviours and being associated with positive psychological outcomes. Thus while shaping one's performance to the requirements of others may avoid their condemnation, this is at a cost.

Quite what that cost can be has been highlighted by recent studies conducted at Johns Hopkins University which have found that bland, emotionally inexpressive people are 16 times more likely to develop cancers than those who feel their emotions intensely and express them. Indeed the stoic, self-denying personality is the most commonly cited factor in the development of cancer (Bahnson, 1975). These people tend to say that all is well with them when it is not. The vast literature on the psychological features of cancer patients characterises their personality in terms of related traits; denial, repression, strong commitment to social norms; and identifies feelings of loss and depression as antecedents to the disease.

People who repress, suppress or depress themselves may from time to time assert themselves, sometimes in explosive outbursts of aggression, against those to whom they too closely strive to conform, but as Storr indicates, after such outbursts they revert to their 'habitual overadaptation to others'. Thus the suppression of anger tends to be significantly associated with feelings of helplessness.

As we have seen, those who constantly adjust to the requirements and demands of others invariably deny their own needs
and fail to express them, and being unaware of their needs are
unable to satisfy them. The American professor of psychology,
Abraham Maslow (1968), drew attention to the unhealthy consequences of such self-denial. He viewed health in its etymological
sense as synonymous with wholeness – as the fulfilment of all
personal needs, physical, psychological and spiritual – and illness as an indication that important needs are being denied.
Accordingly, failure to meet personal needs can result in illness
which manifests at the physical level as psychosomatic disorder,
or at the psychological level as neuroses or psychoses. Moreover, illness is not merely a consequence of unmet needs but
may also be a way – for some people, perhaps the only way –
of fulfilling them.

Physical illness is frequently one of the ways in which people
attempt to manipulate others and the environment for support,
albeit not necessarily consciously. For many people illness is the
only way in which they can meet important needs, define themselves, or prevent others and the outside world encroaching upon
them. People with low self-esteem are more likely to become ill
than those with high self-esteem because illness excuses them
from poor performance and is thus a way of coping with failure
or avoiding evaluative situations (Shuvall et al., 1973). Moreover,
since illness provides an apparently legitimate and acceptable
excuse, people may exaggerate reports of illness and may actually
feel more ill when faced with situations which threaten their self-
esteem (Snyder & Smith, 1982). Indeed, apparent illness which
evokes sympathy may raise self-esteem. Duck and Silver (1992)
illustrate this claim with the case of a woman who was referred
for psychotherapy prior to amputation of an apparently paralysed
leg which had twice failed to respond to surgery and who began
to walk again after it emerged in therapy that she had such low
self-esteem she believed amputation would provide her with an
excuse for being unable to do certain things.

From this perspective much illness can be seen as a self-protec-
tive survival strategy; a means of defending the person against
threats to self-esteem, which, as the case above indicates may be
as or more crippling than physical disability. So illness may be a

useful temporary respite but it can also be a trap for those who find it is the only way to meet their needs. For such people permanent disability may be more attractive than health, although they may not be consciously aware of this. Yet closer examination invariably reveals some underlying inner dis-ease or disintegration, and that the illness represents an unconscious attempt to restore equilibrium and integrity.

BALANCING MOVEMENTS

Fritz Perls viewed health in terms of the satisfaction of needs and homoeostasis as the process by which the organism maintains its health or equilibrium under varying conditions. When a person is unable to change and fixed in an outmoded way of acting, he is less capable of meeting his survival needs, including social needs, and it is then that psychological illness arises. Like Maslow, Perls recognised that human beings have thousands of needs but appear to operate within a hierarchy of values, attending to the most dominant survival need before all others. In gestalt terms, the dominant need of the organism, at any time, becomes the foreground figure and the other needs recede, at least temporarily, into the background. The foreground is that need which presses most sharply for satisfaction, and for the individual to be able to satisfy it he must be able to sense what he needs and know how to manipulate himself and his surroundings, because even purely physiological needs can only be satisfied through interaction with the environment.

Perls observes that man seems to be born with a sense of social and psychological balance as acute as his sense of physical balance, so every movement made on the social or psychological level is in the direction of finding that balance and of establishing equilibrium between his personal needs and those of his society. For Perls the person who can live in contact with society, neither being overwhelmed by it nor withdrawing completely from it, is well integrated and has a well-established identity. As such he is self-supportive because he understands the relationship and the contact boundary between himself and society. He therefore 'renders unto Caesar the things that are Caesar's and retains for himself those things that are his own' (1976a, p. 26). For Perls, therefore, a firm sense of one's autonomous identity depends upon the ability to recognise and maintain boundary distinctions, and the establishment of equilibrium between personal needs and the demands of society. He claims that difficulties arise not from the desire to reject such balance but from misguided movements aimed towards finding and maintaining it.

These movements bring a person into serious conflict with society if through his inability to appreciate the needs of others he impinges too heavily upon them. He tends to see himself as larger than life and society as smaller, and is usually referred to as a criminal. However, when he permits society to impinge too heavily on him, to overwhelm him with its demands, to push and mould him, he is referred to as neurotic. He cannot see his own needs clearly and cannot satisfy them. He cannot distinguish properly between himself and the rest of the world, and thus tends to see society as larger than life and himself as smaller, a perception which is reflected in his low self-esteem. Indeed when presenting self-descriptive information neurotics are found to recall more negative, self-deprecatory features than non-neurotics, and to recall these before positive information (Young & Martin, 1981).

Perls indicates that all neurotic disturbances arise from the individual's inability to find and maintain the proper balance between himself and the rest of the world, and all have in common the fact that the social and environmental boundary is felt as extending too far over the individual. Society impinges too heavily on the neurotic, and his neurosis is a defensive, protective manoeuvre against the threat of being overwhelmed by the world. It is his most effective technique for maintaining balance and his sense of self-regulation in a situation where he feels the odds are against him. The neurosis may manifest psychologically or physically as psychosomatic illness. However, from the perspective of gestalt psychology, all neuroses are ultimately boundary disturbances.

More serious mental disorders such as schizophrenia also arise from a failure to make the distinction between the self and the not-self (Laing, 1960; Mahler, 1968). Moreover, at the physical level this boundary difficulty is manifested in the nature of the cancer cell, which 'in fact, acts as though it were schizophrenic' (Goldberg, 1983, p. 23). A normal cell will, in the process of growth, be impeded through contact with other cells, the separating membranes serving as a barrier against the intrusion of one cell into another. Cells are thus normally permitted to grow, and simultaneously maintain integrity of form and function. The cancer cell, however, fails to respect these boundaries and grows unimpeded by cellular contact inhibition (Lowenstein, 1966), assisted through the collusion of adjoining cells in allowing their barrier membranes to yield to this intrusion. The cancer cells are not qualitatively different from normal cells initially. Normal cells, when young, divide but remain undifferentiated, just as cancer cells do, but at this point cancer cells begin to manifest their pathology. Instead of maturing into a specialised cell with a specialised function the cancer cell remains in a state of undifferentiation. It has thus become stuck in an immature phase. 'As a cancer cell it now defies the laws that would assign it to a rightful and ordered place in the economy of the organism' (Goldberg, p. 24) and defence mechanisms come into play to protect the body from this unwelcome development. Inadequate discrimination of boundaries would therefore appear to be common to psychological disorders or 'mental' illness, and physical illness, and to function in parallel.

BOUNDARY DISTURBANCES

According to Perls boundary difficulties occur when the individual and the group experience differing needs, and the individual is incapable of distinguishing which is dominant. By 'group' Perls is referring to family, state, social circle, co-workers; any or all combinations of persons who have a particular functional relationship with one another at a given time. The individual who is part of the group experiences contact with it as one of his primary needs but problems can arise when, at the same time, he experiences a personal need the satisfaction of which requires withdrawal from the group. In a situation of conflicting needs the individual has to be able to make a clear-cut decision, either to stay in contact with the group or withdraw. If he withdraws he temporarily sacrifices his less dominant need to the more dominant one and neither he nor the environment suffers any severe consequences. When he cannot discriminate, however, cannot make a decision nor feel satisfied with the decision he has made, he can neither make a good contact or withdrawal, and both he and the environment are affected. His concentration is divided and integration is lost – thus his performance breaks down.

NEUROTIC MECHANISMS

Gestalt psychology distinguishes four primary mechanisms for dealing with boundary disturbances: introjection, projection, confluence and retroflection. It does not presume that any single confusion about the boundary, and thus any one disturbance of the balance between the individual and the environment, produces neurosis or is evidence of a neurotic pattern, although it does recognise that instances of sudden or terrifying intrusions of the environment can give rise to defensive patterns, or traumatic neuroses. The boundary disturbances behind most neuroses are much less dramatic than this. 'They are nagging, chronic, daily interferences with the processes of growth and self-recognition through which we reach self-support and maturity. And whatever form these interferences and interruptions of growth may take, they result in the development of continuing confusion between the self and the other' (Perls, 1976a, p. 32).

Introjection

Perls observes that people grow by exercising the capacity to discriminate, which is itself a function of the self/other boundary. They take from the environment and give back to it, accepting or rejecting what it has to offer. However, they can only grow if, in the process of taking, they digest completely and assimilate thoroughly. Something properly assimilated from the environment becomes theirs, to do with as they please. It can be retained, or given back in a new form, having been distilled through them. However, something swallowed whole, accepted indiscriminately, ingested but not digested, is a foreign body. It is not part of the body it is taken into even though it may appear to be so. It remains part of the environment.

> Food which is swallowed whole, which we shove down our
> gullets, not because we want it, but because we have to eat it,
> lies heavily on the stomach. It makes us uncomfortable, we
> want to throw it up and get it out of our systems. If we do
> not, if we suppress our discomfort, nausea and the desire to
> get rid of it, then we finally succeed either in painfully digesting
> it, or else it poisons us.
>
> PERLS 1976a, pp. 32–3

The psychological process of assimilation is much the same as its physical counterpart.

According to Perls the dangers of introjection are twofold. The person who introjects never gets the chance to develop his own personality because he is so busy holding down foreign bodies lodged in his system and the more introjects he has the less room there is for him to discover or express what he himself is. Introjection also contributes to personality disintegration because 'if you swallow whole two incompatible concepts you may find yourself torn to bits in the process of trying to reconcile them' (1976a, p. 34). Introjection is therefore a neurotic mechanism whereby a person incorporates into himself standards, attitudes, ways of acting and thinking, which are not truly his, in a tendency to make the self responsible for what is actually part of the environment. The boundary between the self and the rest of the world is thus moved so far inside the person that there is nothing of himself left.

Projection

Projection is the reverse of introjection. It is the tendency to make the environment responsible for what originates in the self. In projection the boundary between the self and the rest of the world shifts too much in favour of the self in a manner that makes it possible to disown or disavow aspects of personality that are considered difficult, offensive or unattractive. The person who projects uses this mechanism both in dealing with the world and himself, tending to disown those parts of himself in which the unwanted impulses arise. He confers on them an objective existence outside of himself so that they can be made responsible for his troubles without him having to face the fact that they are actually part of him. Thus, instead of being an active participator in his own life, the projector becomes a passive object, the victim of circumstance. When he says 'it' or 'they' he usually means 'I'. This tendency is evident in much illness where the person projects the illness, and often the body parts in which it arises, outside of himself, thinking and speaking of them as though they were external entities. Indeed, while for most people the sense of identity is rooted in the body, this is not always the case. 'Some feel that the body is a kind of appendage to their true self; almost an object in the external world with which they are connected but with which they do not identify. Such people actively dislike or despise their bodies' (Storr, 1990, p. 45).

Introjection and projection frequently occur together. Perls suggests that introjects usually lead to the feelings of self-contempt and self-alienation that produce projection. Introjecting the notion that good manners are more important than the satisfaction of pressing personal needs requires a person to project or expel the latter from himself. He now considers these impulses external activities. 'Like the introjector, he is incapable of distinguishing between those facets of his total personality which are really his and those which are imposed on him from the outside. He sees his introjects as himself and he sees those parts of himself which he would rather be rid of as undigested and indigestible introjects. By projecting, he hopes to rid himself of his fancied introjects, which are, in fact, not introjects at all, but aspects of himself' (1976a, p. 37).

Confluence

Confluence is when an individual senses no boundary between himself and his environment, and feels that he and it are one. This is the normal condition of newly born babies, and it may arise in moments of ecstasy, orgasm or when a person is fully absorbed in an activity. In these circumstances a person may

experience a sensation of total identification with the environment; a feeling that they have transcended personal limits and
boundaries, and merged with the whole of things. This experience
of 'wholiness' or 'holiness' is usually transitory and fleeting, and
may be regarded as a sign of health in its etymological sense
(Maslow, 1968). However, it is a sign of illness when it becomes
chronic and the individual is unable to differentiate himself from
the rest of the world. Such a person has effectively lost all sense
of boundary and of himself. Because he does not know where he
ends and others begin he can neither make contact with others
nor withdraw from them. So, when a person says 'we' it isn't
possible to determine whether he is referring to himself or the rest
of the world.

Retroflection

Whereas the person in confluence has lost the ability to draw the
line between himself and others, the retroflector does know how
to draw the line but does so through the middle of himself,
effectively dividing himself in two. He stops directing his energies
outwards in attempts to act on the environment in such a way as
to satisfy his needs. Instead he redirects his energy inwards and
substitutes himself in place of the environment as a target for his
behaviour. He therefore treats himself as he originally wanted to
treat other persons or objects, effectively splitting himself into
what Perls describes as 'doer and done to', and in so doing
becoming, quite literally, his own worst enemy. Based on this
conception of himself as two different people the retroflector
makes statements such as 'I must control myself'.

The four neurotic styles can be summarised as follows:

> The introjector does as others would like him to do, the
> projector does unto others what he accuses them of doing to
> him, the man in pathological confluence doesn't know who is
> doing what to whom, and the retroflector does to himself
> what he would like to do to others.
>
> PERLS, 1976, p. 40

These mechanisms are reflected in the use of personal pronouns. Introjection is displayed in the use of 'I' when the meaning is 'they'; projection in the use of 'it' or 'they' when the meaning is 'I'; confluence in the use of 'we' when the real meaning is in question; and retroflection in the use of the reflective, 'myself'. Dialogue is therefore a good indication of the manner in which a role is being enacted.

DIALOGUE

In a play the dialogue is normally scripted in advance, and learned by the actor before and during rehearsals. It is generally assumed that by the time he performs in public he will be word perfect, having fully memorised and internalised the script, and that this inner dialogue informs and directs his performance. While this is usually the case it is nevertheless true that during rehearsals many actors negotiate their scripts in various ways, by refusing to say certain lines, rejecting the words put into their mouths as inconsistent with or inappropriate for the character they are portraying; improvising on the written text or making ad lib remarks which are incorporated into the dialogue of the play. In this way actors make their own distinctive stamp on a performance. However, in the final analysis, by whatever means it is contrived, the script dictates the performance.

Similarly, the developing child and adolescent internalise what can be thought of as a number of lifescripts, most of them consequent upon their basic gender script, which guide their performances throughout life. Once internalised, they remain unquestioned and largely unchanged. A compilation of an individual's lifescripts amounts to what Roet (1986) terms *The Book of Shoulds*, and any individual can quote endlessly from it and its companion volume *The Book of Shouldn'ts*. These directives spring unbidden to the mind when certain situations arise and serve as guiding rules of conduct. 'I should do this', 'I shouldn't do that', 'Males shouldn't cry, they should be strong', 'Women shouldn't show anger, they should be calm?', 'I should be taller', 'I should lose weight', 'I shouldn't allow anyone to see me like this'. Admonitions such as these, which have been instilled in the past, and added to continually, usually have little or no relevance to the present, but remain firmly in mind, unexamined, as a reminder of how things should be said, done and felt. If adhered to, these outdated directives impose severe restrictions on the individual, preventing change and thus fixing their character as if it were set in stone.

The previous exercise highlights aspects of character, and in so doing also provides insight into various related factors such as self-concept, self-esteem and attitudes towards the self; the extent to which the individual's self-expression is conditional upon the approval of others and the extent to which the self is concealed. It also indicates, both implicitly and explicitly, some of the directives of an individual's lifescripts and the restrictions they impose. It may also indicate to the person not only the need for, but also the possibility of change. The difficulty for many people is, however, that they are so set in their ways that they do not know how to change and may even doubt that they are capable of it.

It is clear from clinical observations and research, especially with AIDS patients (Solomon & Temoshok, 1987), that people can and do enhance their lives by changing themselves. What this amounts to is freeing oneself from the restrictions and limitations imposed by enacting social roles and constantly playing to an audience, thereby giving expression to the aspects of the self which have been repressed in the process. This involves giving voice to these aspects of the self which normally are not heard and of which the person is largely unconscious, rather than to the scripts imposed by others.

Hypnosis is an effective means of establishing dialogue with the unconscious self. Although widely misrepresented and misunderstood, hypnosis achieves its effects primarily through deep relaxation and imagery; that is, by helping people to relax or let go of the constraints normally imposed on the mind and body by rational, conscious mental processes – the scripts they have internalised through life. Paradoxically, the process exploits one of the fundamental tenets of these scripts, which is the person's belief in the authority and expertise of others, in this case the hypnotist, and the person's willingness to comply with the hypnotist's suggestions. However, these effects are directed not towards the individual's loss of control, as such, but towards the loosening of the rigid control that their conscious mind normally exerts over their being by way of its scripts. So the person is not in any sense handing control over to the hypnotist, but rather, gaining greater self-control of his own functions. Hypnosis can therefore more properly be thought of as guided self-hypnosis, and as such it is highly appropriate to the process of self-actualisation. In the following exercise relaxation and imagery are induced by way of a self-hypnotic technique.

EXERCISE 3

Lying or sitting comfortably, close your eyes and imagine focusing them on a point midway between your eyebrows. It is advisable to remove contact lenses before doing so. If this is not possible then keep your eyes open and focus on a fixed point or object. Having done so begin silently counting backwards from 300. Do not concentrate on distracting thoughts, simply let them go and return your attention to counting downwards, matching your breathing to your counting.

Imagine that you are descending steps and on each one you are progressively letting go of a little more tension in the muscles of your body, so that you are becoming more and more relaxed. When you have reached the bottom of these steps imagine that you are in an underground railway station, standing at the top of a very long descending escalator which is at a standstill so that in order to descend you have to walk down the steps. You begin to do so, descending slowly because the steps are steep and you find yourself silently counting each one of them. After a while you stop counting as you become aware of feeling tired and heavy.

Pausing for a moment you realise that an adjacent escalator is moving downwards and as you look over towards it you become aware of a figure drawing level with you. As it does so it turns momentarily towards you and you recognise it as yourself. What is your reaction? Note your feelings and thoughts as you see yourself, and also details of your appearance, dress, facial expression and manner. Then follow this figure, observing its behaviour as you do so and take the opportunity to speak to it. Notice how this *alter ego* responds as you try to engage it in conversation, and of your impressions and feelings. If you are able to, arrange a future meeting, then part. Having done so you step on to an upward moving escalator, which carries you quickly to the surface, where you open your eyes and return to normal awareness.

Take time to record your experience and any insights derived from it in the first person present tense. Pay close attention to any dialogue between yourself and your double, noting any messages, information or advice conveyed by the latter, and your reactions.

Commentary

Many people are attracted to hypnosis in the mistaken belief that it does not involve them doing anything because they are in the control of the hypnotist. Attitudes to hypnosis are therefore often indicative of an individual's feelings about and perceptions of self-control. When they learn that hypnosis is not being under someone else's control some people are disappointed. Following the above exercise one woman expressed profound disappointment, indicating that she had wanted to be hypnotised because she thought that emotionally she could only cope with a process 'where someone unlocked my consciousness in a state I would be unaware of, emptying it of all grief, bitterness and dark thoughts', and by which she could be rid of trauma without experiencing her hurt again. Another woman expressed disappointment because she wanted to do something outrageous, and abdicate all responsibility for her actions to someone else. Other people are similarly dismayed because they hope hypnosis will 'make' them feel different.

Elements of the exercise also highlight issues of self-control. Some women report being anxious about descending the escalator, admitting to feeling out of control on escalators in 'real' life because of their fears that they may suddenly drop downwards or descend at a very sharp angle. This indicates the extent to which fears and anxieties that are part of our normal, everyday 'scripts' influence and even restrict behaviour at a fantasy level. Men may also share this fear but because of their scripts are very unlikely to articulate it. Although in my experience this anxiety has never prevented a person completing the exercise, it nevertheless influences attitudes to it. In much the same way, a woman who admitted being worried about reaching zero when counting downwards 'because of what might happen then', betrays a view of herself as the passive victim of fate, rather than as a self-determining agent. Another woman reported not wanting to move downstairs because she felt 'nice' where she was. Such a reaction suggests complacency, which frequently is a defence against change; and, when further scrutinised, often betrays a fear that change is beyond one's control, imposed from without rather than directed from within. A man admitted continuing to count the steps as a way of ignoring the other directions, even though he felt foolish and childish. In so doing he realised that his fear and self-doubt about what he might have to confront had complete domination over him and left him 'no choice but to opt out in this way'. A woman who initially enjoyed the exercise because descending stairs had been a favourite childhood pastime became more and more displeased as she went on, and the steps seemed to become steeper and steeper. She explained later that she does not like difficulties in life, especially when they are unexpected, because she might not have learned to cope with them.

Initial reactions to the exercise may also indicate a person's poor self-concept and self-esteem. One woman reported being unable to imagine herself on the escalator, although she was able to see the figure of a young blonde woman on the adjacent escalator. By the time she had realised that it was herself as she had been some 20 years previously, the figure had passed by and she was only able to see the back of its head. She therefore followed, calling out to it, and when it turned she was struck by its beauty and smile, but also by the fact that it looked blank and without signs of recognition. The woman decided that this blonde was 'dumb, stupid, empty-headed and brainless' but friendly, and so wanted to wave her hands in front of her face and shout 'Can you see me' in an attempt to gain her attention. When later she described her experience it was suggested that her dismissive account of the blonde was perhaps unfair; that as she had not experienced herself on the escalator perhaps 'she' wasn't there, or was invisible, and could only be heard and not seen, hence the reaction of the younger version of herself. This struck a chord with the woman, who in the previous exercise had not imagined a sculpture of herself but a huge slab of cement with a chipped jagged corner. She had taken this as an indication that she had an enormous amount of work to do in order to make anything of herself and had later admitted that she had never finished anything she had embarked upon because she was terrified of failure. The present exercise led her to conclude that she had been unable to imagine herself on the escalator because she had not begun to define herself and so was effectively invisible. Several other women have reported seeing 'no one' or 'nothing' on the adjacent escalator, only to reveal subsequently that what they have seen is their 'ordinary' self, which they have dismissed as not worth mentioning. Often they discount this because they believe they *should* imagine something more interesting.

As one young woman descended the stairs they became steeper and steeper, and she shrank. By belittling herself in this way, not only could she not see herself on the adjacent escalator, but, as the steps became more cliff-like in relation to her shrinking self, she also began to fear 'teetering over the edge'. This imagery suggests that the woman (who in the previous exercise fled on seeing the undefined 'mess' of her sculpture) is in danger of being overwhelmed totally by her situation, and of breakdown if she is unable to maintain her grip on the edge or boundary between herself and the world. Another woman who described being unable to see her alter ego nevertheless had a very useful chat with it, in the course of which she learned some very significant things. When asked whether her inability to see her double might indicate a reluctance to face up to herself she wholeheartedly concurred, indicating that while she is prepared to accept the status quo and the aspects of herself she is comfortable with, she does not want to face up to the possibility of change or of confronting unfamiliar aspects of herself.

Another woman, however, interpreted the facelessness of her alter ego as an indication that she does not know herself. An intriguing variation on this theme was presented by a woman who perceived the face of her alter ego completely swathed in bandages and was only able to recognise it as herself from the very distinctively coloured boots worn by this figure. In observing that it looked 'like a mummy', she suggested that the aspects of herself it embodied were obliged to 'keep mum', being able to see and hear, but not speak. She concluded that it might now be the time to 'take the wraps off' these features and give expression to them. Several other people, including a number of men, have reported being unable to see the face of the figure on the adjacent escalator and taken this as an indication that they cannot face themselves. In this connection most people describe being unable to 'face up' to themselves, suggesting that their ordinary or 'actual' self is in some sense inferior to it. Indeed one man saw a very superior being – the pilot of an extra-terrestrial spacecraft – whom he knew to have terrific wisdom, including knowledge of all his problems and their solutions. He was alarmed and saddened by the speed at which this figure was moving away from him, because he wanted to sustain contact with it. Although this being didn't speak it communicated telepathically 'carry on going', suggesting to him that he should not give up in his attempt to make further contact with it and benefit from its wisdom.

Reactions to the other self or alter ego are very mixed. Many people can be observed smiling during the exercise and report afterwards their surprise at the self they have encountered, and what they have learned from it. About two-thirds of the reactions are favourable. Many people are surprised by the energy and vitality of the alter ego. Some see themselves as vivacious, energetic, determined and more youthful, even childlike. Upon seeing herself some 20 years younger, aged about 20, wearing casual clothes and carrying a backpack, one woman felt envious of this energetic character who was free to go where she felt unable to. Indeed, when invited by her double to accompany her, she declined saying she was too old, only to have the younger self grab her hand and take her along with her. The woman reported that she felt liberated by this experience and very much better than she had prior to the exercise. A young woman who saw herself younger, in 'fun clothes', asked the advice of this lively, laughing figure, and was told to 'live life' and not be so serious about it. Similarly, a young man who in the previous exercise had interpreted his statue as an indication that he had 'not made much' of himself, was told by his alter ego, 'get out there and grab at life.

Make something of yourself. You have it in you'. Another young man, seeing his alter ego descending on the moving escalator, found himself thinking 'How come he's speeding along, getting on fast and I'm struggling along', at which point the other self waved to him cheerily. On catching up with him at the bottom of the escalator, and verbalising his earlier thoughts, he was told, 'If you had stopped to look and read the signs at the top of the escalator you would have seen that one was out of order and the other working, and would have made faster progress'. He realised that by rushing into things without thought or attention he often made matters difficult for himself and that the advice implicit in his alter ego's comment,' less haste, more speed', was highly appropriate.

One young woman described herself descending the elevator like Alice in Wonderland, feeling annoyed when she realised that she was on the non-operational escalator while her alter ego was on the working one and thinking 'It always happens to me'. Upon catching up with herself at the bottom of the escalators she initiated conversation by asking the time and initially was unimpressed with the reply, 'Just relax', although this was said in a casual and friendly manner. It was only much later that she recognised its significance, and wrote: 'I know that if I don't slow down I'll burn out but it's hard to put that into operation sometimes. It is curious to wonder if I was not Alice at all but a certain White Rabbit who is always late'. Another woman, seeing her alter ego descending quickly on the adjacent escalator climbed on to it and realised in so doing that she is always trying to 'keep up' by failing to keep to the strict deadlines she imposes on herself. By comparison, a man whose alter ego asked him to climb over to his escalator so that he might travel more quickly declined to do so, explaining later that although he tends to fall behind with his work he refuses to be rushed. Another man who was dashing down the escalator as quickly as possible was advised by his alter ego to 'slow down and take it easy', but he ignored him and pressed on regardless. He later admitted that because he believes he should be achieving he is constantly 'on the go' and pushes himself too hard in the race to get on. This pressure to 'get on' in life is very evident in the accounts of many men and reflects their belief that they *should* achieve, whereas in many cases women's accounts reflect the opposite belief that they should not achieve, are too old, or incapable of doing so. Not uncommonly women appear to believe that while they should not necessarily *do* anything, they should *be* perfect.

One young woman attributed the vagueness in her description of her alter ego to the fact that she had deliberately not looked at it in case it was less than perfect and she could see defects that might shatter her illusions about herself. Similarly, she had not tried to engage it in conversation because she did not want to hear any 'home truths'. Another woman described her horror at the prospect of seeing herself because she tended to compare her actual self with an ideal or perfect self that she believed to be her alter ego. On seeing the latter she felt anger, but decided to suppress this and be friendly, so reached out and touched it on the arm. She was delighted when it replied positively with the message 'You're OK'. This made her realise that it might be easier to get on with herself if she were not so judgemental and self-critical, and she wrote herself another lifescript – 'You're OK.', instead of her usual 'You're not OK'. She subsequently discovered that by not expecting perfection from herself she was more relaxed and approachable.

Another woman discovered that by accepting the parts of herself she had previously hated she had effected a healing. This woman saw her alter ego as a child of seven or eight years of age wearing a white nightdress. When she spoke to the child it was to tell her simply 'You're OK' and she received a smile in reply. This was of great significance to this woman, who between the ages of seven and nine had been subjected to sexual abuse by her aggressive older brother, who had threatened to kill her if she told anyone. This, and her belief that no one would believe her, had led her to remain silent about the abuse until she was 16, when she told her mother about it and was disbelieved until the brother finally admitted it 2 years later. Before this exercise she had hated the part of her that 'didn't tell anyone, and let everything happen', the part she used to blame. So she was delighted to see this childish part of herself smiling in response to her affirmation, wearing a white nightdress, which she saw as a sign of innocence as opposed to the dirtiness she had long attributed to herself.

Some people are surprised by the obvious confidence of their alter ego or its other positive features. A woman whose statue in the previous exercise had appeared very depressed, was pleasantly surprised to see a 'lovely cheerful' figure in bright clothes on the adjacent escalator. She recognised it as how she used to be and how she would now like to be. Together they went for a day's pleasure trip, which made her feel 'great' and very happy. However, she later doubted the validity of the image, questioning whether she was deluding herself into thinking that being herself could be so easy. When asked what makes it so difficult to be herself, she realised that she normally stops herself feeling 'great' by putting herself down. A young woman who saw her other self as larger than life, bigger, brighter, luminous, sparkly and with an angelic quality, described her reaction as 'Gosh!', but felt jealous of this being who seemed self-confident without being arrogant, very happy, self-accepting and free from pressure.

Some people do not like the figure they see on the adjacent escalator or are afraid of it, which may reflect their dislike or fear of those aspects of themselves that are normally repressed. Many believe that these shadowy aspects of themselves are undesirable and best avoided. A young woman who described being frightened descending the escalator in the dark indicated that this may be because she feels able 'to shed little light' on herself. Although unable to see her alter ego she sensed it next to her, describing it as 'a featureless black orb in a monk's cowl', which she would not engage in dialogue, preferring to remain in the dark about this unknown and frightening aspect of herself.

Another woman who saw a little woman dressed in black initially reacted fearfully to this image of herself, thinking it might signify death. However, this gave way to her feeling the strong presence of her dead mother and as she did so her alter ego asked her to look at herself, whereupon she did so and discovered that she was a child. Her alter ego observed that she had now outgrown childhood and was, like her, adult, and it was time for them to merge. They did and the woman subsequently described feeling 'great', and knowing that a real healing had taken place as she integrated these formerly separate aspects of herself. Another woman reported initially being terrified of her alter ego, claiming it was 'mad', rushing past her into the distance. Nevertheless, despite being scared by it she found herself calling out 'Just a minute. Where are you going?' in a challenging voice. As she did so she realised that she didn't sound in any way fearful or timid, although this was how she normally thought of herself and that she did not sound very inviting either. This surprising awareness led her to recognise that she repressed certain aspects of herself because of her authoritarian 'personality'.

Some people are disappointed by the appearance of their alter ego. One woman who saw herself in her usual clothes, described her reaction at how bland, dull and unimaginative she looked as 'Yuk!' During the exercise she began to accept herself, despite her apparent dullness and to feel comfortable with it. However, when later she compared her alter ego with that of others during group discussion, she returned to her original assessment of herself, revealing her beliefs about what she 'should' be rather than acceptance of herself as she is.

Some people react tearfully, although not necessarily emotionally, to this exercise. Perplexed by having burst into tears while feeling no sadness whatever, one woman repeated this exercise on going to bed one night. She fell asleep in the course of it but in her ensuing dream was told by someone she could not identify that what she needed was grievance counselling, not bereavement counselling. On waking she realised that this was quite true and that she needed to shed anger not tears following the death of her partner. This incident highlights a common experience, that people are frequently unaware of the true nature of their needs and misled by others into thinking they are quite different to what they really are. The belief instilled by others that a person should feel sadness after a loss, especially a bereavement, usually prevents a person examining their true feelings. However, if articulated, the latter might be along the lines, 'If he were alive now I'd kill him', reflecting the anger a person may feel about the grief occasioned by a loved one's death; the difficulties it has led to, such as responsibilities for dependants; or how the loss occurred, such as reckless, risky or selfish behaviour, or suicide. This woman's experience also shows that our real needs and feelings are often communicated to us in dreams, another vehicle for imagery, and that when a person begins to stimulate their imagination through exercises like these this is often reflected in their dreams, which may become richer in imagery, more vivid, frequent and memorable. So if you are interested in and committed to discovering yourself fully you can work with your dreams as profitably as imaginary exercises, and in just the same way (see Chapter 11).

Many people find themselves acting impulsively toward their alter ego, often feeling urged to ask its advice on specific or more general issues. A woman who felt impelled to embrace an identical alter ego, found on doing so that this changed into an older woman, who seemed strong, serene and wise, and advised her 'to make the best of what you have now'. Such advice is mostly regarded as highly significant and appropriate, but sometimes it may seem unremarkable and even trivial. One man initially considered his conversation with himself quite banal. He first enquired 'How are you?' and received the reply 'I'm really well'. It had not occurred to him that he might need to know this information, although he admitted that he often worried that he might not be 'all right'. Some receive advice or information from themselves and disregard it, as did the man who failed to slow down when advised to by his alter ego. One young man saw himself engrossed in reading a book as he descended the steps of the escalator and, resenting the arrival of his alter ego on the adjacent escalator, he refused to speak to him. Nevertheless his other self spoke to him, telling him that he lacked energy because he wasn't using it correctly. The young man ignored him and carried on reading, only to question later whether reading and study represent an escape from himself, and whether they are an appropriate use of his energies.

A number of people find their attempts to engage their alter ego in conversation fail. In some instances, as has been noted, this is because it seems to be retreating from the person's authoritarian or didactic manner. Some people are quite alarmed to glimpse themselves only briefly. One woman described excitedly chasing after herself 'as though I hadn't seen her for years'. Many experience a sense of loss or sadness, which spurs them to follow the figure and establish contact with it. It may take them some time to do so, however. One woman imagined following herself, with some difficulty, through the crowds at Leicester Square tube station and through the streets of London before finally managing to catch up with herself in a coffee shop in Covent Garden, where she was pleasantly surprised by the friendly response she received; while a young man had to run miles over undulating countryside in order to receive the enigmatic comments of his quarry. Some people follow their alter ego, observing its behaviour before making contact. One woman reported watching hers in a bookshop, noting what books she selected before speaking to it. Others, however, feel a sense of relief when they lose themselves in the crowds or distance. To her great surprise, one woman burst into tears when she saw herself draw away in this manner, but felt no sadness. Puzzled by this she invited the observations of fellow group members, who suggested that while consciously she might be cutting herself off from feeling emotion, unconsciously she might be reacting to the loss of some aspect of herself. Subsequently she realised that she had never fully expressed grief at the death of her father during childhood, telling herself what she had been told by others, that she would have come to terms with it.

Some cannot think of anything to say and experience a sense of panic as they realise that they may miss an opportunity to establish contact with themselves. One man described feeling very embarrassed when, having greeted his alter ego, he had no idea of what to say because they did not know each other. This concerned him because he realised that if he were in touch with himself communication and understanding would be easier. Just as anxiety may prevent inner dialogue, denial also occurs, as in the case of the man who insisted that the person he imagined on the opposite escalator was not an aspect of himself but someone imposed from outside; or the woman who emphatically denied that the identical person on the other escalator was her because she couldn't see herself as such a 'smart' person.

Sometimes it is the alter ego that initiates conversation, as in the case of a woman who was asked somewhat aggressively 'Why don't you play any more?' Instead of expressing surprise she found herself promising to do so and becoming aware that she was angry with herself for not having played her saxophone for 18 months. She realised that since beginning to study music, playing had become a pressure rather than a pleasure, and emphasis on style and technique – on what she should and should not do – prevented her expressing herself. Previously, playing the instrument had released emotions she found difficult to express verbally, and resuming play after the exercise helped her greatly in dealing with emotions of sadness and depression. Another woman, who described being frozen rigid and unable to speak but desperate to listen to her alter ego when it reached out and touched her, experienced total dismay when the escalator moved on after momentarily stopping alongside her. As they drew apart she heard her alter ego say 'Just listen to yourself', whereupon she raced down to catch her up and spent some time discussing her worrying addiction to cigarettes and need for self-control. She found subsequently that, without consciously trying, she had reduced appreciably her heavy smoking habit.

Some people report that the alter ego gives them insight as to how they appear to others by reflecting their usual manner and behaviour. In this way they have recognised their aloofness, stony faces, coldness, 'shortness' and 'sharpness' towards others; features which invariably reinforce the impression conveyed by their sculpture in Exercise 2. These features have to be overcome before they can establish contact and dialogue with themselves, and sometimes there are indications of conflict and hostility. One young woman felt that she was 'courting' her alter ego, who appeared to be 'playing hard to get'. Clearly, some people are not at ease with themselves and don't want to have to reconcile their different features. Others are surprised to find that they like themselves and to discover how well they get along together. As one woman explained, 'It is almost as though I have a good friend in myself'. Some feel bereft when, after establishing contact with themselves, they are directed to part. Some simply refuse to. Others make arrangements to meet again or stay in contact. Many determine to become firm friends with themselves. Some, however, prefer to remain strangers and to keep their distance, believing perhaps that:

> To approach the stranger is to invite the unexpected. It is to start a train of events beyond your control.

T.S. ELIOT

CHAPTER FOUR

Understanding Dis-ease

> Life can only be understood backwards but it has to be
> lived forwards.
>
> KIERKEGAARD

Friends are persons well known to each other, and regarded with liking, affection and loyalty. They are:

> people who are liked, whose company is enjoyed, who share interests and activities, who are helpful and understanding, who can be trusted, with whom one feels comfortable, and who will be emotionally supportive.
>
> ARGYLE & HENDERSON, 1985. p. 64

Friendships are generally assumed to be established on the basis of mutual liking and esteem. However, friendship is determined by various other factors, both personal and situational, notably proximity, familiarity and similarity. People who are 'close' or similar to each other physically, socially and psychologically, and thus fairly alike in appearance, interests, attitudes and personality tend to be friends, as do people who are spatially close and see each other fairly frequently. So you tend to become friends with people who live or work nearby. Proximity increases familiarity, which, rather than breeding contempt as we are led to expect, increases liking (Zajonc, 1968). We tend to like what we know and many friendships do not survive distance.

Another widely held misconception is that opposites attract.

They don't. Friends tend to be like each other and to like being with each other, most probably because by validating and providing support for each other's opinions, beliefs, attitudes, preferences, choices and feelings, they bolster their self-esteem.

A further factor in the development of friendship is self-disclosure; baring one's soul – making one's real self known or visible to another (Jourard, 1971). Mutual self-disclosure, whereby people allow each other to know one another apace, is a feature of successful friendships and marriages. Accordingly, people who know, identify with and accept each other tend to become friends. This is also true of those people who are on friendly terms with themselves. They are likely to be familiar and in touch with themselves; self-accepting; to have positive self-regard and self-esteem.

STRANGE SYMPTOMS

It is clear, however, from Exercise 3, that many people do not possess these features. They are not in touch with or accepting of themselves; having low self-regard and placing little value on their own worth. As a result many people are self-alienated; strangers to themselves. Furthermore, many do not want to make their own acquaintance. It is perhaps true to say that the majority of people are not on the best of terms with themselves. Indeed, as the psychologist Sidney Jourard (1971) observed, self-alienation is so widespread that no one recognises it.

Carl Jung referred to the 'alien' or 'stranger' within us as the 'shadow', describing it as the personification of everything we refuse to acknowledge about ourselves: 'the inferior part of the personality, the sum of all personal and collective psychic elements, which because of their incompatibility with their chosen conscious attitude, are denied expression in life and therefore coalesce into a relatively autonomous "splinter personality" with contrary tendencies in the unconscious' (1972, p. 417).

Jung observed that people tend to view their shadow as sinful or evil, and try and rid themselves of it, most usually by projecting their faults on to others. However, as he indicated, the shadow has many positive features, such as normal instincts, appropriate reactions, realistic insights and creative impulses.

Nevertheless, fearing its apparent strangeness and menace, people tend to defend themselves against it in various ways. One defensive reaction is repression, whereby potentially painful or dangerous thoughts and desires are excluded from consciousness. It is well illustrated by Laing's account of a very embarrassing experience that occurred when he was 13 years old.

> About two minutes after it happened, I caught myself in the process of putting it out of my mind. I had already more than half forgotten it. To be more precise, I was in the process of sealing off the whole operation by forgetting that I had forgotten it. How many times I had done this before I cannot say. It may have been many times because I cannot remember many embarrassing experiences before that one, and I have no memory of such an act of forgetting I was forgetting before thirteen. I am sure this was not the first time I had done that trick, and not the last, but most of these occasions, so I believe, are still so effectively repressed that I have still forgotten that I have forgotten them.
>
> 1978, p. 87

To all intents and purposes, therefore, these aspects of the self are lost or hidden away out of awareness. Indeed, Jung considered that repression of the self leads to one-sided development and eventually to neurotic dissociation. Jung thus conceived of psychotherapy as concerned with helping a person to explore the hinterland of his mind, and to grow by confronting and making contact with the dissociated aspects of himself. He claimed that assimilation of the shadow, 'gives man body', making him substantial, whole and therefore healthy, and that in order for the shadow to be confronted it must be brought into consciousness so it can be recognised. The alien must therefore be brought into the open, as it were. Otherwise, 'if this rediscovery of . . . wholeness remains private, it will only restore the earlier condition from which the neurosis i.e. the split-off complex, sprang' (1954, Vol. 13, p .238).

The goal of Jungian psychotherapy is therefore 'not merely intellectual recognition of the facts with the head but confirmation by the heart and the actual release of emotion' (Vol. 16). However, as Hamachek (1972, p. 18) observes, 'we utilize defence mechanisms to change the so-called 'facts' so that the self is protected'. These defence mechanisms have to be overcome if the suppressed emotion is to be released.

DEFENCES AGAINST DIS-EASE

Various mechanisms are thought to operate within the psyche to defend the person against the threat that the inner alien or shadow poses to his integrity and sense of personal worth. These defence mechanisms or 'devices to avoid becoming known' (Jourard, 1971, p. 32), include repression, confluence, introjection, projection and retroflection, which have been examined above and previously (see Chapter 3); and also a number of others, some of which are relatively simple, while others are more complex, involving two or more operations.

BECOMING AN INVALID

Laing considered the principal functions of all these operations to be the production and maintenance of experience that is at best desired, at least tolerated, by others, most notably within the family. These operations, which inevitably lead to self-alienation, are therefore done by a person to himself in response to others. This, according to Laing, is because every relationship implies definition of the self by the other and definition of the other by the self. This is achieved through the attribution of characteristics to a person, which, by telling him what he is, i.e. 'good' or 'bad', define him. Thus a person's own identity cannot be completely abstracted from his identity for others.

By indicating what a person is, these attributions are 'in effect, an instruction for a drama: a scenario' (Laing, 1978, p. 71), which casts him in a role. Thus a child might be cast as 'naughty' in a particular family drama. As Laing indicates, such a drama is a continuous production, hence motives, agency, intention and experiences are attributed to the child in this role all the time. In this way attributions facilitate the development of a sense of self or self-identity, because what others attribute to him implicitly or explicitly necessarily plays a decisive part in forming the child's sense of his own agency, perceptions, motives and intentions. However, they may also undermine development of a sense of self when they convey contradictory or paradoxical identities, because 'it is difficult to establish a consistent identity for oneself, that is, to see oneself consistently, if definitions of oneself by others are inconsistent or mutually exclusive' (1972, p. 87). To 'fit in with' or repudiate them all may be impossible, and so conflict and confusion is inevitable.

Some attributions can be confirmed or otherwise by the person. You can reject another's claim that you are lying by stating that you are not, but there are some attributions which you cannot confirm or disconfirm yourself, such as whether or not you are 'worthless' and their validity can only be tested by seeking the consensus of others.

Laing pointed out that total confirmation of one person by another is an ideal possibility seldom achieved, but all interaction is more or less, and in different ways, confirmatory or disconfirmatory. Confirmation or disconfirmation can be by way of speech, a look or facial expression, touch or gesture, by listening or not listening; and can vary in intensity, extensity, quality and quantity. Thus cool, 'lukewarm', imperious or disdainful reactions endorse certain aspects of a person, while failing to endorse others.

The qualities and capacities confirmed or disconfirmed by parents, siblings, friends and other significant acquaintances may differ widely, so that an aspect of yourself negated by one person may be endorsed by another. Moreover, there may be different periods in life when you experience more confirmation or disconfirmation than at others. Indeed, 'at different periods of life, the practical or felt need for, and modes of confirmation or disconfirmation vary, both as to the aspects of the person's being in question and as to the modes of confirming or disconfirming particular aspects' (Laing, 1972, p. 100). Therefore responses adequate to an infant will not be appropriate to an older child or adult.

If one's self doesn't receive confirmation through its contacts with others, or if the attributions others ascribe to it are contradictory, it becomes untenable and it may break down. Ultimately, therefore, those aspects of the self not endorsed or validated by others become invalid and the person becomes an invalid rather than a fully functioning autonomous being.

Jourard (1971, pp. 183–4) describes the process as follows:

> When roles and/or self-concepts exclude too much 'real self', a
> person soon experiences certain symptoms, viz. vague anxiety,
> depression and boredom, and if the person has come to neglect
> the needs and feelings of his body, then such physical symptoms
> as unwarranted fatigue, headache and digestive upsets will
> arise. In short, failure or inability to know and be one's real
> self can make one sick. In extreme cases, where the real self
> has been well-nigh strangulated, it may happen that there is a
> 'breakthrough', and the person suffers a 'nervous breakdown'.

Accordingly, self-alienation or dis-ease with the self is ultimately the cause of ill-health and invalidity. Certainly this is the view of psychotherapist and healer Barbara Brennan, who observes (1987, p. 110), 'The basic malady I have found in all the people I have ever worked with is self-hatred. Self-hatred is, in my opinion, the basic inner illness in all of us'.

Some people are more sensitive than others to not being confirmed by their fellows. Laing (1972, p. 106) observed that if someone is *very* sensitive in this respect, they stand a good chance of being diagnosed as 'schizophrenic'. He indicated that in many families there is little genuine confirmation of parents by each other and of the child by each parent, separately or together, and interactions are marked by pseudo-confirmation; by acts that masquerade as confirming but are counterfeit. A false, rather than actual self, is confirmed. Features or aspects of a child that are 'false' may be confirmed actively and persistently by one or both parents, or even by all significant others at the same time. Thus what is confirmed in the child is counterfeit; it is inauthentic, not genuine. As Jourard suggests therefore, the crucial 'break' in schizophrenia is with *sincerity*, not reality. Accordingly, the characteristic family pattern of schizophrenics:

> . . . does not so much involve a child who is subject to outright

neglect or even to obvious trauma, but a child who has been subjected to subtle but persistent disconfirmation, usually unwittingly. For many years lack of genuine confirmation takes the form of actively confirming a false self, so that the person whose false self is confirmed and real self disconfirmed is placed in a false position. Someone in a false position *feels guilt, shame or anxiety at not being false.* Confirmation of a false self goes on without anyone in the family being aware that this is the state of affairs.

LAING, 1972, p. 100

Indeed, as Jourard observes, 'Day after day for years, family members go to sleep with their family drama patterned in one way, a way that perhaps satisfies none – too close, too distant, boring, suffocating, – and on awakening next morning, they reinvent the same roles, the same relationships, the same plot, the same scenery, the same victims' (p. 104).

Any attempt to change oneself within such a set piece is likely to prove very difficult, as Jourard (1971, p. 105) explains,

> If I begin to change my ways of being myself, I feel strange; I feel I am not myself. The different ways of being may make me anxious or guilty. And so I revert to the familiar, but stultifying, ways of being myself. If I persist in my efforts to reinvent myself, they may become angered or affrighted. They don't recognise me. And they may punish me in ways at their disposal for changing a part of their world – viz., myself – without first 'clearing it' with them. Much invaluable growth and change in persons has been invalidated and destroyed by the untoward reactions of well-intentioned others.

REGAINING SELF-CONTROL

Each of us gives away authority over ourself to others to the extent that we rely on their confirmation, endorsement or validation of our thoughts, feelings, actions, beliefs and opinions. This means that others have authority and power over us, and that we are not fully in control of ourselves and our lives.

Caroline Myss (1991) insists that most people compulsively give authority away to others, always looking to them for approval, advice and guidance, because they neither like nor trust themselves and are not accustomed to listening to themselves with any respect. They therefore listen to and trust others, who are often in no better position themselves. Ironically, therefore, they are listening 'to data from people who aren't listening to their own data'.

Myss observes that most people don't consider themselves worth listening to because they lack self-esteem. She therefore defines self-esteem as the ability to listen to oneself and recognise its authority. More fundamentally, perhaps, self-esteem is considering yourself worth listening to. It determines the extent to which you are in control of, and have authority over, your life. Failure to listen to your own data or self-knowledge, and to follow your own advice and instructions – literally, your in-tuitions – leads to disempowerment and dis-ease.

Jourard has indicated the way in which failure to listen to oneself leads to the neglect of bodily needs and thus to sickness, both physical and mental. Similar observations have been made by researchers in the health field whose experience leads them to the conclusion that people who suffer from serious illnesses such as coronary heart disease typically ignore or undervalue their intuition and that cancer patients may have become completely cut off from their inner resources. Certainly many of those who have recovered from such conditions view their illness as, in part, a message to pay more attention to their unconscious self and its needs rather than the demands of others (Simonton et al., 1978).

Accordingly taking control of your life and of your health involves acquiring self-esteem, which amounts to taking power back from outside yourself and thus effectively shifting your locus of control from the outer world to the inner. In order to take power back to yourself, every circumstance and situation that disempowers you has to be dealt with. Regaining self-control thus necessitates confrontation with the world which has power over you in order to establish where you lose power and why; and how you give it away to others. Myss describes the process as identifying the voices that have control over you and allowing your own voice to emerge. Berne (1974, p. 26) has indicated that these voices, or scripts, as he termed them, are usually based on childlike illusions which may persist throughout an entire lifetime. He noted that in some people these dissolve one by one, leading to various crises including the adolescent reappraisal of parents, the often bizarre protests of middle age and the emergence of personal philosophies after that. In others, however, overly desperate attempts to maintain the illusions in later life lead to depression, while the abandonment of all illusions may lead to despair. In order to gain control of your life it is therefore necessary to dissolve these illusions by confronting them directly.

The first step in initiating self-control is to take your need for approval back from others and to give it to yourself, so that the only approval you ever need is your own. Myss indicates that in order to do so you have to identify those aspects of yourself that look for validation or endorsement from the outside world and thus the features of the world that have control of you. Parents, family members, neighbours, friends, partners, teachers, acquaintances, business and other associates, all the people you try to please or whom you begrudge, all have authority over you, not only in the past, but also in the present.

Indeed it is necessary to establish how much power the past has over you in the present and how much of your power or energy goes into maintaining the past – its memories, experiences, relationships, unfinished business, wounds, regrets and resentments – and how much remains active in the present, and has an influence on moods, health and what you create. The more authority the past retains over you, the less control or power is available in the present. Myss observes that when 80 per cent of your energies go into fuelling the past, only 20 per cent is available to you in the present. Therefore, in order to increase power in the present you should turn the past into passive history so that it has no power over you. The events of your past then become mere facts rather than emotionally charged facts. She describes this process as 'unplugging from the past', indicating that it provides a great upsurge in power because it releases the power or energy trapped in the past and brings it into the present. She suggests that, in effect, this requires a rebirthing of self, a going back to one's source, to what one really is. This involves a journey into yourself, attempting to shed light on and thereby rediscover those aspects which have been repressed or hidden away, walled off, in an attempt to defend against challenges to self-esteem; that is, against feelings that you are worth less than others.

The following exercise facilitates this journey.

EXERCISE 4

Take a few moments to make yourself comfortable and to withdraw your attention from your surroundings, and bring it to your inner self, closing your eyes as you do so.

Imagine that it is the afternoon of a warm summer's day which you have spent most enjoyably at a leisure park. You have tried most of the rides and activities, and are feeling quite tired, but still open to new experiences, so you are delighted to see a sign for a ride you have not yet been on, which reads *Back to the Future: a voyage on the river of time.*

There is no queue and you find yourself almost immediately stepping into a small boat, which begins to move along an underground waterway into a series of caves. Within a few moments you come upon an illuminated recess in the cavern wall, where you see yourself in the leisure park and all the events of the day as they unfold. As you pass you observe yourself as you appear now, noting every detail of the situation and your reactions to it.

Moving on you come upon another illuminated recess in which is depicted a scene from your recent life, complete in all its detail, which you observe, noting your reactions as it unfolds.

Passing on to another illuminated recess you see there a scene from your distant past, before moving on to a further illuminated recess where you observe a scene from your early childhood, observing both in detail, and your reactions to them.

As you move away from the last scene the boat continues to move forward and you have some time to consider the impact of the events depicted here upon your self-development. You are now approaching the end of the waterway, which is signposted *The Source of Your Self*, and wider, enabling the boat to turn around slowly. As it does so you notice all its details and features, and your feeling and thoughts about it.

Having turned around, the boat returns in the direction from which it has come, enabling you to review the scenes from your life and your feelings about them.

As the boat passes the last of these, the waterway opens out into a wide channel signposted *The Caves of Now*. As you look around, noting your feelings and reactions, you see leading from the caves of now, a channel directly ahead and signposted *The Caves of the Future*, which the boat approaches. The boat does not follow the sign, however, turning at the last moment towards a landing platform, where you leave the boat and walk outside, and then back into your present surroundings, where you open your eyes.

Having done so, take a few moments to record your experience in as much detail as possible and in the first person present tense.

Commentary

Very few people have difficulty in imagining themselves in a leisure park, which may be an old-style funfair or amusement park, or a more modern theme park such as Alton Towers or Disneyworld. A tiny minority express anxiety or discomfort at being in such a place, either because they are frightened by the kinds of rides there or because they dislike this kind of amenity. One young woman claimed not to be able to imagine such a place, having never been to one, which again highlights the limits on some individuals' imagination or creativity. Einstein had never been into outer space but this did not prevent him imagining it, to the great benefit of modern science.

Most people are quite excited by the prospect of a voyage on the river of time, but some sense danger, feeling anxious and threatened, and likening it to a 'ghost train' or other 'horror' trip and, in one instance, to a nightmare. One young woman felt such dread of the unknown, which she recognised as herself, that she did not want to get into the boat; another felt nauseous.

Negative attitudes and expectations are also suggested in various details of a person's imagery such as unpleasant smells, low, dark ceilings and cold, slimy walls. One man imagined that the ride was very drab and falling apart. Another man described a heavy wooden door at the entrance of the ride which, when pushed open, revealed a dark, cold, damp tunnel with a low ceiling. A woman described everything as black and depressing; a smelly canal, which, she admitted 'seemed to be the precursor of something I was not ready to discover'. One man described the deafening roar of water that threatened to overwhelm him.

Features of the boat may also be significant. People describe all kinds of craft, some of which are rowing boats, some motorised or mechanised, one being described as on rollers. The boats may be barges, gondolas, dinghies, canoes, pedalos, punts, of varying construction, some being wooden, some metal, others plastic. They may be personalised, carrying the individual's name – and indeed, whether or not the person initially imagines being in the company of others, everyone appears to undertake the voyage alone, although some have a sense of the boat being propelled by a vague figure behind, which they may glimpse fleetingly. Several people have described gondolas propelled by hooded or faceless gondoliers. Others have described rowing the boat themselves. This may be a defensive reaction against being out of control, as was the case for one man who indicated that he started to row the boat because he felt that he had to control what he would eventually discover, and for a woman who interpreted her insistence on steering the boat from the tiller at the rear as an indication of her need to be in total control of her life.

The appearance and performance of the boat are also potentially significant. One man described a huge, 'awesome' black and gold gondola lined with red cushions, which seemed to him to be 'kind of wicked', suggesting perhaps that the experience was exciting and somewhat self-indulgent; or, more literally, bad, injurious and potentially harmful. Others have described how the wooden seats of the boat made the ride 'hard' for them.

Some boats do not appear to be safe or sound. One woman discovered upon getting into her boat that it was holed and letting in water. Indeed, she described 'being sunk' at one point; and able to complete the voyage only by climbing into another boat. Other people have described falling into the water, and discovering, to their surprise, that the water was only a few inches or a few feet deep, apparently having assumed that they were in 'really deep water'. A man who fell out of his boat several times, described it as rocking violently. Certainly for many people the exercise is of the 'boat-rocking' variety in that it troubles or disturbs them by challenging the status quo. Moreover, it does so from the outset, suggesting that what troubles or disturbs them is embarking upon a voyage of self-discovery. Many people find that the boat rocks, dips or rolls as they get into it, making them feel anxious and insecure. However, one young woman whose old-fashioned rowing boat did not sink, despite being made of freshly cut light wood that was neither varnished nor waterproof, saw this as a sign of her recent determination to 'sail through' things undeterred by her feelings of vulnerability and lack of experience.

For many people the initial instability of the boat results from their attempts to find a seat. While most people sit in the boat facing forwards, others sit 'back to front', appearing unwilling to face what is to come and this in itself may give some indication of their 'approach' to life. Some people cause the boat to rock by shifting their position in the boat, often preferring to 'take a back seat' rather than to be 'up front'; or by turning around when they realise they can't see where they are going. Those who attempt to maintain control over what they see and discover by rowing the boat themselves will be facing backwards in the direction of what they already know and where they have already been; whereas those who 'paddle their own canoe' or otherwise propel themselves will face forward into the unknown.

While some people assume that the water is deep, others see that it is shallow and may trail their fingers in it or even their feet. Those who do so usually describe the water as clear or brightly coloured. By comparison, others reveal rather negative attitudes towards the water, describing it as black, dirty, murky, smelly; and in one instance as having a serpent swimming in it. Occasionally the water is described as turbulent and the boat as 'making waves' or 'churning it up' as it moves. One woman saw no water, however, her boat being engulfed by flames.

The boat's ease of passage along the waterway is very variable. In the majority of cases the boat proceeds without difficulty, moving smoothly and steadily; but sometimes the passageway is so narrow and the ceiling so low that it is difficult to negotiate, and gives rise to anxiety in the passenger. One woman described joining a long queue of boats all obstructing each other's progress, yet feeling that she was in the way of others who wanted to pass her by. Not only does this suggest a low self-esteem but also a tendency to block self-awareness. Indeed she subsequently saw nothing in any of the caves and was bored by the experience or lack of it.

The manner in which images are seen varies. Some people 'see' static or moving images as though projected on screens or rock faces; others describe them as having been painted or drawn in the manner of cave paintings. Some see the events occurring as though within the substance of the rock, whereas others see tableaux, miniaturised 'models' or real-life dramas, staged within caves or grottoes; or photographs. Some see only one scene from a particular period of life, whereas others see a whole series of flashback episodes.

The woman described above concluded that because she did not see anything in any of the caves, that there was nothing there to be seen and that she had been deceived. The possibility that she was deceiving herself, just as she had been blocking herself, did not occur to her. However, others are well aware that they have deliberately defended themselves against painful past experiences by not allowing them to be seen.

Most commonly, people describe 'switching off'; as though they are turning off the illumination they could shed on themselves or a projector. Having done so, one woman described feeling bitter and resentful towards herself for not being willing to tackle the issues of her inner life. Other people describe 'blanking out' all or some of the scenes. Frequently these relate to issues that a person thought had been resolved, but which they realise have not. One woman, for example, thought that she had come to terms with the death of her father in childhood but realised during this exercise that she had not and began crying copiously. Having done so she described feeling that a great weight had been lifted from her, as though a barrier had been removed allowing her to make contact with an area of herself previously blocked off. Several people have acknowledged 'blocking off' periods of their life, as did a man who could not 'see' anything of his life before the age of 7; unlike another man, who blamed his 'cold' for a similar oversight, thereby ignoring the fact that it hadn't prevented him imagining scenes from the 40 years or so up to that time.

The tendency is for people to 'blank out' or 'block off' the more distant scenes from their past rather than those from their recent past or present. This is possibly because earlier hurts are more deep-seated and painful, and therefore more likely to be defended and repressed. The insights provided by present and recent events may, however, be highly enlightening.

Present day events

Many people's view of themselves reveals their poor self-image and low self-esteem; their self-doubt and uncertainty. One young man saw himself very small and far away, out of reach on a ferris wheel. He took this as indicating his tendency to belittle himself; that he was out of touch with himself and 'going around in circles'. A young woman saw herself riding a roller-coaster, screaming, which she felt represented her current way of life, 'flying by the seat of my pants' out of control. To another woman the events of the day were like a circus. She saw a lion on a stand and, looking for herself, found that she had her head in its mouth. She didn't know whether or not she was the lion tamer, but nevertheless initially felt that the lion was in control, which she took to be an indication that she was not controlling current events very well. She then realised that this could be an act; that she might in fact be in control of the situation and could handle it. Her uncertainty about whether she was dangerously out of control or merely acting as though she were provided her with a good deal to think about.

One young woman saw herself standing still and isolated in the leisure park while all moved on around her. Similarly, a young man saw himself sitting alone on a bench eating an ice-cream and watching a group of people play crazy golf. They seemed to be having a really good time and he wanted to be able to join them, but could not think how he could. He realised that the ice-cream gave him an excuse for watching them and that without it they might wonder what he wanted from them and take offence at his being there. His presence was, in effect, being legitimised by an ice-cream. By contrast, a woman saw herself in the present as a child being shouted at, and hence invalidated, by someone in the distance. Another woman, looking for herself in the present, saw a figure made indistinguishable by 100 per cent burns.

However, not everyone imagines their present to be so bleak. One 42 year old woman saw herself as emerging from a cocoon. She saw this as representing herself at an age when she can let go of her children and marriage, and put behind her all the anxieties and social conditioning of her earlier life. She felt exhilarated and positive as she realised that 'now is the time to fly'.

Recent events

Having experienced a pleasant 'first' scene some people 'switch off' when the next one is less enjoyable. One woman imagined climbing out of the boat and into the darkness in order to avoid seeing the rape she 'knew would be there', and which would be extremely painful and disturbing to her. Others have wanted to avoid reliving painful arguments and other 'bad dream' experiences in which they had been hurt and upset, but were unsuccessful in doing so. One woman, seeing water all around her, recognised this as an indication that she had been 'adrift' for a long time and that emotional confusion had long preceded the recent break-up with her boyfriend. Moreover, she realised that her inability to see herself clearly in the scene with him reflected her current self-image. Another woman saw herself, anxious and agitated, telling her boyfriend that she couldn't cope with events in her life, and, in so doing, realised the extent to which she relied on him for support, rather than on herself.

Distant events

The further back in time people go the more intense are the emotions evoked by the imagined scenes. One woman described these scenes as depicting 'tender spots' – areas of life that hurt and have not been fully healed. These are generally hurt or painful feelings that are very deep seated and long standing, responses to events that may not have been consciously remembered or thought about for many years. They are often hurts that a person has believed to be long healed and their discovery may come as a surprise. Almost invariably the initial hurt has been covered up, often very quickly, rather than being exposed and aired, and, as in the case of a hastily applied dressing, contaminating factors may have been sealed in and buried. Thus, although on the surface the issue appears to have been dealt with, real healing has not taken place. In many cases the wound has continued to fester beneath the skin, sometimes producing problems out of all proportion to the original hurt. These may erupt much later and not be recognised as having any connection with the original trauma or they may simply poison the whole system. Inevitably the unhealed wound will give rise to sensitivity, whether localised or more generalised, against which the person will try to protect themselves consciously or unconsciously.

Thus one woman wanted to remove herself from the situation when, instead of her earlier feeling of excitement, she began to feel hurt, fearful, hateful, lonely and lost as scenes from her distant past began to 'flash up' that she didn't want to see, most notably that of being raped on a cold bathroom floor by her brother; while she, feeling petrified, suffocated, choked and thinking 'no one cares', tried to blot him out by staring at the pattern on the vinyl floor covering.

Another woman looking back upon a situation in which she was apparently frightened speechless, felt she wanted to be swallowed up by the chair of the psychiatrist to whom she had been referred. One woman was very disturbed by an event that she had completely forgotten, that of herself, aged eight, arguing with her younger sister as to which of them should put the finishing touches to a snowman they had built with their father. She was shocked by the hurt and resentment she still felt towards her sister who had eventually been lifted up by their father to put the nose on the snowman. She felt that by 'elevating' her sister in this way, her father had, in effect, 'put her down'.

Similarly, hurt and anger were felt by a man at seeing himself as a child being beaten by another boy; and hurt and resentment were felt by a woman towards a headteacher for humiliating her and causing her to lose face in front of other children. Another woman felt hurt at being told by her mother that her parents intended to divorce. The people who re-experienced these incidents all interpreted them as implying that they are worth less than others.

Early childhood events

However salient these images from the distant past may be, for most people early childhood events are more poignant. Most of these occur before the age of seven and whether the events perceived appear happy or not, all seem to have a bearing on current life issues. Thus happy scenes appear to highlight that which is missing in later or present life – emotional warmth, closeness, fun, security, protection, reassurance, acceptance.

Feelings of loss, rejection or abandonment are very commonly reactivated by these incidents. Grieving may have taken place, albeit cursorily, at the time of the loss so that it appears to have been dealt with, but anger or guilt relating to it may not have been discharged. These unexpressed emotions then fester as resentment towards others or the self. For many people, therefore, resentment develops because they have never aired their feelings appropriately in the first place, usually because they have learned that they 'should not' express emotion or that it is inappropriate. They have internalised scripts which include directives such as 'men and boys don't cry'; 'girls and "ladies" don't express anger'.

Many people realise that they have repressed their grief at the death of a parent, grandparent or sibling during early childhood and that they still miss the person deeply. Those who have what they describe as 'a good cry' report feeling very much better for it, and invariably admit that they did not cry, or cried very little at the time of their loss. This is also frequently true in cases where the person did not die but was still lost to the child, as in the case of divorce or separation. One woman who pictured her father leaving home, saw herself searching frantically around the house for him, and continued to be bombarded for several days afterwards by childhood events she hadn't thought of in years and long suppressed emotions. These included feelings of guilt that she might have been the cause of his departure. This rebound into consciousness of previously repressed material is quite usual and its intensity may be an indication of the degree to which it was repressed initially.

As indicated previously, the hurt felt by an individual may appear disproportional to the apparent trauma they initially experienced. Thus emotions arising from a temporary loss or an apparently trivial incident may be repressed. One man, for example, felt a sense of great loss when his mother went into hospital to give birth to his brother and resentment towards his father who was holding him back from her. Indeed, for some people, as Simonton has suggested, such painful early experiences may become a template for similar experiences throughout their life; almost as though this isolated incident has defined them. Hence, people who have suffered a loss in early childhood may come to define themselves as a loser, even though they have repressed all memory of the incident which triggered this conviction or those which subsequently appear to confirm it.

In this way various emotional and behavioural patterns may become established. Many people can therefore identify a clear similarity or trend in the scenes they picture which highlight unresolved issues stemming from their early years. Thus, a woman, who saw herself as a young child lost, carefree and happy on a beach, until her mother found her and, shouting angrily, began to hit her, saw herself being shouted down by others in scenes throughout her life. Another woman's experience of alienation seemed to stem from a feeling in early childhood that, as the youngest member of a much older family, she was excluded from its activities, and thus an outsider, which is how she appeared in the various scenes from her life. Another young woman who as a child had to escape from her parents' control in order to play as she wanted to, realised that in every subsequent scene from her life she was engaged in 'escapist' activities, apparently out of control, skiing 'crazily' down a mountain, 'raving', that is, dancing frenetically under the influence of drugs, and screaming 'wildly' on a roller-coaster.

Other repressed feelings which may emerge in relation to early childhood events include that of being controlled by others or restrained by them and thus being incapable of independent action. One man related the frustration he felt at being held in reins by his mother; and a woman reported her feelings of sadness at being able as a seven-year-old child to identify with a donkey on a treadmill. One young woman resented being told by her father that she had to climb to the top of a mountain and bribed by the promise of some chocolate. Others have resented being punished or having to be secretive in order to avoid punishment.

The most graphic illustration of the lifelong effects of a repressed emotional pattern comes from a woman who was reared
by her mother alone during the Second World War when her
father was serving overseas. She saw herself aged between three
and four years of age refusing to do as her mother told her and go
to bed. Eventually her mother resorted to threats, putting on her
coat and saying 'I shall go away and leave you' as she went
outside into the garden. The woman remembered her terror and
panic as a child, screaming into the garden 'Please come back',
and in so doing realised that this childhood anxiety about losing
her mother had dominated her life ever since, accounting for her
inexplicable anxiety during otherwise pleasurable family activities
and her fear of losing those she loved. Indeed, one of her great
fears was that her children would go out into the garden and not
return. Ironically she lived and worked in a 'nursery', growing
plants commercially within a walled garden. Not only did she
suffer from often incapacitating and apparently inexplicable anxiety but also from guilt, always feeling herself to be at fault. She
realised that she felt herself to be to blame for the childhood
incident and also guilty of disloyalty to her mother by relating
this event, of which until then she had no conscious memory.

The source of the self

Irrespective of what has gone before, most people feel very
positive towards their 'source' and this is reflected in their imagery; which has included rising suns, sparkling stars, other
heavenly bodies and heavenly music, gems of stunning beauty,
magnificent crystal caves, huge colourful flowers, rainbow colours, a shimmering gold curtain, beautiful perfumes. These images
have been associated with feelings of great warmth, security,
peace, bliss, satisfaction, stillness, happiness, calm and weightless-
ness. Many people admit wanting to remain at their source and to
hold on to the feelings they experienced there. The imagery often
conveys great energy, potential or impetus, as in the case of a
beating heart, vigorous sperm, a chrysalis bursting open, water-
falls, rushing water and continuous lightning. Birth and pre-birth
images are very commonly reported, people seeing themselves as
embryos or unborn babies. One woman reported being frightened
by the booming sound in her head until she realised that it was

one of the sensations of being born. Many people have a sense that their future will lead back to their source, and describe the feelings of wholeness, completion and continuity thus evoked as very uplifting. Their experience is reminiscent of lines from T.S. Eliot's *Four Quartets*:

> *The end of all our exploring*
> *Will be to arrive where we started*
> *And know the place for the first time.*

Not everyone has positive imagery, however. A woman who saw fire in every scene came upon metal sliding doors like those in a lift, which when forced apart, also revealed flames. Being unclear as to the significance of this powerful and frightening imagery, she began to consider various possibilities – that something, perhaps herself – had been consumed, engulfed, 'gone up' in flames; has burning desires, great intensity or has burnt itself out. Another woman, seeing only blackness, and feeling that she didn't know what she was looking for acknowledged that this might be because she has no sense of herself, and no idea where she is coming from.

Only rarely does a person feel unable to tolerate being at their source, as was the case for one woman who upon seeing herself in her mother's womb, felt enclosed and so desperate to be free that she 'shot out' and back to the present without looking again at any of the scenes on the way, all of which, she realised, showed her to be trapped in various ways.

Sometimes, however, people are eager to return to the present so that they can begin to implement some of the insights they have gained by going back to their source. Somewhat ironically, this was true of a man who, while realising that difficulties in his past had arisen because of his impetuosity, could not wait to act on this awareness and improve relationships in his present life.

The return journey

After having encountered their source most people seem to change their reactions to previously witnessed events. Thus the return journey often affords a quite different perspective on life events, especially those previously perceived as negative or traumatic. For many people reviewing these events is much less painful. One man observed that it enabled him to feel that life wasn't so bad after all and a woman claimed that 'the greatest benefit of this exercise was to help me face what I have been through'. Several see features, often positive features, that they have missed on the outward journey. One man admitted having felt resentment throughout his life towards people because of their censorious attitudes towards actions of his he thought were amusing. However, having reappraised some of these, he could now appreciate that they had been highly irritating or frightening for others. Similarly, on reassessing her encounter with a psychiatrist, the woman who previously had viewed herself as frightened speechless saw herself talking to him intelligently, confidently and with animation. Indeed, this was a situation in which she had taken control, rather than one in which she had lost it, as she had previously thought.

However, on review some people find scenes more painful than previously. Thus one woman described feeling choked by events that had left her relatively unmoved initially. Similarly, others have admitted feeling uncomfortable viewing scenes that previously had seemed non-threatening. A young male student, who initially saw a series of pleasant, family scenes, felt upon reviewing them that they were scenes from someone else's history. He concluded that he needed to distance himself from his family in order to become autonomous and make his own way in the world; and that if he were to return to the comfortable home depicted in his initial scenes he would never leave it, and would remain dependent on his family for ever.

A woman who on the outward journey saw a series of reasonably pleasant scenes realised on reviewing them that they were 'cheap, nasty, set-up commercial scenes; public, posed pictures; everything a facade and unreal' – all pointing to her inauthenticity and superficiality. Even her source was, in reality, a folly – a place where she had once been able to feel relaxed and at ease, until the occasion when, only a few hours after she left, a vicious murder took place and she could never again feel comfortable there. This imagery suggests, perhaps, that her real self had narrowly avoided being killed off early in life, hence the subsequent pretence or defence against realness. This is further suggested by the woman's assessment of her imagery: 'It seems to say that although I think my inner self seems OK, it's not a place I can retreat to without feeling threatened'. Subsequently she reported feeling better able to like herself and to allow other people to like her.

In some instances the person cannot bring themselves to look at the scenes on their return. This was true of the woman who had been disturbed by the long-forgotten snowman incident. She reported reversing back quickly through the caverns, feeling sick, dizzy and panicky. Although initially relieved to get off the ride she was subsequently bad-tempered and upset by the realisation that, in a family which valued intelligence more than any other attribute, she felt worth less than and profoundly jealous of her more intelligent younger sister, to whom she was not reconciled, but resentful.

The caves of now

Those who find the return trip disturbing are usually relieved to return to the 'caves of now', which are often described as safe, secure, comforting and familiar. It is a place that some people do not want to leave. However, this is not always the case. Some people find them unpleasantly cold, dark or featureless and want to escape into the future, as did the man who described now as 'empty but filled with loneliness'. One young woman attributed her desire to escape from the present to 'all sorts of things going on in my life now' and another claimed this was because of the confusion in her present life. Others describe being bored and wanting to move on, and often feel disappointed, frustrated and angry, even furious at not being able to.

The caves of the future

Some of those who are eager to move into the future take the view that it cannot be worse than the present and therefore must be better. Others, such as the woman who earlier witnessed herself emerging from a cocoon, are excited by the prospect of the future. Indeed her boat had already progressed in that direction and was obliged to turn back, much to her disappointment. Some people have described dashing to get into the future, 'rowing like mad' and even, in some instances, leaping from the boat and swimming towards it. Others, who normally view the future with anxiety, are surprised to find themselves exhilarated or excited at the prospect. These are often people who realise that it leads to where they have already been, to their source, and that they have nothing to fear.

There are those who are fearful at the prospect of the future. One woman claimed that this was the only aspect of the exercise she found frightening. Like several others she did not wish to know about it, considering it to hold unknown terrors, thereby reflecting a very negative outlook and also an idea that the future is created for one, rather than by one, and thus without the participation of oneself. One woman described being able to see 'a light at the end of the tunnel', but not wanting to get there. Another woman saw the waterway ahead disappearing into a small trickle and thus found herself without a future to go into, had she wanted to, which she emphatically did not. She wanted everything to remain as 'it now is', apparently unaware that nothing stays the same. It is therefore never possible to step twice into the same river:

> We go down twice into the same river, and yet into a different river.
>
> HERACLITUS

Combating Dis-ease

Whatever the public blames you for, cultivate it – it's yourself.

JEAN COCTEAU

Edward Bach, the distinguished Harley Street physician, defined health as listening to one's inner voice. He believed that by listening to its teaching, a person hears what is needed in order to be healthy. However, most of us do not listen to our intuition. We listen instead to others and what we hear, generally, is not what we need but what others want of, for and from us. Indeed we are all conditioned into believing that we need what others want us to and as a result we tend to confuse our needs with their wants.

The latter are imposed upon us throughout life and in some cases even before birth. The psychiatrist Eric Berne (1974) has observed that in many cases the name and/or nickname bestowed upon us indicates what is wanted by our parents and where they want us to go in life. As such, names can be script indicators, identifying the role we are expected to play in life.

Parents who name their child after a film, rock or sporting star – and in some cases the whole band or team – identify the child in a very specific way, as do those who name their children after historical or political characters, kings and emperors. Berne suggests that naming a child after its mother or father is also usually a purposeful act on the part of a parent which imposes an obligation on the offspring that he or she may not be able or care to fulfil. The person may actively rebel against the obligations thus imposed so that his or her life is permeated with a slight bitterness or active resentment. This may also be the case where the child's name is the same as that of the opposite sex parent or its diminutive and implies a preference for a child of the opposite sex or is ambiguous. Berne observes that names as script indicators are most likely to take hold in school, where we learn about famous namesakes in myth and history, or where classmates bring home to us with more or less brutality the hidden meanings in our names. Hence the traumas and torments that shaped the destiny of 'a boy named Sue', as portrayed by the country singer Johnny Cash, may also have influenced Nigellas, Edwinas, Martinas and Evelyns. It is therefore perhaps more appropriate to consider 'wants in a name' rather than the more usual question of 'what's in a name'.

Having been provided with a more or less subtle script indicator by way of your name, your lifescript begins to unfold as others tell you, more or less subtly, what is wanted of you. Even before a child can understand language the family begins to transmit society's messages, because 'it is the function of the family to transmit to offspring the prescribed, permitted and proscribed values of the society and the acceptable and unacceptable means of achieving goals' (Lidz, 1975, p. 22). These are the 'givens' of a person's existence, provided by others and society, irrespective of whether they meet the person's needs. Indeed, this is not their purpose, which is to meet the needs of others. It is therefore not surprising that most of us find it difficult to distinguish our needs from the needs and wants of others, or to perceive how much of our time and energy are taken up with the latter. As a result of paying attention to messages from others, we fail to hear their own voice, much less listen to what it has to convey about our needs. Not surprisingly, therefore, a good deal of illness is inevitable.

Constant listening to what others want can be sickening and also maddening. Professor of psychiatry Theodore Lidz observes that a common pattern among schizophrenics is that their emergence as individuals is thwarted by subservience to parental needs. Typically, boundaries are not established between parent(s) and child so parental feelings and needs are not differentiated from those of the offspring. The child's energies and attention therefore go primarily into meeting parental needs rather than his own. So the world as the child should come to perceive it is denied and invalidated as events are distorted to fit into the pattern required by the parent(s) who are impervious to the needs of the child and extremely intrusive.

PRESCRIPTIONS FOR HEALTH

In cases where a person is incapable of distinguishing his needs from other people's wants, judgements about needs tend to be made by policy makers and professional observers rather than the individuals whose needs are being assessed. Unfortunately these professionals are frequently in no better position than the individuals themselves because they too invariably make assumptions about a person's needs on the basis of what they and society want for them, rather than what is appropriate.

What then are the 'real' needs of an individual? Maslow identified two broad classes of need: *deficiency needs* – extrinsic requirements the person lacks which must be provided in order for growth and development to occur; and *growth needs* which must be met in order for development to be achieved. The former include physical needs for air, water, food, shelter and sleep; and emotional needs for safety, security, support, belonging, love, affection, appreciation, esteem, respect and recognition. Growth needs are those which must be fulfilled in order for a person's intrinsic potentials and capabilities to be realised or actualised. These can be considered as spiritual needs insofar as they provide meaning and purpose in life, and are essential to the activating principle of a person.

Maslow conceived of these needs as organised within a hierarchy based upon physical needs, which must be met before psychological needs; which, in turn, must be met before spiritual needs. Thus, according to Maslow each need can only be attended to when a lower one is met and the more basic it is the more vital is the necessity to fulfil it. He considered the healthy development of a person as a progression through this hierarchy towards the fulfilment of all needs or self-actualisation. As such it is a movement in the direction of autonomy or self-control and away from dependence on others.

At birth, and for some years afterwards, a child is totally dependent on others for the satisfaction of its needs. Clearly, if a child's physical needs for air, water, food, sleep, hygiene and housing are not met it is unlikely to thrive, and likely to become ill. Fortunately, in the majority of cases, these needs are met, if only incidentally to the wants of others. Parents tell their children that they *need* sleep, because they want a few hours in the evening free of them; that they *need* to eat their meals because they do not want to throw food away; that they *need* fresh air because they want them out of the house on a Saturday afternoon.

However, these 'needs' may translate into others, such as a certain kind of cot, bed or baby carriage; diet, living accommodation with a garden and so on. In this way a child's actual needs may be sacrificed to its parents' wants, because by working all hours to earn money to provide for these 'needs' they may rarely see the child, much less spend time with it.

'Needs' such as these are reinforced and exploited through advertising and the mass media, and a vast industry has thus grown up around baby needs. The message is that parents who do not provide appropriately for their offspring (i.e. as the industry wants them to) do not love or care for them. As parents *want* to be seen to be loving and caring, it therefore behoves them to feed, dress and equip their children in the appropriate manner, and to send them to appropriate schools, camps and entertainments.

Such prescriptions are the norm in a materialistic society which focuses upon all things physical, and thus on services and facilities, rather than psychological, emotional and spiritual factors. Consequently it is not readily recognised that failure to meet non-physical needs can result in dis-ease, which may manifest as psychological or physical illness.

CULTIVATING ATTACHMENTS

During the 1950s psychologist John Bowlby drew attention to both these outcomes. He claimed that a child's fundamental need is for a loving relationship with its mother, explaining this in terms of what he saw as the child's tendency to become attached primarily to this one figure; and his belief that this attachment is qualitatively different from all others. He saw mother love as absolutely essential to the normal healthy development of the child, arguing that any separation from the mother, particularly during the first five years, gives rise to a deficiency of love resulting in disorders like infantile autism, dwarfism, intellectual retardation, mental illness and delinquency. He supported these claims by reference to a depressive response observable in babies who have lost their mothers, and evidence from the 1940s that found poor health, high death rates, low intelligence and mental retardation in the foundling hospitals and orphanages of that period.

Bowlby's views on 'maternal deprivation' were exploited politically in the post-war years when, in attempts to restore women to their place in the home rather than factories, the closure of crêches and day nurseries was justified in terms of the adverse consequences to children of working mothers, who, with their so-called 'latchkey' children, were stigmatised. This led some people to place an almost mystical importance on the mother and to regard maternal love as the only element in child-rearing. The child's attachment to the father was ignored, as was the possibility of 'paternal deprivation' and his participation in child-rearing was discouraged. Indeed, only relatively recently has the child's attachment to the father, and its implications for development, been given serious consideration. In the mean time, every social ill from delinquency to mental illness was laid at the mother's door.

Subsequently, however, Bowlby's theories on attachment were subjected to serious criticism and research showed them to be misguided. Maslow observed that apart from the obvious difficulty in defining what is meant by love in operational terms, Bowlby's logic was flawed. He spoke of love in such a way as to suggest that if it were not available constantly the child would suffer a deficiency which inevitably would result in adverse consequences. Such a view was very potent at a time when it had recently been established that rickets, a disease mainly of children characterised by softening and bowing of developing bones and liver enlargement, resulted from vitamin D deficiency. However, as Maslow, indicated, while vitamin D prevents rickets it does not follow that it has to be given constantly to avoid the disease. Indeed such overdosing with the vitamin could give rise to as many problems as its deprivation. A decade later feminists would take up this argument, claiming that an exclusive mother–child relationship can be stultifying to the child, depriving them of much-needed stimulation which may result in emotional and intellectual deficits; and that other people, notably the father, have an important role in child-rearing.

Subsequent research has borne out these claims (Rutter, 1981). It has been established that there is a distress syndrome following a young child's separation from its mother, which, where it occurs, is most marked in children under five. However, one-third of all children under five are separated from their mothers for periods of a week or more without showing any ill effects. It is also clear that children of all ages differ greatly in their response to separation, which tends to be more severe in males than females and less so in children who remain in familiar surroundings after separation. However, as regards long-term effects, separation does not inevitably give rise to psychopathology; a finding Bowlby was subsequently obliged to accept, although he remained adamant that prolonged separation from the mother under the age of five is deterimental to the development of the child and that the child's attachment to the mother is all important.

Research since the 1950s does not support either position. It reveals that the term 'maternal deprivation' is, in fact, a misnomer and that distress following separation from the mother is not the effect of her loss *per se*, but of disruptions in the process of mothering – that is, of patterns of care, and that if these disruptions can be minimised so can the resulting trauma.

Growing awareness that it is not the loss of the mother that is important but the loss of what the mother does, has led to a focus on what mothering actually comprises. This has been greatly facilitated by the development of audio-visual recording techniques which enable mother–child interactions to be carefully monitored. As a result it has become clear that the activities of the newly-born child are not random, but carefully articulated to serve its survival needs. Immediately after birth the baby is highly active, scanning its environment and emitting clear signals of need which are recognisable by those who perceive them as attempts at communication. The person's attempt to respond to these signals is the first stage in attachment or bonding. It is also the fundamental feature in the care of the child, since if the signals are not responded to its needs will not be met. Clearly, the person who does not see these signals, for whatever reason, is unable to respond to or care for the child, and a child whose needs are not attended to because they are not monitored will fail to thrive, hence many of the consequences, such as dwarfism, attributed to maternal deprivation by Bowlby.

Mothers usually have an advantage over others in the establishment of an early relationship with the child because they are the one person guaranteed to be present at the birth. Nevertheless, although present many mothers may not be conscious, as for instance following a Caesarean birth, or may be conscious but unable to relate to a child which has been removed to a special baby care unit, as in the case of very premature babies. In either case the establishment of the early mother–child relationship is disrupted, and this is believed to contribute towards post-natal depression in the mother and a greater tendency to reject the child (Klaus et al., 1972). Mothers separated from their babies in this way tend to hold them at a greater distance, rarely look them in the face and generally touch them less than those who have not experienced separation. Moreover, these differences are discernible 12 months later, as is the tendency for mothers who have been separated from their infants immediately after birth to chastise them physically. This is considered particularly significant given statistics which suggest that premature babies represent 30 to 40 per cent of physically abused children, although they constitute only 8 per cent of the live birth total (Kempe & Kempe, 1978).

However, anyone who is able to perceive the baby's signals and is capable of responding to them is, in so doing, establishing a relationship or bond with the child. Fathers, traditionally excluded from birth and early child-rearing, were thus precluded from forming this bond. Nevertheless, the child can and will form multiple attachments with those who respond to their signals of need and, providing these needs are met adequately, no ill effects will ensue, irrespective of how many carers there are, their gender or biological relationship to the child.

Recognition of these factors has led to the view that mothering, rather than being in any way mystical, is in fact a skill – that of recognising and responding to the infant's attempts to communicate its needs. Mothering is therefore monitoring and, just like any other skill, it can be learned. Accordingly, psychologists now refer to deprivation of care rather than maternal deprivation and to the child's attachment to its primary caretakers rather than to the mother alone. Moreover, there is a general acceptance that the carer's attachment to the child is not instant and instinctive, but develops slowly, as in any other relationship, and in most cases surely, given time, physical closeness and appropriate encouragement.

Indeed, one of the most unfortunate aspects of Bowlby's ideas on attachment was that the importance of early mother–child bonding became prescribed dogma among health care professionals. So misguided ideas as to what constitutes good mothering have led in many cases to severe harassment of mothers who have difficulty relating to their babies in the early stages of motherhood, and proved counterproductive because the feelings of guilt, anxiety, inadequacy and depression engendered are not conducive to the development of good mother–child relationships (Sluckin et al., 1983).

Mothers and other caretakers learn to make certain responses to the child's signals of need, and the quality of care they deliver depends to a great extent on the opportunities for this learning and its appropriateness. If the mother fails to respond to the child's needs, over time the child will stop attempting to communicate them, and this would appear to account for the subsequent impoverishment of social and emotional development noted by Bowlby in uncared for babies, and for autistic and other pathological behaviour. Audio-visual analyses of the behaviours of very young children have shown that they are highly sensitive to the attentions of others and react initially to disruptions of attention by becoming more active in an attempt to regain this attention. However, if and when these fail, and attention is not restored, the child ceases to try and gain attention, and progressively becomes passive, unreactive and inert – the characteristic features of the autistic and depressed children observed by Bowlby.

Furthermore, as a consequence of the disrupted attention the child is likely to receive reduced social, perceptual and physical stimulation, known to be a crucial factor in stimulating the intellectual development of the child. Indeed it is now recognised that the mental retardation often observed in orphanage children of the 1940s, wrongly attributed by Bowlby to lack of maternal love, resulted from lack of environmental and interpersonal stimulation, these children usually having been left in cots staring at the walls all day. It is therefore now accepted that multiple attachments are highly advantageous to the child because they increase the amount and diversity of stimulation, which enhances emotional and intellectual development; and that an exclusive mother–child relationship can be a source of deprivation to the child.

Although many of Bowlby's claims have been discredited, his focus on the mother–child relationship has served to highlight the importance of psychological and emotional needs other than love. More precisely, perhaps, it has shed light on what the components of love are: attention, care, stimulation, contact, touch, security and communication, and in so doing has provided broad empirical support for the basic needs identified by Maslow. However, doubt has been cast on Maslow's notion of a need hierarchy that the fulfilment of a child's physical needs appears to be contingent on the extent to which psychological and emotional needs are met, rather than vice versa; both being intrinsic to and interdependent within the carer–child relationship. This finds further support in studies reported by Siegel (1990) which suggest that survival involves the simultaneous satisfaction of physical and psychological needs.

CULTIVATING DETACHMENT

The whole issue of attachment is something of a paradox because it is through interaction with its caretakers that a child gains its first experience of its own distinctness from them, and this ability to distinguish itself from others is, as we have seen (Chapter 2), fundamental to its subsequent mental health. Moreover, the child's ability to discriminate and detach itself from its caretakers is to a great extent determined by the strength of the initial attachment.

Studies have suggested that the security of early attachments has an important effect on later development and health. Boys identified as insecure in their attachments at the age of one have been found to show more pathology at the age of six than those identified as securely attached. Intriguingly no relationship between attachment and later pathology has been observed for girls (Lewis et al., 1984). Attachment style also appears to exert a pervasive influence on people's relationships with others and upon their self-esteem (Feeny & Noller, 1990); and to be related to their orientation to work. Securely attached individuals approach their work with confidence, relatively unburdened by feelings of failure and don't allow interpersonal relationships to interfere with work or vice versa, whereas insecurely attached individuals are more influenced by praise and fear of rejection at work, and allow love concerns to interfere with work performance (Hazan & Shaver, 1990).

As noted in Chapter 2 the baby initially learns to distinguish itself from others and its environment through touch. In this way it establishes its body boundaries and develops a rudimentary body image which forms the basis of its concept of self. This process is subsequently elaborated through various interactions with others, notably by them indicating and naming objects in the world, and the child learning to use personal pronouns.

Sigmund Freud's theory of personality development, at its simplest, focuses on this fundamental self/other discrimination at the physical level, and highlights the interaction between physical and psychological development. Freud drew attention to those orifices – the mouth, anus and genitals – by way of which the external world and others can impose themselves on the individual, and vice versa. Much of the child's early socialisation therefore focuses on messages relating to these boundaries. The child learns that its basic needs and pleasures are associated with these areas, and that it can be controlled and manipulated, and can control and manipulate others, by way of them.

According to Freud, during different phases of development

states of tension focus on the body's orifices which the child needs to discharge. Appropriate discharge of these tensions is gratifying or pleasurable, whereas failure to do so gives rise to frustration. When this occurs the child begins to engage in various strategies in order to deal with the crisis. These may persist if the child becomes stuck or fixated in a stage of its development, and manifest in later adult behaviour. Thus, in its bodily interactions with others and its environment, the child is learning strategies for meeting basic needs which it will tend to generalise throughout life to other situations. What a child learns in relation to these areas therefore becomes a template for later behaviours, which come to characterise him and constitute his identity. According to Freud, therefore, personal identity or personality emerges from dealing with developmental crises.

Indeed, in order to meet its needs effectively the developing child must have an emerging sense of who and what it is, as opposed to who and what others are. So it needs to define its own boundaries – what Freud termed the ego boundaries, which are being established and tested in every contact the child has with its social environment. The self or ego that emerges in this process was conceived by Freud as constituting a balance between the primitive, innate and instinctual pleasure-seeking urges of what he referred to as the id, which are always striving for immediate gratification, and the controlling forces of the social world as mediated by the so-called superego, which is virtually synonymous with conscience. Its function is to express and satisfy the id in accordance with reality and the demands of the superego. The balance between these processes will therefore differ from person to person as a consequence of their various experiences of the social world. Freud therefore placed great emphasis on the challenges to the pleasure principle within the first five years of a child's life, and thus upon oral, anal and genital phases of development.

Subsequently the psychoanalyst Erik Erikson argued that the child's learning in relation to these phases has a lasting impact on character not simply because they are the focus of pleasure but because they present the child with its first experiences of conflict between its needs and the wants of others. These stages involve significant social situations that have important implications for the development of the child's self-identity. He suggests that in the feeding situation a relationship of basic trust or mistrust develops between the child and its carer. Subsequently, during toilet training the child may develop a sense of autonomy or succumb to shame and self-doubt; and later still as the child develops sexually it may develop initiative or guilt about assertiveness, competitiveness and success.

The way in which feeding, toilet and moral training are handled by the child's caretakers will therefore determine to a great extent his attitudes to the world around him and also to himself. This is true also of the disciplinary practices they adopt, which may take various forms, not only in respect of the chosen rewards and punishments, but also the manner in which they are given. Tangible rewards, deprivation of privileges, physical punishments, praise and withdrawal of love are all effective in producing socially conformist behaviour. However, they also produce different kinds of child, depending on which is favoured. Mothers who regularly resort to physical punishment report more feeding problems with their young children than those who use such punishment rarely or occasionally, and those who show affectionate warmth to their children have fewer feeding problems than those who tend to be cold and hostile (Sears et al., 1957). However, parents who discipline by means of physical punishment tend to raise children with low self-esteem (Coopersmith, 1967). Children who have a highly developed conscience (which may be thought of as being highly controlled by others) tend to be disciplined by withdrawal of love (Sears et al., 1957). Such children may come to believe that being loved or lovable is conditional upon certain kinds of behaviour and feelings, and lead them to repress, deny and distort those behaviours and feelings not positively regarded by others, unlike children whose caretakers show acceptance of them even when disapproving of particular kinds of behaviour. The difference, essentially, is between saying 'I don't like what you are doing' and 'I don't like you'. In the former the caretaker is accepting the child while not approving its behaviour; whereas in the latter the caretaker is telling the child, verbally or in other ways, that it and its behaviour are bad.

Erikson (1950) points out that the quality and nature of the parental nurturance a child receives will profoundly influence his emotional development – his vulnerability to frustration, and the anger, aggression, anxiety, hopelessness and helplessness he experiences in various conditions. It influences the quality of the basic trust he develops in both others and himself; his sense of autonomy and the clarity of the boundaries that are established between himself and others, and contributes to his self-esteem. It therefore forms the basis for further growth.

GROWING CONDITIONS

Various studies have suggested that accepting, democratic parental attitudes do indeed enable the most intellectual and emotional growth in children. Children of parents with these attitudes show accelerated intellectual development, originality, emotional security and control when compared with children of rejecting, authoritarian parents (Pervin, 1993). However, the most significant factor to emerge from research is the critical importance of children's perceptions of their parents' appraisals of them. If they feel these are positive they will tend to feel positive about themselves and their bodies, and if negative they will develop negative feelings about themselves and their bodies, and insecurity. So a child's view of its own worth is determined by the amount of respectful, accepting and concerned treatment it receives from significant others in its life: 'In effect we value ourselves as we are valued' (Coopersmith, 1967, p. 37).

Children with high self-esteem are more assertive, independent and creative, less likely to accept social definitions of reality unless they accord with their own experience, more flexible and imaginative, and more capable of finding original solutions to problems than children with low self-esteem, who tend to be more submissive and withdrawn, and less independent (Coopersmith, 1967). This research also confirms that self-esteem originates in the degree of acceptance, interest, affection and warmth expressed towards the child, and reveals that mothers of children with high self-esteem are more loving and have closer relationships with their children than mothers of children with low self-esteem. Paternal attention and concern is also important. Adolescents who have closer relationships with their fathers are higher in self-esteem than those with more distant, impersonal relationships.

Parents' interest appears to be interpreted by children as an indication that they are worthy of the concern, attention and time of significant others, and thus significant in their own right.

Another determinant of self-esteem relates to permissiveness and punishment. Parents of children with high self-esteem establish and enforce clear guidelines as to conduct, and reward desired behaviour. By contrast, parents of children with low self-esteem give little guidance to their children and are harsh in their treatment of them, tending to use force and withdrawal of love as punishment rather than reward. While parents of children with high esteem establish and enforce an extensive set of rules, within the defined limits they are non-coercive, recognising the rights and opinions of the child. Parents of children with low self-esteem set few and poorly defined limits, and are autocratic, dictatorial, rejecting and uncompromising in their methods of control. These findings can be summarised as follows:

> The most general statement about the origins of self-esteem can be given in terms of three conditions: total or nearly total *acceptance* of the children by their parents, clearly defined and enforced *limits*, and the *respect* and latitude for individual action that exist within the defined limits.
>
> COOPERSMITH, 1967, p, 236

Self-esteem is a personal measure of worthiness. It is the evaluation you make and customarily maintain with regard to yourself, and is as such a general personality characteristic or enduring trait, rather than a momentary attitude or an attitude specific to individual situations. Therefore the sense of whether or not you are worth caring for and attending to is likely to persist throughout life. It follows that if you judge yourself unworthy you will be less likely to care for or attend to yourself, less likely to address your needs and more likely to become ill as a result. Self-esteem thus emerges as a fundamental growth need essential to health.

Certainly people who seek psychological help frequently suffer from feelings of unworthiness, inadequacy, incompetence, inferiority and insignificance which are the basis for sadness, depression and anxiety (Coopersmith, 1967). The question arises, therefore, as to whether it is possible for a person to develop self-esteem if its antecedent conditions have not been present in early life. Carl Rogers, while insisting that the potential for health, wholeness, integration or self-actualisation resides within the person, claimed that the conditions for facilitating its development can exist within a therapeutic relationship that is close, emotionally warm and accepting, free from threat and evaluation, and where the individual has the freedom to be himself – in other words, which provides precisely those conditions known to promote self-esteem in the parent–child relationship: 'I can state the overall hypothesis in one sentence, as follows: If I can provide a certain type of relationship, the other person will discover within himself the capacity to use that relationship for growth; and change and personal development will occur' (Rogers, 1961, p. 33).

The type of therapeutic relationship Rogers sought to provide has three particularly significant qualities, the first of which is the authenticity or genuineness of the therapist. To achieve this the therapist must be aware of his feelings in as far as is possible and be able to express these where appropriate rather than present any facade.

The second quality required in the therapist is unconditional positive regard for the person – the ability to value, respect and care for them irrespective of their condition, behaviour, attitudes and feelings. The third quality is empathic understanding or genuine listening; the continuing desire to understand the feelings and meanings which the other person is experiencing.

Rogers claims that within such a relationship there is an implicit freedom to explore the self at both the conscious and unconscious levels, and that under such conditions the person moves from fear and defence of inner feelings to acceptance and expression of them; from being out of touch with feelings to greater awareness of them; from living life by the introjected values of others to those experienced by the self in the present; from distrust of spontaneous aspects of the self to trust in them; and towards greater freedom and more responsible choices. Essentially, Rogerian therapy affords a situation in which the individual learns to be free from the controls of others.

Rogers's concept of therapy is close to the original Greek word *therapeia* meaning attendance, in that the therapist is an attendant, who attends to a person. Simply being attentive, caring, open and genuine is, in Rogers's view, therapeutic, bringing about positive changes and growth which move a person in the direction of wholeness and health.

Exactly the same conditions and outcomes are relevant to self-healing or therapy, in that if you attend to yourself in an open and caring way, and with respect, genuinely listening to yourself without judging, allowing freedom to explore both your conscious and unconscious aspects, and attempting to understand the feelings and personal meanings you experience, growth and a move in the direction of health will be facilitated. The following exercise is directed towards the promotion of growth.

EXERCISE 5

Imagine sitting or lying under the sun feeling its warmth penetrating your skin, and soothing away tensions, aches and pains. Imagine these areas of tension, pain or discomfort as ice being melted by the sun's rays, and dripping or flowing through and out of your body, leaving it feeling warm, heavy and pleasantly relaxed. Notice any areas where the ice appears especially thick, massive or resistant to the warmth from the sun, and focus your attention on dissolving the tensions there. Then imagine the sun's warmth also dissolving your mental tensions, concerns and conflicts, leaving your mind empty. Having done so allow yourself some time to enjoy relaxing in the sun.

Now imagine you are a seed planted in some kind of medium. What kind of seed are you? What size, shape, colour, texture? What kind of medium are you planted in? What colour is it? Is it heavy or light in texture, rich or poor, wet or dry? Does the medium provide adequate conditions for growth?

Now observe your roots; their number, colour, length, direction of growth and how easily they penetrate the medium. Are they deep or shallow, widespread or localised, strong or weak? Do they come up against any obstacles? If so what are they and what is their effect on the growth of the roots?

Now observe your seed putting out a shoot or shoots. How

easy or difficult does this seem? How much resistance is
encountered and from what? How many shoots are there?
Notice their colour, texture and other details. Do they grow
straight or distorted? How easily do they reach the surface and
how many shoots fail to do so? How many shoots emerge
from the medium and in what manner?

Observe the context and the conditions in which the newly
emerged plant begins to grow, and the process of growth.
Does this environment meet the growth needs of the plant? In
what way does the plant grow? Is it supported and, if so, in
what way?

Now pay attention to the plant itself. Notice whether or not
it is in flower or bud, or is fruiting; and the size, colour and
condition of these features.

Notice also the size, colour and condition of the leaves, and
whether they are healthy, diseased or pest ridden. Notice the
colour, number, strength and condition of the stem or stems.

How healthy is this plant? What does it need for its
potentials to fruit and flower? Are its needs being met? If not,
how can they be met?

Now observe the plant completing its lifespan, dying and
withering. What, if anything, does it leave? What are your
feelings as you watch it?

Allow the image to fade. When it has done so take time to
record your experience and any insights derived from it, noting
particularly what you may be able to learn from it about what
you need in order to be healthy and achieve your full
potential.

Commentary

The seed

A seed is a mature fertilised plant ovule consisting of an embryo
and its food store surrounded by a protective seed coat, which
has the capacity to develop into a plant. It is therefore the source
of a plant, and possesses its potentialities or latent and inherent
abilities for growth. It can be a potent symbol of the latent
potentials and capacities of a person, and its examination may
reveal what is needed for these potentials and capacities to be

fulfilled. Irrespective of the kind of seed imagined, each has its own distinctive character and potentials, and different growth requirements, so conditions suitable for one seed variety may not be right for another.

All kinds of seeds are imagined in response to the above exercise, including various kinds of nuts, fruit pits or stones, corms and bulbs. Acorns, corn, sunflower, bean, melon, orange, apple and cress are all quite common, although the list of possibilities is endless. Each has to be considered in terms of its own unique character, as a species of seed and as an individual example of that particular variety. Given the uniqueness of each seed it is not possible to consider one kind of seed as being better than another, although it may be possible to regard a seed of a particular variety as less viable, robust or prolific than others of the same kind, or those of a different variety. However, certain features apply to all seeds, notably the potential they possess for growth in general and for the development of special characteristics, and a degree of protection of these qualities. Examination of these features may therefore yield insight into the possibilities for personal expression.

One man described a chickpea seed, fat and stored with food, which he took to be a sign of abundant potential. Another man regarded the image of a very tough seed planted in a moist, well-aereated soil which met its growth needs, as an indication that his capacity to realise his potential is hard to maximise. One woman described herself as a secure and content seed that didn't want to put out roots: 'I felt as if I were nicely tucked in, closed in on myself a bit, and I didn't like having to spread out'. As is often the case in imagework it is possible to discern in this response that complacency is a defence against growth and change, in this case growth and development of a fairly basic nature, and a resistance to any expression of personal potential. Moreover, here, as in other instances, fear emerges as the underlying difficulty, the woman describing herself as the seed 'having to look over my shoulder to see who might see, interrupt or intrude upon me'.

Some people by-pass the seed stage, seeing themselves immediately as plants. One man interpreted this as typical of his impetuosity and impatience to reach his objectives, but realised that without regard for its seed his plant 'never had a chance' to do so. Indeed many people who imagine a plant but no seed realise in so doing that they have no idea of where they are coming from; no idea of who and what they really are, and thus of the true nature of their potentials.

Some people imagine a seed but have no idea what kind it is until it grows, when they often describe their surprise at the outcome. This suggests that they are looking for an identity, trying to find out who and what they are, and that, to the extent that they are unaware of these factors, they do not know how adequately their needs are being met. Other people wrongly identify the seed, as they discover when what they have taken to be a tulip grows into a daffodil. This may be regarded as an understandable mistake, given the similarity of the bulbs and the nature of the plants, but in cases where the seeds are very different in appearance and the resulting plants very different in nature this may be more perplexing, as when a person imagines herself to be a sunflower which grows into an oak tree. Although manifestly different, these plants nevertheless have similar characteristics such as height, strength, shade, durability, practicality and fruitfulness, albeit different growing requirements and conditions.

Sometimes the potential product of the seed is very different to that imagined by a person: a grass or corn seed grows into a decorative flower, or perhaps a weed, rather than a productive crop plant. This may reflect a person's basic confusion about his identity and the nature of his potentials. Confusion often occurs at a later stage of growth when the disparity between the identity attributed to the seed and the actual plant becomes apparent or it may be a feature of early development, when it is experienced as anxiety. The latter often promotes uncertainty and self-doubt, as is indicated by the woman who reported constantly asking herself 'Is this what I am?' at every phase of her development; whereas the former may give rise to shock, denial and rejection. Such was the case for a woman who was convinced her seed was a strong sunflower, only to discover subsequently that it put out shoots of mustard cress. She refused to acknowledge this as a true reflection of her potential or identity and imagined throwing it into the sea because she thought it useless. She saw subsequently that she had spent a good deal of her life submerged in tears (salt water), resenting the loss of potentials she never had, while not allowing those she had to develop. One woman who kept telling herself it was 'time' she knew what she was grew into an unidentified flower which eventually produced a dandelion-type 'clock'.

In some instances the 'seed' may not be recognisable as such. One young man imagined something like a teardrop on its side, which instead of roots produced fins that enabled the seed to move around and gradually transform into a fish. This suggested to him that he was not tied down, as a plant would be, but free and fast, and so could escape quickly from danger.

The feelings and thoughts evoked by these seed images may be of considerable significance in relation to a person's physical and emotional growth and development. Barbara Levine (1991) identifies catalysts for physical and emotional responses which she terms 'seedthoughts'. These she defines as thoughts a person thinks frequently that either come from or create their core beliefs. 'Just as the apple core contains seeds that sprout into an apple tree, you have at your core beliefs that shape you' (p. 49). These core beliefs, she suggests, are the basic assumptions and ideas upon which everyday thoughts and actions are based. According to Levine, therefore, a seedthought is an idea planted in the mind that grows into manifestation within the person. It may or may not be positive and health promoting. Indeed the examples provided above are both potentially unhealthy in that the woman's problem about her identity translates into a concern with time, which is a major contributory factor to stress and stress-related disorders or so-called 'hurry sickness' (Graham, 1990). Similarly, the man with the 'fishy' seed anticipates danger, which is suggestive of anxiety, in this instance that of 'the free-floating' variety, where the person is unable to relate his state of tension to an external object. This anxiety alerts the ego or self to danger so that it can act, and by so doing maintains the person in a state of psychological and physical readiness constituting a continual stress, and an inevitable drain on personal resources.

The growth medium

According to Levine the attitudes surrounding the seedthought determine its potency, just as the soil around a seed determines the strength and vitality of a plant. Certainly the medium in which the seed is planted is generally interpreted by people in terms of the attitudes and emotions surrounding them in early life, and usually relates to what can be thought of as the family culture. It is clear from their accounts that these experiences are very potent determinants of personal development.

The growth medium may be perceived as positive, as in the case of the woman who described 'a soft warm medium which gave me everything without my having to ask for it' and enabled her to establish firm roots. She described herself as a delicate child, feeling totally dependent on her family for survival and, although now no longer vulnerable, still reliant upon it for support.

The medium described by most people, however, typically fails to provide for the needs of the seed in some way, even where it is fundamentally sound. So, a woman who imagined her seed growing in good, peaty soil beneath a chalk layer considered the latter to reflect her view that her family life in late childhood was not as healthy as previously, having changed when her father died after a long illness when she was aged ten. Similarly, another woman imagined the good nutritious soil in which her seed was planted retreating, leaving her roots exposed and insecure. The soil could not be retained around the roots, and as a result the plant withered and failed to produce fruit. The great potential of the seed was therefore not realised despite the good quality of the initial growth medium, which was withdrawn.

In some cases the growth medium is deficient in only one particular requirement. One young woman described her seed planted in a light, loamy soil with plentiful nutrients, that offered little resistance to growing roots and enabled a broad root system to become established. She considered this to be consistent with her early life, having been reared by happily married parents who gave their children a great deal of respect and love. She was then surprised to imagine this soil as slightly dry, but related this to a period in her mid-teens when she 'went through a difficult phase', rebelling against authority at home and school. On reflection she considered that she had 'too much of a good life, too much attention and love, and insufficient discipline'. Her soil related to this lack of discipline and her reactions to it, which had left her feeling guilty about her behaviour towards her family.

The dryness or aridity of the growth medium is a commonly identified feature. (For reasons which are examined in Chapter 9 this usually relates to the emotional aspects of a person's experience.) In some cases this shortcoming is overcome with external assistance. One woman imagined her seed set in sand, where it took root and grew into a date palm, helped by 'others' who watered it. The providers of much-needed moisture are sometimes specified, as in the case of the woman who described her seed growing in 'well laid out formal gardens', well watered by her mother.

Sometimes the dryness of the growth medium is overcome by the seed itself. An apple pip planted in a huge desert was able to obtain water by way of hundreds of roots which extended for miles and supported the seed. However, although the seed survived these conditions, it produced no plant. Similarly, a woman who found her seed planted in an arid, windswept and insecure sand dune, imagined it adapting to its situation. Indeed, she found that by putting out deep, wide roots it not only withstood the situation but actually secured the dune rather than being carried away by it. By extending, the roots could also obtain and store water for particularly dry periods. This image suggests that by drawing support from further afield during her development she provided security in an insecure and arid situation, effectively holding it together rather than allowing it to drift apart.

In contrast to those whose growth medium is too dry, some imagine it to be too wet. One woman described herself as a seed planted on its own in the middle of a huge muddy field which made her feel suffocated and want to escape. She saw the sodden empty field as representing the bitterness and resentment she feels towards her parents for the lack of attention she received from them as a child. (Interestingly the word 'sodden' derives from *soden*, the past participle of *seethe*. Figuratively speaking, therefore, this woman is still seething with resentment at being ignored in childhood by her family.) Indeed, many people resent having been 'soiled' or 'muddied' by their past.

Some of those people who are initially concerned to find their seed waterlogged, subsequently discover that this is appropriate to the plant, as is the case with watercress and various flowers such as water iris. A few people are alarmed to find themselves at sea, believing sea water to be deadly to plants, only to discover that their seed is a kind of seaweed. In fact water is a very commonly reported growth medium.

It is possible for a seed to be in a wet environment without being in water, as is illustrated by a young woman who saw herself as a seed in a wet, sweet orange and 'loved it', recognising the thick skin of the fruit as a protection against her insecurities and an indication of her desire to protect herself against emotional injury.

The growth medium may have shortcomings other than in relation to its moisture content, notably lack of or excess warmth. Most people indicate that warmth is essential to the growth of their seed. Many people specify that the medium is too cold to enable easy germination, whereas others indicate that its warmth has quickly promoted growth. In certain 'barren environments' heat has caused seeds or the germinating shoots to shrivel.

Another requirement of the growth medium is the availability and adequacy of nutrients. One woman indicated that hers needed more fertiliser. A rather more 'down-to-earth' man who described his as needing manure, subsequently realised that 'the shit I have to deal with at work is actually necessary to my growth and development'. This reflects an important feature of this imagery in that growth needs not met by the family culture often have to be provided for at later stages of development. People who imagine the growth medium as minimal, as in the case of those who describe seeds growing on flannel or cotton wool, usually realise that it is insufficient to sustain continued development. So, a woman who imagined her seed growing on cotton wool realised that although her childhood had been warm and comfortable it was also extremely overprotective, and had not prepared her to cope adequately with the challenges of later life. However, a man who saw his seed germinating in nothingness, and surviving rather than thriving, realised that he was a survivor with the potential to thrive in a less vacuous context.

Roots

The *Collins English Dictionary* defines 'root' variously as the 'organ of a higher plant that anchors the rest of the plant in the ground, absorbs water and mineral salts from the soil'; 'the essential, fundamental or primary part or nature of something'; 'origin or derivation, especially as a source of growth, vitality or existence'; and 'a person's sense of belonging in a community, place, etc., especially the one in which he was born or brought up.' In the context of the present exercise roots tend to be an indication of a person's sense of security or groundedness within the initial growth medium or culture.

Seeds or plants may be imagined without roots. Invariably those who do so report feeling little or no sense of security or belonging. A woman who imagined herself as a cutting in a glass of water said that she had been informally adopted shortly after birth in somewhat unusual circumstances and had never felt a member of her 'adoptive' or any other family. Others claim their roots are 'not worth talking about', being short, weak, pale and insignificant. One man related the inadequacy of his roots to feelings about his family, indicating that after his parents' divorce in his early childhood, since when he has had no contact with his father or paternal grandparents, his only substantial relationships have been with his mother and sister.

Some people have difficulty imagining the seed putting out roots. A woman who described her roots being chewed by ducks was reminded of battles with her parents, who constantly argued with her and each other. Feelings of anxiety tend to be associated with shallow or inadequate roots, especially when the plants are tall and substantial such as sunflowers or cypress; or in certain circumstances, such as high wind, pressure, or being grazed or pushed by animals. Short roots may be a sign of impermanence. Not uncommonly people from itinerant families, especially those who have travelled to many countries, describe short roots as an indication that they have never put down roots anywhere. A woman who could only imagine lateral roots perceived this as reflecting her belief that her roots were in a foreign country and not in the British soil beneath her.

Indeed, many problems in relation to roots come about because people perceive them as growing in the wrong place. This is particularly true of trees, large shrubs and other outdoor plants grown in tubs, window boxes and other containers, sometimes indoors, rather than in open ground. These receptacles are usually synonymous with security and safety but also restrictiveness, entrapment and stunted growth. One man described feeling 'up against it' and 'with nowhere else to go' on realising that his roots were restricted in a heavy, cumbersome red pot despite a vast expanse of space around him. He felt the need to 'smash' his way out of the container in order to breathe. Others who have felt their roots to be pot-bound have also felt it necessary to burst out or to escape through holes in the bottom of the pot. One female student recognised the large black pot she imagined growing in as her family trapping her. She felt this to be particularly true of one family member who, by providing her with money, was freeing her from financial worries but also imposing pressure on her to produce good results and obliging her to work hard. However, as a result of the exercise she was able to talk to this person about the situation and subsequently felt greatly relieved.

Many people describe roots which are trapped and pot-bound but are unable to break free from their containers. They are reliant on others for transplantation so their lives are controlled by them. In most cases where transplantation occurs subsequent growth is rapid and satisfactory, but the upheaval caused by several moves of this kind can be traumatic. Numerous people identify the difficulties associated with being uprooted in this way, whether by being sent away to boarding school or changing schools, moving to different homes or areas, or into different families.

There may be impediments to growth other than confinement or relocation, both within and around the growth medium. Thus one man described pushing through obstacles in the soil until he learned to grow around them and recognised this as a reflection of his stubbornness.

By comparison to those people who describe restrictions upon their roots, many who imagine themselves growing in water discover a great sense of freedom. One woman, who initially tried to remove her seed from water, realised that it presented no restrictions, allowing her 'to go in whatever direction' she chose. A man decribed the advantages of floating in water with free-moving roots as being 'able to move freely and seek areas with the highest nutrient content'.

A sense of freedom is also highlighted by a woman who imagined an airborne seed floating across a field before falling to the ground and putting down roots. However, there are some people who imagine airplants or epiphytes, as opposed to airborne plants, which grow upon other plants or structures. While these are not necessarily parasitic they are nevertheless reliant on these other structures and tend to be circumscribed by them rather than free.

Emergent needs

Emerging from the medium in which they are growing represents for most people the first contact with the world beyond the immediate family. For some this is traumatic, as is reflected in their imagery. A man whose shoots had difficulty reaching the surface because of heavy soil, admitted that he had experienced great pressure in school and later in adolescence. In some instances exposure to a wider environment than the family challenges the person's existing self-concept. Thus a red-haired woman who initially thought she was a melon – exotic, warm, soft and very sweet, was shocked on reaching the surface to discover that she was a carrot – ordinary, earthy, hard, rather less sweet and identifiable as such by her 'carrot–top'.

Some shoots emerge at the surface weak, spindly and clearly not thriving, indicating that their needs have not been met and that they are at risk. Whether or not they thrive depends on the extent to which their growth needs are met by the wider environment. In some cases the risk is considerable. One man described his one shoot emerging in a very dangerous place – on a football field where a match was in progress. The football players care-lessly trampled and crushed the little shoot, but despite being damaged it continued to grow into a leafy bush with a woody stem, which made it impossible to play on the pitch. He accounted for this imagery in terms of his vulnerability as a child, describing himself as 'not at all tough', but little, sensitive, lively and imaginative. He saw the shoot's emergence on the playing field as representing his emergence from a sheltered home into the 'big wide world'; and its subsequent development as an indication of his persistence and inner strength. Badly scarred by his early experiences he became a rigid and insecure adolescent, tough and hard, but following a crisis in late adolescence he began to blossom into a quite different kind of person and, as his subsequent imagery revealed, a very different kind of plant. Similarly, a woman who described emerging from the ground as cress and being cut down, overcame this setback and grew as an apple tree.

Conditions in the external world can make it difficult for some people to establish an identity, as in the case of a woman who couldn't determine whether she was an acorn or a sunflower because all the shoots put out by her seed shrivelled in a hostile environment. By comparison one young woman who imagined herself as a plant growing in rich peaty soil in a large well-kept garden where she was 'not given freedom to run wild' saw this as a reflection of a very happy and sheltered, albeit rather strict childhood, in which she had been protected from the harsh realities of life, to the extent that she never heard anyone swear until she was in her late teens.

The plant

As the shoots begin to grow many of the conditions for the plant's growth transfer to its wider environment and surroundings. The condition of the plant is therefore an indication of the extent to which its requirements are being met. A very frail woman, suffering from myeloencephalopathy (ME), who imagined herself as a dwarf sunflower (someone suggested it was a bonzai version!) lacking sufficient warmth in the soil and environment realised in so doing that she always looks to others for positive encouragement rather than provide it herself. Others have described their plants as limp and unhealthy, with yellowing or dropping leaves. A man who described his plant as having been stunted in the past, realised that the disease with which it was afflicted – his past hurts and resentment – had not been totally eradicated and needed excising.

Sunflowers appear to be the best and most common expression of the human life force and potential, being vital, vibrant, strong, vigorous, striking, colourful, capable of reaching great heights, dignified, independent, impressive, versatile, useful, prolific and fruitful. In many cases, however, they are imagined as stunted, shrivelled, distorted, thwarted, undernourished, cold and non-productive. They also appear more likely than any other plant to be converted into something else during growth. In almost every instance where this occurs the seed or plant is described as lacking necessary warmth.

One young woman saw herself as a sunflower with a face, two arms and legs in a large black tub filled with good soil. Initially she thought it funny until she recognised that it represented her tendency not to take herself seriously and to undermine her potentials. She realised that the feeling of not being quite good enough shapes most of her responses and that the sunflower face's missing mouth signifies her difficulty in telling others how she feels. Another woman saw herself as the only sunflower among tomatoes. She observed, 'As for being an intruder, I'm certainly the black sheep of the family', and attributed the height of the sunflower to her desire to grow away from her family influence.

Other people have imagined themselves as plants growing in the wrong place. One young woman saw herself as a foxglove, grown indoors where it was unable to fulfil its purpose and attract bees. Unable to grow well in this situation, she was moved outdoors, close to the house. From there she tried to take steps towards a wood, but was unable to because she was still rooted in the family context she wanted to be rid of.

Some people recognise that the plant they imagine is a disappointment to others. One man saw himself as a trailing houseplant on a windowsill, which he described as 'totally useless' but very attractive and pretty, and a reflection of his desire to cultivate himself rather than the roles imposed upon him by others. In so doing he also realised and deeply resented, 'exactly what my parents wanted me to be – a potato', spending life outdoors, underground in the dark (perhaps in a pit), not enjoying life, but ultimately being useful.

A similar conflict is conveyed by the imagery of a woman who imagined a tulip bud alongside a piece of corn. The latter represented her farming family – true 'hearts of corn' – and the expectation planted in her at an early age by it that she would

sway with the wind when young it will not taper properly, that is, grow thickest at the base, which aids the tree's stability in windy conditions. Nor does it make an extensive anchoring root system. Research workers maintain that, with certain exceptions such as 'weeping' trees, most young trees require only the base of the stem to be supported and then only for a limited time. Eighteen months is thought quite ample in all but the most exposed positions, by which they mean gale-lashed coasts. Buchan concludes; 'It may seem a harsh tenet, but the sooner a tree is allowed to stand on its own roots the better . . . The best chance we can offer our trees is the chance to bend without harm before the storm'. She therefore urges gardeners 'to spend time checking whether you, or rather your trees, really need those stakes'. This advice would seem equally applicable to the imaginary variety.

Leaves

It sounds almost too trite to suggest that leaves may relate to 'leaving', but there are indications that, in some cases at least, this is so. One man described a plant which grew plenty of leaves low down on shoots which appeared above ground quickly. He considered that they reflected the fact that from the age of 12 he needed to grow up quickly, being obliged to be more mature and take on more responsibility in a single parent family than friends of the same age in 'normal' families. Another young man described himself as ivy growing in the shade of a tree, but quite uncharacteristically for this plant, growing away from the tree, the leaves progressing in an arrow-like formation but without any growth in the stem – simply a profusion of arrow-shaped leaves in one large arrow-like configuration, pointing away from the tree. He felt that this clearly signifies that his future path lies in a different direction from home, but that he is not yet ready to leave its security.

Growing to fruition

The flowers and fruit of a plant represent its lifetime achievements, and its seeds contain promise for the future, even after its death. While most people imagine a plant fruiting and flowering, many do not. Some describe their flowers being nipped in the bud or express concern about this possibility, as in the case of the woman previously referred to whose budding tulip had grown alongside corn. Others regard few flowers as the sign of under-achievement; thus a man who imagined only three flowers on his particular plant considered this to be an indication that he doesn't work hard enough to achieve his potential; claiming that if he were more ambitious his would be a beautiful plant with numer-ous large exotic flowers. A woman whose flowers opened one at a time considered this to mean that she opens herself up to one focus at a time; while another, who described a plant with one tulip-like flower which kept moving in different directions just as a human head might move, saw this as representing over-concern about her audience. A bean with numerous small flowers reflected one woman's belief that despite having potential in a number of areas she has done little to bring them to fruition, tending to start a number of things with great enthusiasm and then lose interest when application is needed, reflecting a lack of self-discipline she attributes to a lack of parental discipline in early life. Another woman who described emerging from a 'good growing environ-ment' nevertheless imagined her sunflower producing only leaves and flowers but not seeds.

This is a difficulty reported by a number of people and some find it distressing, as in the case of a woman who saw her infertile or non-existent seeds in relation to her inability to become preg-nant. This was particularly frustrating for her, because as she explained, 'after all, one of the best things about a sunflower is that one planted seed yields so many hundreds of new seeds'. Certainly there is something incongruous and possibly unhealthy about a sunflower that fails to produce seeds, but within the context of imagery this is very common. The woman previously referred to as suffering from ME and a 'bonzai' sunflower de-scribed the latter as unable to produce seeds, and decided that like her plant she needed encouragement to stretch herself higher and obtain what is necessary to bring her potentials to fruition.

It is not only sunflowers that fail to bear fruit. An elderly woman who imagined an evening primrose that failed to produce seed attributed this to her feelings of having achieved nothing of value in her life. Similarly a man who admitted to being dull and stuffy, and who looked much older than his years, described himself as an anonymous bush with a single stout trunk; a long-lived, tidy indoor plant, without flowers or fruit, the leaves of which yellowed and fell off the plant before it died, concluding in doing so that this indicated a long and ultimately fruitless life.

By contrast some people feel that they have 'gone to seed' too quickly. This tends to be true of several men who have produced families in early life and have felt their youth rush by almost unnoticed. Such a view is also echoed by the man who claimed he had 'no more fruits to bear, having given them all to others'.

Death and dying

Some people consider their death 'premature', as in the case of a woman who described her date palm being cut down in its prime and used by others for their own purposes, its fronds being chopped off for roofing material, half its trunk for support struts and the remainder for a dugout boat. However, in the process a child discovered a sucker that was protected and nurtured to grow again. Her imagery betrays a mixture of attitudes and emotions: resentment towards others after a lifetime of service, and an awareness of some continuity and remembrance after death. A rather different emotional tone is suggested in a man's imagery of an apple tree which had borne lovely blossom and fruit, and at its death experienced a very positive and fulfilling sense of having served and been a provider. Indeed it died leaving a beautiful legacy, having just shed its blossom. Another man considered that his death would leave a big gap, as indicated by his tree, which upon falling over left a huge crater. Many others describe feeling good about having achieved their purpose, even in death feeding insects on a dung heap and disintegrating into compost or feeding the ground.

Much imagery suggests a continuity after death – whether as plants regenerating by way of their seeds or in the form of long-lasting artefacts. Many people do not envisage their plants dying as such, but recycling year after year, as is best illustrated by a woman's snowdrop whose withering and death did not concern her because 'I left everybody looking forward to summer, and knowing that I would be back next year to mark the end of winter yet again'. Some imagery conveys a sense of regret and of missed opportunities. One man saw three beans remaining on his plant after it had shrivelled. He interpreted this as something positive he was holding on to; potential which had not been realised, having needed something to release it and enable it to flower. It is tempting to suggest that this image is less that of a 'has been' than a 'could have been'.

Some of the attitudes revealed in the imagery are not very positive and may be quite alarming. One young man imagined a tree in a forest being drawn progressively towards the edge, leaving the other trees behind as it did so, and then falling over the edge and dying, feeling great resentment at having been killed off too soon when enjoying life. He acknowledged that this imagery reflects his tendency to be drawn to the edge in a variety of ways and to become progressively distant from others, although he refused to be 'drawn' on the possible consequences of this tendency. Some people feel that their imagined plants are relieved to die. The man who saw his rootless plant as 'never having a chance', felt relief when it was dead and its suffering over. Another man saw his plant die peacefully, 'relieved after a busy life'.

Others resist death or even the idea of it. One woman found the idea difficult to accept because her plant had produced no fruits. She believed this reflects her sense of not having achieved anything in life or left her mark, and her fear of not capitalising on her potential and living to regret it in old age. Another woman didn't want her plant to die but found that its dying leaves fed the birds and the soil, and she realised that it would grow again after a period of retreat in the soil. A woman who imagined herself as an orange tree resisted death, 'holding on' to life as long as she could. Another plant refused to die – a fern, which interestingly does not die in a conventional sense but continuously recycles itself through a complex regenerative process. Nevertheless, this imaginary fern fell down, having suffered a massive heart attack.

Other plants do not die in any ordinary sense of the word; one shrank 'like a video running backwards to the same seed, alive and able to grow again'. Another reversed its telescopic-expansive process of growth in a 'gentle retreat to a state from which it could grow again', reflecting its creator's belief in reincarnation. Indeed, many people consider that their imagery reflects their belief in the latter or life after death or, indeed, the lack of such beliefs. Fears of death and dying are also sometimes revealed in negative and terrible images, such as burning, but this is quite unusual.

However, the deaths envisioned in the imagery are not necessarily referring to some final ultimate death but to what the psychiatrist Elisabeth Kübler-Ross refers to as the 'little deaths' of existence; the transitions and changes, losses and failures, disappointments and downfalls of everyday life. This is illustrated in the case of a woman coming to terms with major life changes. She imagined her plant toppling over and dying, but, in doing so, dropping a seed into the rich fertile earth produced by its own decay, which began to grow in a better situation and to reach its potential. She described this as her feeling true to herself, having learned from her past and made a new beginning. Like many people she had perhaps grown to realise the wisdom of André Gide's observation that:

It is better to be hated for what you are than loved for what you are not.

CHAPTER SIX

Raising
One's Spirit

A dunce once searched for a fire with a lighted lantern.
Had he known what fire was he could have cooked his
rice sooner.

FROM *The Gateless Gate*, J MURRAY, 1934

SOUL-SICKNESS

Abraham Maslow described a condition which he called 'the
psychopathology of the average' – the normal state of dis-ease or
literal soul-sickness (from the Greek *psyche*: soul and *pathos*:
suffering) that results from unmet needs for authenticity and self-
expression; needs which are spiritual inasmuch that they relate to
the very essence, inner core or spirit of a person; to the self or
soul. This, he claimed, is 'so undramatic and so widely spread
that we don't even notice it ordinarily' (1968, p. 16). Nevertheless,
as Jourard (1971, p. 31) indicated, 'Everywhere we see people
who have sold their souls (or their real selves) for roles'.

For the Ancient Greeks the spirit, soul or psyche was the very
source and essence of life; a dynamic life force synonymous with
the self. Human experience was conceived by the Greeks in terms
of paired opposite qualities and the soul as the overall balance or
harmony between them. Maintaining a sense of proportion or
proper balance was thus central to their world view and way of
life. When proportion or balance was lost so also was the integrity
of the soul which became unbalanced, irrational or fragmented
(from the Greek *ratio* – to break into fragments) and it was the
tragic consequences of human irrationality of losing a sense of

proportion – that were so dramatically depicted in Greek theatre. All human problems were seen as disharmony or dis-ease of the soul and all illness as symptomatic of this underlying psychopathology or soul-sickness, and therefore fundamentally spiritual in origin. Accordingly treatment was directed to the cure of the soul or psychotherapy, through restoration of its balance and harmony. The study of the soul, or psychology, was therefore essential to Greek culture.

This concern with the soul and its development was common to all the cultures of the ancient world. The ethnopsychologist Holger Kalweit (1988, p. 21) observed, 'if mankind has one thing in common it is surely the belief in the existence of a soul . . . This notion can be found almost without exception among all traditional peoples and cultures and indeed also in modern civilisation, albeit only in subcultural groups'. Certainly the idea of the soul as an animating, separable, surviving entity; the vehicle of individual personal existence, is continuous throughout Western history from antiquity to the present. Jung has indicated that the history of Western psychology until the seventeenth century consists essentially in the enumeration of doctrines concerning the soul and throughout the same period medicine was largely the application of this knowledge concerning the soul to healing. Accordingly traditional healers made no distinctions between religion and medicine.

However, the advent of Christianity affected the practice of medicine quite dramatically. All that was pagan was systematically eliminated, including the practices of medicine. From the Renaissance onwards Western culture acknowledged the soul less and less. By the nineteenth century science had become the ultimate authority within Western culture, and the values and meanings formerly provided by organised religions were progressively eroded. With the rise of economic materialism and a mechanistic, purely object-oriented science, modern culture came to look upon the psyche as a conglomeration of biological, physiological and sociocultural factors, with the result that the soul was regarded as no more than a primitive and superstitious notion without any content or reality. Consequently, 'the modern belief in the primacy of physical explanations has led to a psychology without a psyche' or soul. 'As for a modern scientific psychology which starts from the spirit, there simply is none' (Jung, 1960, p. 344).

The emergence of soul-less psychology can be attributed in good measure to the influence of Sigmund Freud who, in his attempts to develop a psychology consistent with the scientific thinking of the time, created 'a model of human consciousness which dispensed with spiritual aspirations and made them disreputable' (Jackson, 1992, p. 13). Freud was a self-proclaimed enemy of religion, viewing it as a universal obsessional neurosis; an illusion preventing man from reaching maturity and independence.

Such a view is not entirely without foundation since as the theologian Paul Tillich (1952) observed, religion can reduce the openness of man to reality and above all the reality which is himself. He acknowledged that in this way religion can protect and feed a potentially neurotic state, although religion as such does not lead to or directly support pathological self-reduction.

The psychiatrist Viktor Frankl (1969) considered that many people in contemporary society live in an existential and spiritual vacuum which arises because of the gulf between their need for meaning in life on the one hand and the lack of any perceived meanings on the other. He claimed that as a result of this frustration of their desire for meaning many people suffer from what he termed a 'noogenic neurosis', the remedy for which is the discovery or rediscovery of meaning in life. Such a view is shared by many psychotherapists and psychiatrists, including R.D. Laing who considered much mental illness to be a spiritual striving for meaning which is often misunderstood, misrepresented and thwarted.

Although the impressions of clinicians do not constitute firm evidence they do suggest that meaning in life is an important human need. American professor of psychiatry Irving Yalom relates this need to fundamental perceptual processes demonstrated by the gestalt psychologists whereby incoming stimuli are instantaneously organised into patterns or gestalten in the manner outlined in Chapter 1.

Thus, when presented with random dots on wallpaper, one organizes them into figure and ground; when confronted with

a broken circle, one automatically perceives it as complete;
when presented with diverse behavioral data – for example, a
strange noise at night, an unusual facial expression, a senseless
international incident – one makes 'sense' out of it by fitting it
into a familiar explanatory framework. When any of these
stimuli or situations do not lend themselves to patterning, one
feels tense, annoyed and dissatisfied. This dysphoria persists
until a more complete understanding permits one to fit the
situation into some larger, recognizable pattern.

YALOM, 1980, p. 462

It is clear from gestalt studies that man needs to make sense of
the random stimuli and events in his everyday world, and tries to
impose meaning or coherence on them. Yalom suggests that man
also approaches his existential situation in much the same way,
searching for patterns, explanations and meanings of existence in
an attempt to overcome his feelings of dis-ease in the face of an
indifferent and unpatterned world. So man's search for meaning
in life is necessary to relieve the anxiety that comes from facing a
life and world without an ordained comforting structure.

According to Yalom, man also needs meaning because it gives
rise to values – necessary guidelines or principles by which to live.
These not only provide a blueprint for personal action but also
make it possible for individuals to live in groups: 'Social norms
emanate from a meaning schema that has the consensus of the
group, and provide the predictability necessary for social trust
and cohesion. A shared belief system not only tells individuals
what they ought to do but what others will probably do as well'
(1980, p. 464).

Meaning therefore reduces uncertainty and the anxiety that this
gives rise to. There are, however, different levels of meaning, as
Yalom observes:

'What is the meaning of life?' is an enquiry about *cosmic
meaning*, about life in general, or at least about whether
human life fits into some overall coherent pattern. What is the
meaning of *my* life? is a different inquiry and refers to what
some philosophers term 'terrestrial meaning'. Terrestrial
meaning ('the meaning of my life') embraces purpose: one who

possesses a sense of meaning experiences life as having some purpose or function to be fulfilled, some overriding goal or goals to which to apply oneself.

1980, p. 423

As defined above, cosmic meaning implies some design existing outside and superior to the person, and invariably refers to some magical or spiritual ordering of the universe, whereas terrestrial meaning may have foundations that are entirely secular. Yalom identifies various secular activities that provide human beings with a sense of life purpose. These include the following.

Altruism	'Leaving the world a better place to live in', serving others and participation in charity
Dedication to a cause	The family, the state, politics, religion, artistic or scientific endeavour, and so on
Creativity	
Hedonism	Living life fully, searching for pleasure in the deepest possible sense
Self-actualisation	Dedicating oneself to realizing one's inbuilt potentials
Self-transcendence	Transcending self-interest and striving towards something greater than oneself

An individual may therefore have a personal sense of meaning without a cosmic sense of meaning. Yalom indicates that a person who possesses a sense of cosmic meaning generally experiences a corresponding sense of terrestrial meaning in that the latter consists of fulfilling or harmonising with that cosmic meaning. Traditionally, cosmic meaning has been provided by religions which have permitted a vast number of interpretations of individual life purpose.

THE CURE OF SOULS

The secularisation of society has profound implications for the Western perspective of the human spirit or soul. This was first replaced by mind and then by brain functions, which, for a materialist culture, have a more reassuring physical basis. Psychopathology thus came to be seen as 'mental' illness and psychotherapy, its treatment, within the province of the 'brain' sciences. Accordingly doctors, psychiatrists and psychologists inherited what Frankl (1969a) has termed 'a medical ministry', for which they have no specialised expertise or training and accordingly are frequently unable to fulfil. It has therefore fallen to them to wrestle with the task of reconciling the spiritual and psychical with the material and medical – a venture doomed to fail, since as Jung (1978) has observed Western science has paid no attention to spiritual needs and aspirations, at least, that is, until relatively recently. Even so, it is now widely acknowledged within medicine that as much as two-thirds of all patients seen by doctors are suffering, not from any physical or organic pathology as such, but from what might loosely be called 'problems in living', which formerly would have been dealt with by the priest, pastor or rabbi.

> In the past hundred years in particular what might be called 'the religious answer' has progressively lost its punch, with more and more people turning to the textbooks of science in an attempt at understanding the strange physical and mental environment we live in . . . unfortunately where the answers provided by religion fail to satisfy, science frequently has no suitable alternative.
>
> EVANS, 1974, P. 9

Inevitably therefore the loss of traditional explanations created for many people a vacuum, an emptiness and a meaninglessness, and prompted an active search for new meanings and answers which is reflected in a growing fascination with alternative and unfamiliar views of the human predicament, especially those provided by different ages and cultures.

Over the past 30 years, as church attendance and commitment has declined, there has been a dramatic upsurge of interest in the spiritual traditions of antiquity and the East, in all forms of shamanism and traditional healing, mysticism, magic, the supernatural and the occult. Whereas until recently mysticism was seen as symptomatic of mental disturbance it is now recognised as representing an expression of yearning, and both disillusionment and dissatisfaction with scientific truth. Indeed the US Group for the Advancment of Psychiatry reached the conclusion (reported in *The Practitioner* in 1977) that 'the comfort and satiation of the consumer society may create a need for non-material satisfaction, and the material advances of science and technology a desire for experience that transcends the rational'.

The quest for meaning has also led to the emergence of numerous cults and quasi-religions, many of which have met with strenuous opposition, especially in the aftermath of the Waco tragedy of 1993 in Texas, in which 86 followers of the so-called Branch Davidian cult perished. However, although the fanatical adherence of some people to some of these cults might be pathological there can be little doubt that they represent peripheral manifestations of a valid need for meaning in existence and a reaffirmation of identity in a world from which humankind has come to feel alienated.

The upsurge in religious interest has prompted commentators to declare the late twentieth century an era of religious revival and renewal of faith. Others regard the climate of the times as therapeutic rather than religious in that there has been a dramatic increase in both the number of available psychotherapies and those who have sought them. Any such distinction is, however, somewhat arbitrary given that psychotherapies of any denomination are in many cases treating the very same condition, or disease, to which religion traditionally responds. 'Not only Christianity with its symbols of salvation, but all religions including the primitive with their magical rituals are forms of psychotherapy which treat and heal the suffering of the soul, and the suffering of the body caused by the soul' (Jung, 1954, Vol. 16, p. 16). This 'soul-sickness' now frequently leads many people to seek help from counsellors, psychologists and psychiatrists where before they might have sought clerical guidance.

Psychotherapists . . . are increasingly confronted by would-be patients who do not manifest any of the more objective hallmarks of a neurotic problem, who do not complain of failures of productivity or achievement, who do not suffer from serious interpersonal conflicts, who are free of functional somatic complaints, who are not incapacitated by anxiety, or tormented by obsessions, whose objective life circumstances they confess are close to optimal. These seekers for help suffer a freedom from complaint. The absence of conflicts, frustrations and symptoms brings a painful awareness of absence – the absence of faith, of commitment, of meaning, of the need to search out personal, ultimate values, or the need to live comfortably and meaningfully each day in the face of final uncertainty.

SCHOFIELD, 1964, p. 150

Schofield suggests that for increasing numbers of rational, educated and thoughtful people the central struggle becomes one of finding and keeping an emotional and psychological balance between 'the pain of doubt' and the 'luxury of faith'. Accordingly psychotherapists become their principal allies in the struggle for composure and peace of mind, and it is to them that people often turn in the hope of achieving the modern equivalent of salvation – 'mental health'.

THE PEAK OF HEALTH

At the forefront of this mental health movement was Abraham Maslow, for whom health was equivalent with self-actualisation, the characteristic features of which 'peak' in an ability for mystical or spiritual experiences which he regarded as evidence of man's ability to transcend present personal experience to some ultimate experience or reality. According to Maslow the meaning and purpose of human life is the fulfilment or actualisation of its potentials, and the values by which to live are those intrinsic to this end that the individual will discover intuitively if he or she trusts to his or her organismic wisdom. 'Authentic selfhood can be defined in part as being able to hear these impulse-voices within oneself, i.e., to know what one really wants or doesn't want, what one is fit for and what one is *not* fit for' (1968, p. 191).

Maslow's views share much in common with Eastern psychological traditions, notably Buddhism, Hinduism and Taoism. The psychiatrist Erich Fromm (1951) has identified these as 'humanistic' religions, in contradistinction to what he terms the 'authoritarian' religions of Western culture, in which God is viewed as the supreme power or force over man, who is utterly powerless. Within this tradition God is also viewed as external to man which, Fromm suggests, leads to man's alienation from himself and his own powers, which are projected on to God, making him both slavishly dependent on God and bad or sinful to the extent that he transgresses against God's will. Indeed, according to the Judeo-Christian tradition the entire human race was punished for Adam's original sin of disobedience by its fall from God's favour and consequent loss of Paradise.

By contrast the humanistic religions of the East are centrally concerned with man's innate potential for transcendence, for inasmuch that they are theistic, God is viewed not as external to man, but as residing within him. Man is seen as a manifestation of God and emphasis is upon him realising, in his own nature, his godliness. God is therefore a symbol of man's personal powers, that he should strive to realise in his life, and not a symbol of force and domination. The aim of such religion is to achieve the greatest strength, not the greatest powerlessness. Virtue is self-realisation, not obedience; faith is conviction based on one's own experience rather than the propositions and dogma of others, and the prevailing mood is joy rather than sorrow or guilt. Fundamentally therefore, humanistic religions emphasise man's belief in himself and his basic goodness, whereas the authoritarian religions encourage a belief in man as basically bad or evil, which makes it difficult for people to believe in or trust themselves and their impulses.

Jung was influenced by Eastern religions and within his psychology the self can be considered as the God within, and the individual, in seeking self-realisation, unity and wholeness, the means by which, as he put it, 'God seeks his goal'.

The aims, objectives and values of Eastern religious traditions also underpin the 'humanistic' psychology Maslow inspired during the 1960s. This is concerned not only with self-actualisation and personal growth as fundamental objectives but also aspects of human experience such as creativity, spontaneity, spirituality, higher values, intuitive processes and transcendent states that have little or no place in the predominant psychological approaches and therapies. It subsequently spawned the so-called 'human potential movement' and a proliferation of 'humanistic' psychotherapies, notably the person-centred therapy of Carl Rogers.

Rogers did not actually acknowledge the spiritual aspect of his work until quite late in life and when he did so (1980) it was to recognise spirituality in much the same way as Maslow, that is, as the outcome of the actualising tendency. He also identified it as an important quality in the therapist and thus as an intrinsic feature of the healing relationship.

> I find that when I am closest to my inner, intuitive self, when I
> am somehow in touch with the unknown in me, when perhaps
> I am in a slightly altered state of consciousness, then whatever
> I do seems to be full of healing. Then, simply my *presence* is
> releasing and helpful to the other . . . it seems that my inner
> spirit has reached out and touched the inner spirit of the other.
> Our relationship transcends itself and becomes a part of
> something larger.
>
> ROGERS, 1980, p. 129

He indicated that this kind of transcendent phenomenon had also been experienced within group therapy, changing the lives of some of those involved and concluded: 'Our experiences in therapy and in groups, it is clear, involve the transcendent, the indescribable, the spiritual. I am compelled to believe that I, like many others, have underestimated the importance of this mystical, spiritual dimension' (1980, p. 130).

Recognition of this aspect of psychotherapy prompted the professor of psychiatry Thomas Szasz to define it as 'the religion of the formally irreligious' (1979, p. 9). While this may not be a view all psychotherapists would share, especially those with a Freudian or a behavioural orientation, it is a not unjustifiable claim in the light of Maslow's observation that the more humanistic approaches 'give promise of developing into the life-philosophy, the religion-surrogate, the value-system, the life-program that these people have been missing' (1968, pp. iii–iv). Indeed, he considered these to be transitional; a preparation for a transpersonal, transhuman psychology 'centred in the cosmos rather than in human needs and interest, going beyond humanness, identity, self-actualization, and the like'. Certainly during the 1970s transpersonal psychology developed into a fully-fledged movement which emphasised the empirical, scientific study of spiritual experience and altered states of consciousness.

Throughout the 1980s transpersonal psychology had grown alongside research into altered states of consciousness, drug-induced experience and Eastern religions, which reflected the growing interest in and experimentation with these within Western culture. Disappointment with the limited answers revealed by science led many people to turn increasingly towards themselves for answers to their questions of the spirit. This may be seen as an attempt to regain a lost perspective in Western culture, that of human experience. It prompted a return to fundamental concerns such as the nature of mind and consciousness, which increasingly are being addressed within fields of scientific enquiry, including that most physical of sciences, physics. Therefore neither Freud nor the scientific world view has succeeded in eliminating the concept of soul from the thinking of the populace or contemporary theorising.

Indeed quite the contrary is the case. The psychologist Margaret Donaldson (1992) has provided a new structure for looking at the human mind in which religious and mystical experience find a niche as a fourth and transcendent mode of mind, thereby legitimising spirituality, ultimate values and self-transcendence as areas of concern for 'scientific' psychology. That these are not simply legitimate but necessary concerns for science is most evident in the declaration of the Third International Symposium on Science and Consciousness held, appropriately, at ancient Olympia, Greece in January 1993, and attended by 100 scientists from 20 countries, to the effect that the development of spiritual values and understanding of consciousness are vital if mankind is to survive the ecological and social crises gripping the world.

We believe it is vital to recognize that the basic problem behind these crises is the lack of understanding of more profound aspects of human consciousness and a dangerous denial of spiritual values. We speak especially of the realization of our fundamental inter-connectedness and interdependence and the deep values of cooperation which arise from this realization. Therefore, we of the Third International Symposium on Science and Consciousness call for intense, world-wide efforts by all people, especially scientists, educators and decision makers, to foster the development of spiritual values in our lives. IF WE DO NOT DO SO WE ARE UNLIKELY TO SURVIVE.

CITED IN CADUCEUS, 1993, 20, p. 43

Increasingly, therefore, it is being recognised that failure to acknowledge and meet spiritual needs and values jeopardises not only the health of the individual and society, but also the planet itself. Advocacy of spirituality as the key to healing is therefore becoming more commonplace.

MEANINGFUL RESEARCH

Moreover, empirical evidence for these claims, although limited, is increasing. The relationship between health and religion has received attention from health professionals, epidemiologists and public health researchers, although much of this is quite recent (Vaux, 1976; Levin & Markides, 1986, 1987) as sociologists of religion have become alerted to the potential for the empirical study of health outcomes, and health professionals reconsider the relevance of religious beliefs and practices for health promotion and disease prevention. The relationship between religion and cancer mortality has been the focus of numerous published articles which generally suggest that religious participation and affiliation influences health behaviour, and reduces cancer mortality rates. Specifically, frequency of church attendance and general commitment have been identified as important predictors of cancer mortality among those who profess some religious affiliation (Enstrom, 1975, 1978).

Religion is linked to health predominantly by way of dietary or lifestyle prescriptions or proscriptions. Religious attitudes and behaviours can therefore have different effects on health-related activities ranging from drinking, smoking and multiple sexual contacts, to nutrition. Religion not only influences health and mortality by way of specific health practices but also through variables such as group membership, social networks and support. It has been established that religion has a powerful effect on the way many people live, on the quality of their lives and on the length of time they live to experience that quality (Jarvis & Northcott, 1987). Moreover, there is evidence that the general population in an area with a high concentration of religious participants may experience health benefits resulting from diminished exposure or increased social disapproval of behaviours relating to cancer mortality. Research shows that religion has a significant impact on mortality rates for all malignancies combined, and for digestive and respiratory cancer in particular (Dwyer et al., 1990).

It has also indicated that religious belief is a very potent factor in reducing death anxiety in both healthy individuals and those who are terminally ill, and that 'it is a powerful sustaining force and one that those in the helping professions . . . must be able to appreciate and implement to the patient's greatest benefit' (Gibbs & Achterberg-Lawlis 1978, p. 568). A report published by the Spiritual Care Work Group of the International Work Group on Death, Dying and Bereavement (1990) also emphasises the importance of respecting a person's spiritual beliefs and helping him to meet his spiritual needs, but indicates that the spiritual dimension of patients is too often neglected because health care professionals do not recognise the spiritual component of health care; that dying and death are spiritual rather than simply physical events, and that the search for spirituality may be heightened as a person approaches death.

The problem, for both health care professionals and researchers, is to differentiate adequately between religious belief or affiliation and spirituality. While the former generally encompasses the latter it is not necessarily the case that the reverse is true, and it cannot be assumed that religious belief and spirituality are equivalent. Many formally non-religious people are highly spiritual and many people who profess a religious belief are markedly a-spiritual. Attempts to clarify the concept of spirituality for exploratory study have led to the emergence of a construct of spiritual well-being and the Spiritual Well-being Scale of Measurement (Poloutzian & Ellison, 1982; Ellison, 1983). This incorporates features of what Davidson (1972) has referred to as the 'horizontal' or 'this worldly' dimension of spirituality that includes perception of life's purpose and satisfaction, apart from any specifically religious reference; and features of the 'vertical' or 'other worldly' dimension identified by Davidson, that includes specifically religious issues like the perception of well-being in relation to a higher being or entity. In a study using the Spiritual Well-being Scale Kaczorowski (1989) demonstrated that irrespective of age or gender there is among adults diagnosed with cancer an inverse relationship between anxiety and spiritual well-being such that when the latter is high anxiety is low. This, she considers, lends support to the claim that spirituality reduces anxiety.

Another measure, the Purpose in Life Test or PIL, was developed in 1964 by two psychologists, James Crumbaugh and Leonard Maholick, for the assessment of the 'horizontal' dimension of spirituality and it has since been widely used as a research tool. Studies have shown that there is a significant relationship between high PIL scores and strong religious beliefs, idealism and self-transcendence; that is, interests that extend beyond the individual's material and mental well-being; and also that high PIL scores are associated with low death anxiety. High PIL scores are also associated with involvement in organised groups, whether religious, ethnic, political or community based; community service, sports and hobbies.

Generally, patient populations have a lower PIL score than non-patient populations, and the average score of hospital in-patients is significantly lower than hospital out-patients. Delinquent adolescents and students who abuse drugs have been shown to have low PIL scores, as have patients hospitalised for chronic alcoholism and severe mental disorders. Highly neurotic individuals have low PIL scores, and sexually frustrated and maladjusted students have lower scores than normal students, as do students who have not made vocational choices.

The research findings lend support to the observations of

numerous clinicians who, like Yalom (1980, p. 431), have noted 'that those patients who experience a deep sense of meaning in their lives appear to live more fully and to face death with less despair than those whose lives are devoid of meaning'. They broadly support Maslow's claims by suggesting a roughly linear association between a lack of meaning in life and psychopathology such that the less the sense of meaning the greater the severity of the psychopathology. They also suggest an association not only between a positive sense of meaning in life and deeply held religious beliefs, but also self-transcendent values, membership of groups, community service, dedication to some cause and the adoption of clear life goals; that is, secular activities cited by Yalom as providing life meaning and purpose.

Taken as a whole therefore the results of research lend support to the proposition that some sense of meaning or purpose in life, however this is achieved, is an important factor in personal well-being, health and healing; and that 'meaning makes a great many things endurable – perhaps everything' (Jung, cited by Yalom, 1980, p. 432).

The following exercise is directed towards exploration of meaning and purpose in life.

EXERCISE 6

Imagine that it is a warm evening and that you are sitting, comfortable and relaxed, on a hillside above a town. You remain sitting as dusk begins to fall, watching the lights as they go on in the town below and the patterns they make. Suddenly you become aware of a non-threatening, reassuring presence and a figure which intuitively you recognise as the wise hermit who, according to local folklore, lives on the hill.

Approaching you the hermit says, 'If you go down into the town tonight you will find whatever you are looking for in life', and having done so walks away with no explanations and with no time for you to ask questions.

How do you react to this statement? What are you thoughts and feelings? Do you want to go into the town or stay where you are?

Irrespective of your initial reactions, you feel impelled to go into the town. Be aware of your feelings as you do so. Seek out the place, person or situation to which you feel drawn. Don't go merely where you think you should. Follow the dictates of your heart and see where it leads you.

Where do your feelings lead you? What do you find there? What occurs as you find it? How do you react? What, if anything, changes? How do you feel? What do you do then?

If you can't find what you are looking for, just let go of all ideas of what you might find and take what comes, noting your reactions and feeling as you do so.

Allow yourself to return to normal awareness. Then record your experience in the first person present tense, noting what you have learned from the experience.

Commentary

Many people have found the above experience extremely powerful in focusing attention on the direction, or lack of it, in their lives, and in prompting them to question their aims and values. In some instances it has provided a significant impetus for change, clarified important decisions and resolved inner conflicts. It has also yielded other significant insights, some of which are not directly or apparently related to the central issue of meaning in life. Some of these insights have arisen in relation to the hermit.

The hermit on the hill

This figure presents in many guises. Very commonly it reflects stereotypical notions about hermits and recluses, often being of shabby and possibly unkempt appearance, sometimes dwarfish or troll-like, with long hair and/or beard, and wearing long robes in the manner of a monk or other monastic person, or a 'hippy' from the 1960s. It may be an historical sage like Socrates or Plato, a mythical or fictional character, a cartoon figure, or even a famous celebrity. A woman dismissed the hermit as silly because she saw it as the actor Sir Alec Guinness and, having failed to find anything in her imaginary 'town', was inclined to regard the exercise as meaningless for her. However, in the course of the next week she suddenly understood its meaning when she realised that the actor had appeared as Obi-Wan Kenobi, the great sage in the *Star Wars* films, and that it was he or rather his guidance in understanding the 'force' – the life force or energy of which he was a master – that she was looking for to provide her with meaning in life; a non-religious, spiritual understanding which she had been searching for throughout her life but had not previously recognised.

Another woman imagined the hermit as that from the Tarot pack, who gives the choice between following him to live the reclusive life or going down the path of life which he lights with his lantern. She chose the latter, but a man, whose imagery was very similar, refused it because the lantern didn't shed enough light on issues and fears lurking in the dark beyond. However, this man did accept the hermit's offer of an apple and a comb, which he associated with those used by the Wicked Witch in her attempt to poison Snow White. He identified these with his attempt to break off a romance and to 'kill off' his girlfriend. When pointed out to him that poisoning is a cowardly act he acknowledged that he could not show anger or aggression to her or to others directly, and that the 'poisonous' feelings he could not confront her with manifested in frightening dreams, physical sensations and pain. It was therefore necessary for him to be able to deal with these feelings in order to have the 'meaningful' relationships he desired.

For a significant number of people the hermit appears as a much loved or respected grandparent, now dead; for others it may appear as a guardian angel. It may be a bird or animal; and in some cases, as with Obi-Wan Kenobi, the hermit and the 'discovery' are the same. For one young woman they appeared as a black snake which she identified as a symbol of her sexuality and as a recurrent image of terrifying dreams in which it chased her away from a group of children towards whom she felt very positive. However, as she explained, in this exercise the snake's menace was reduced because it was knotted and therefore unable to chase her, and no longer positioned between her and the children as in her dreams, but beyond them. She realised that fear of sexuality stood between her and the children she wanted in life, and that as they were tied up together she needed to resolve the conflict between sexuality and creativity.

Reactions to the hermit vary greatly. Some people are frightened by it. Others are reassured, as in the case of a young woman who imagined the hermit to be her grandfather, whom she had been unable to visualise since his death and whom she felt was looking after her. Some people refuse to take their hermit seriously, perhaps a reflection of their attitude towards their intuition or inner wisdom, or a more general approach to life. Thus a man who didn't take his hermit seriously still went into the town because he had 'nothing better to do'.

Viktor Frankl has suggested that when free time makes a person aware of the fact that there is nothing they *want* to do they are suffering a crisis of meaninglessness that is typically characterised by feelings of boredom, apathy, emptiness, cynicism, aimlessness and a sense of the pointlessness of life's activities. He claimed that depression, obsessionalism, delinquency, promiscuity and various forms of addiction rush in to fill 'the existential vacuum' created by this meaninglessness syndrome, giving rise to existential or 'noogenic' neurosis, which is also reflected in conformist and submissive behaviours as the person does what others do or what they are told to do, in the absence of any clear idea as to what he wants to do or traditional guidance as to what he should do.

Like Frankl the psychiatrist Salvador Maddi considers that much current psychopathology emanates from a sense of meaninglessness. He has identified 'crusadism', which he defines as the compulsive engagement in activities arising out of an individual's deep sense of purposelessness, as one form of existential sickness. This is characterised by a powerful inclination to seek out and dedicate oneself almost indiscriminately to a cause or issue, irrespective of content or danger, or one's belief in it. In the present exercise crusadism may manifest in responses where the hermit's guidance is not taken seriously but is followed 'just for the hell of it' or out of a sense of adventure.

Others take the hermit's guidance seriously but are reluctant to act upon it or do so only grudgingly. In some cases this may be an indication of complacency and a dread of change. One woman described not wanting to go down into the town and feeling horrible, awful and hateful when she realised that she must leave the comfort of the hillside. Another did not want to go into the town because she believed that everything she wanted in life was on the hill, only to be proved wrong when she did venture into the town. Another hesitated because she was not sure she wanted to find what she is looking for in life.

This reluctance to discover what is being sought often arises from a fear of disappointment or failure and from negative attitudes of the 'I never get what I want so why bother trying' variety. Such reactions negate the biblical injunction to 'ask, and it shall be given you; seek, and you shall find; knock, and it shall be opened to you. For every one that asketh, receiveth; and he that seeketh, findeth; and to him that knocketh, it shall be opened' (Matthew, vii, 7–8), and justify lack of effort on the person's behalf.

Maddi has identified this inability to believe in the usefulness or value of endeavour in life as vegetativeness, claiming that it is the most extreme form of purposelessness and very widespread in contemporary culture. He indicates that if this 'why bother?' syndrome continues unchecked it can lead to a severe state of apathy and aimlessness, culminating in total indifference and depression, and possible withdrawal from life. He suggests that many institutionalised psychiatric patients suffer from this condition. Indications of this tendency can be found in some responses to the present exercise, such as that of the woman who was hoping to find friendship in life, although ordinarily she cannot be bothered to look for friends or act in a friendly way, expecting others to come to her offering friendship, companionship and acceptance.

Maddi has also identified another form of existential sickness, nihilism, whereby a person frustrates attempts to discover meaning, thereby justifying the futility of trying to find meaning in anything. Maddi attributes this to despair and claims that it is so commonplace it is not even recognised as a problem, and is sometimes regarded as a sophisticated approach to life. There are indications of this tendency in the reactions of some individuals to the present exercise. One person insisted that it was impossible to descend the hillside where she imagined herself sitting as there were no paths up or down it and no point in attempting to as there was no town below. Several people do go down towards the town but claim not to be able to penetrate the darkness or find anything other than darkness itself. One woman justified not looking for anything because of her fear of being raped in the blackness. A doorway that another woman located in the darkness began to shrink in the manner of that in Lewis Carroll's *Alice in Wonderland*, and when she attempted to get through it a shutter came down, barring her way altogether. She recognised in this her tendency to keep reducing the possibilities for discovering what she is looking for. Other people, upon realising that the approach road constantly bends and winds or zig-zags, so that they never reach the town, frequently acknowledge that they are distancing themselves from whatever is to be found there, and that usually they tend to put obstacles between themselves and their objectives.

The town

This tendency towards nihilism also manifests in a person's attitude towards the town and the way it is imagined. One woman claimed that she knew from the outset that she would find nothing in the town. Another imagined herself trapped in a grim, dark town lacking all signs of life. The layout of the town was maze-like and, as she wandered its short streets, turning corner after corner in an attempt to find her way out, she felt she would never discover anywhere different. She could see no gap or alleyway between the buildings, no people and no lights, being able to see only by the reflection of the moon in puddles which seemed to be on the walls of the buildings and the ground, although it was not raining.

Similarly, a man imagined himself as the 'Third Man' in the drab, shadowy surroundings of post-war Vienna. He described being able to hear violin music mocking him as he walked endlessly trying to find what he was looking for; the tempo of the music quickening the harder he looked. He felt cheated and very depressed when he could find nothing. Afterwards he indicated that he feels bitter about the end of a three-year relationship and, with no direction in his life, no one to guide him and no beliefs to motivate him, spiritually empty.

An even more profound sense of meaninglessness emerges in the account of a woman who imagined herself in a Transylvanian town, full of apparently happy people in festive mood. Despite the high spirits of those around her she experienced a sense of foreboding, which she described as if 'everyone was waiting for something to happen; having a last party before all hell broke loose'. To make matters worse, she was on the lookout for vampires, convinced of their existence and that she was to be the next victim. She felt scared and trapped, believing that there was nothing beyond the town except darkness. There are several nihilistic features in this account: feelings of alienation, futility and despair; the tendency to view the activities of others as senseless or meaningless; and a strong sense that the hell about to break loose is that of the principal figure, the woman herself. Moreover, it highlights another feature of the nihilist as identified by Maddi: the quickness to doubt the positive in man and to point to 'the monster' concealed beneath a thin veneer of civilisation.

While some people can find no point in looking, others appear half-hearted, lacking conviction in and commitment to what they are doing. It is as though they want to but can't quite allow themselves to believe that there is something worth looking for. Frequently they don't give themselves enough time and they tend to give up easily. A typical example of this tendency is the woman who decided there was nothing for her in the few shops she looked in and went home, disappointed but unsurprised. Apathy and indifference may also be indicated, as in the case of a woman who went into a bookshop and took the first book she saw, being apparently willing to settle for anything so that she no longer had to continue to search.

Others search fairly enthusiastically but nevertheless thwart possibilities for any meaningful discovery. One woman went into a town full of 'lovely' shops looking for an open cheque to spend. Deciding against this, she went instead to a bistro full of handsome men and, failing to find what she was looking for there, went to a maternity hospital looking for a baby. Upon deciding not to have a baby, she found herself on a wide open road leading to an unknown destination, which she did not follow 'because of being a woman alone at night'.

This reluctance to look beyond conventional ideas of what she should be seeking and stereotypical constraints about women 'going it alone' are also indicated in the reactions of a woman who imagined finding her family as they had been a year or so previously. She found them carrying on happily without her and felt very depressed to realise that although they had been her purpose in life, they were no longer and she still had not found what she was looking for. Nevertheless, despite profound feelings of depression, she remained with her family rather than go in search of a new purpose. Similarly, another woman went looking for her husband because she didn't want to be alone, believing that she could not find what she wanted from life on her own.

Many people look to others to provide them with meaning and purpose in life rather than find it for themselves. They may look to books or other prescriptions, as in the case of a young woman who imagined herself among the cobbled streets of what she described as a 'Shakespearean-type town', where she found a theatre and what she presumed to be a Shakespeare play in progress. She asked for a programme and when she looked inside discovered that all the pages were blank. When she protested to the programme-seller he said 'All you need to know in life, and all that you are looking for is in those pages. The rest is up to you'. Initially this scared her but she then realised 'that we write our own lives and in those blank pages I have to write my own destiny'. She later wrote, 'We are the only ones who can control our lives, and when it comes down to it, we are in charge of ourselves. We can have help but when it comes to the crunch we are the only ones who can sort ourselves out'.

A similar realisation came to a woman who went into a library looking for a specific book, only to discover on opening it that all the pages were blank. Although initially shocked, she recognised that there is no book of rules for life and no easy answers to her questions. However, she was even more surprised on describing her experiences within a group to be told by a man that he actually had such a book, which subsequently he brought to show her. This amazing book is the subject of traditional Persian folklore, as is related by Idries Shah (1969) in the brief introduction to its blank pages and its effect on the would-be reader is difficult to convey. It feels rather like being hit around the head in the manner favoured by zen masters in their attempts to bring pupils to their senses.

A similar challenge to logic and rationality was experienced by a young man who, in response to the exercise being presently considered, imagined himself in a foreign town descending steep steps to a square which kept falling away under him until he was clutching at a vertical wall with only some sort of horizontal struts to hold on to. As the square dropped away below him he could not decide whether to continue making his way downwards or return to the top, both of which were equally difficult. He became very frustrated and reported thinking, 'No. It shouldn't be like this. It's not supposed to be difficult to get into the town. I'm doing it wrong'. At the moment of his greatest frustration he let go, challenging himself to fall, only to find himself floating over the rooftops, feeling warm, happy and free.

Writing about this later, he interpreted the experience as like solving a zen koan – a riddle or puzzle that admits no logical solution; or completing a Grail quest in which a naïve student meets a wise master who sets him an impossible goal or task, and where the more he tries the more difficult the task becomes until, at the moment of his greatest confusion, something snaps and he is spontaneously liberated from the problem. He realised as a result of the exercise that the assumption that he could solve rationally or logically the problem of how to proceed in order to discover what he is looking for is invalid, as is his assumption that he is looking for some*thing* to fulfil all he wants from his life. Once he relinquished these beliefs and the struggle they gave rise to he found himself free of the problem, which he interpreted as meaning that he should learn to let go of rational and logical assumptions and approaches, and become free. He had therefore gained an insight into a favourite maxim of Fritz Perls: 'lose your head and come to your senses'.

As a result of the experience he gained another important insight. Having previously cured himself of a throat infection by using visualisation he attempted to do so again, only to realise that this time he felt differently. Before he had known that he would do it, whereas this time he lacked faith and was merely setting himself a goal, telling himself that because he had done it before, he should be able to do it again. He tried all the same things as previously and none of them worked. He then realised that trying is useless; a rational 'superficial' process implying a degree of doubt, whereas healing is not a trying 'but just doing it' and comes from 'deeper down ... and a peculiar sense of certainty'. He concluded that 'this is what brings about positive attitudes and expectations and allows healthy processes to take effect', and that 'the certain belief that I can get well is identical with getting well itself – it is the very same event'.

Others have made similar discoveries. A woman who could not find what she was looking for despite travelling all over town by car, train and bus, finally discovered peace in a small park when she gave up the search. Another woman imagined that she was searching the apparently empty stalls of an Israeli market town. She experienced frustration not only at being unable to find anything but also because she couldn't see what was forming ahead of her. Eventually she gave up the search and just wandered the streets only to make the important discovery that by so doing she experienced a feeling of great calmness. She interpreted this as suggesting that she should 'just wander through life', dealing with issues as she encounters them rather than worrying about what lies ahead. She concluded that she had found peace of mind and the confidence to walk through life without needing any purpose other than simply being alive.

For many people expectations about what they are or should be looking for in life act as a set of blinkers so that they don't see other possibilities, and upon not finding what they are seeking they assume they have failed to find anything at all, or that they have not been going about doing so correctly. One woman assumed the latter because she imagined two beaches, one from childhood and one where she presently lives. When it was suggested to her that they might represent what she is looking for she acknowledged that the feelings of freedom and naturalness she associates with them are entirely positive and satisfying, and quite inconsistent with those she experiences in her current life situation.

Very commonly what a person thinks is 'right' for them and looks for in this exercise, proves not to be so on closer scrutiny. Thus a rather 'Sloaney' type of young woman felt that the image of a simple artisan's shop she located in a North African town could not be 'right' and had meaning only as a holiday memory. When asked what feelings this memory evoked she said that the simplicity and creativity she associated with this place gave rise to greater feelings of fulfilment than her chosen career in company law.

Some people, like the dunce in the opening quotation of this chapter, realise that they already have what they are looking for. Thus a man found part of himself he had lost sight of for some time; aspects he knew he needed badly and had sorely missed – his faith in himself, and a warm and positive attitude to his life and those of others. Another man, a self-declared aetheist, who felt lonely wandering aimlessly in a town which he thought held nothing for him, was profoundly shocked to rediscover God – bumping into him as he turned a street corner.

Occasionally people have a clear idea of what they want from life but appear to be looking for it in the wrong place, as in the case of a woman purporting to look for peace and quiet in a noisy market place. However, sometimes what a person is seeking is found in an unlikely place. Not regarding myself as a particularly materialistic person I was surprised to imagine myself looking down on Monte Carlo from the High Corniche and even more astonished to find myself driving down into the town in a red Ferrari because it was a long walk. However, on finding myself down in the town I was not even remotely interested in the riches and luxuries of what is described in the Fodor guidebook as a 'sybarites' haven'. Ignoring them totally I went to the bathing resort of Larvotto and sat alone on the rocks in the dark looking out over the navy blue and completely serene Mediterranean, feeling in its movement the rhythm of the universe and wanting to be immersed in it. I was aware of the hotels and apartments that rose in columns stacked to the sky behind me only because of the light they shed on the water. Initially I regarded this literally as 'turning my back on the bright lights' and the values of a society made loathsome by its insatiable greed for material wealth. Subsequently, however, I recognised in it a deeper and more significant search for 'oceanic experience'. In a similar vein a woman who imagined herself in a primitive town lit entirely by candles realised she was looking for 'enlightenment'.

Many people come to realise that their discovery is nothing, as such; nothing material or even nothing at all. For some the discovery of nothing is all important. One woman who could find nothing in her town became aware that she was walking alone and feeling good about it. She then realised that this is what she is looking for in life. Another woman, finding herself in a boring town 'with nothing there and nothing lively about it', walked on and eventually came to a little wood full of new grass and spring flowers. Subsequently she realised that it signified that her marriage was over – dead – and that she wanted to go on to pastures new and a new life, which she did.

Wanting to find a way out of a town that appears to offer nothing is very common and often highly revealing. A young woman found herself wandering along the streets of her home town and realising that it held nothing for her. She continued to look, however, until she heard the instructions to those who had not found what they were looking for to let go of their preconceived ideas and expectations, and just take what comes. Immediately she imagined some balloons which she grasped and was lifted out of the place, grinning with delight, feeling elated and aware that she must move away from her home town. Another woman who found herself in her small home town realised her fear of never being able to leave it, and move on to bigger and better things. Unable to find what she was looking for she began to walk out of town but eventually came to a level crossing and was able to go no further. As she stood there leaves of paper fell from the sky and landed at her feet, making her realise that she had to take steps in order to find what she was looking for in life but that she cannot leave until she has the right pieces of paper – written qualifications. By contrast a woman found herself feeling peaceful, easy and with a sense of belonging in a town she had left many years previously, and realised that she must return to it.

Many people discover new paths and ways of escape from the town. One woman imagined herself in a Wild West town, deserted except for a solitary horse tied to a post. She gained a sense of freedom from stroking the horse, and so untied and mounted it, and rode off at a gallop, later describing the effect as 'absolutely breathtaking'. She realised in doing so that she wants to escape from the restrictions of her present life but cannot do so by herself and needs an aid or a means to escape.

Finding himself in a town with nothing to offer, a young man jumped into a large hole in the road and slid into a volcano. He took this as meaning that he should look for meaning in life 'away from the ordinary run of things'. However, the distinctly dangerous element of this imagery, together with the impulsivity, could be an indication of the crusadism Maddi has identified as an unhealthy response to meaninglessness.

The themes of wanting to move on in life and/or leave certain of its features behind are quite commonly reflected in a person's imagery. One woman imagined leading her children along the street of a holiday town and leaving them in a McDonald's restaurant while she went into a library where she was pushed aside by others at the catalogue desk while looking for the book she wanted. Although she did not find the book she took the imagery as an indication that her newly discovered interest in education is part of her search for meaning at a time in her life when she is able to leave her family in order to do so. The fact of other people pushing in at the catalogue desk also made her appreciate that she has to compete with others in order to get what she wants from life.

Another woman, who in real life was awaiting the outcome of an important job application, imagined herself in the idyllic, pretty and peaceful part of an old town where she remained quite happily, in no hurry to enter the newer part of the town with its cars and modern supermarkets. However, she took this as representing an approaching life transition and her lack of fear as an indication that she isn't frightened of new challenges.

Freedom is something that many people discover, even though they were not consciously seeking it. This may be freedom from emotional ties or from worry, especially the specific worry that they may not find what they are looking for in life. Others describe a sense of relief from the tensions and stresses of everyday reality and urban life. Some find relief in a return to basic values and traditions. Many discover feelings of peace, happiness, serenity, safety, friendship, belonging and community. Some discover themselves or the time and space alone simply to be. One man found himself with time to spare, the one thing he lacks in his everyday life.

Some discover specific people. Thus a man who expressed difficulty in forming and maintaining relationships found a beautiful girl with whom he had a great deal in common, felt safe and wanted to stay for ever. A young woman met her mother who hugged her and walked around the town with her. This was a particularly significant discovery for this woman who had been very badly affected by the death of her mother during her early teens, since when she had been unable to visualise her face and had felt that her mother was completely lost to her. To be able to 'see' her and feel close to her again was extremely powerful for her at a time in her life when she was in need of support and direction.

Occasionally people discover a specific vocation, as in the case of the woman who discovered the importance of working with her hands and another who realised that she has the gift of healing. Relatively few people find any*thing* as such, and some people feel cheated and disappointed by this. One woman expressed disappointment at discovering 'only' feelings rather than being guided to find a specific thing. Another felt cheated because she expected to be led to a guide or guru who would tell her what she most desired in life. She declared that she 'expected to find treasure, at the very least'.

It is therefore interesting to compare her reactions with those of a man who went looking for treasure. What he found everywhere he looked were very smart, well-dressed, apparently happy yet very stressed people who were not being themselves but were conforming to social pressures. He saw unhappy people in cars, all seemingly preoccupied with problems in life they couldn't let go of. He began to realise that these people in cars, appearing to be going somewhere, were taking their troubles with them everywhere. He decided that he should not allow himself to be stressed by others or to be so self-conscious; that he should be himself and not 'wear masks'; and that life is too short to worry about and be preoccupied with trivial problems. Suddenly he understood that although he had not found anything he had discovered something of great value – himself. In so doing he had stumbled upon the wisdom of the Little Prince:

'Men' said the Little Prince, 'set out on their way in express trains, but they do not know what they are looking for. Then they rush about, and get excited, and turn round and round ... And' he added 'it is not worth the trouble ... what they are looking for could be found in one single rose, or in a little water . . . but the eyes are blind. One must look with the heart'.

ANTOINE DE SAINT EXUPÉRY, *The Little Prince*

❧ CHAPTER SEVEN ❧

Inspiring Health

They bought one Pinch, a hungry lean-faced villain,
A mere anatomy, a mountebank,
A threadbare juggler and fortune-teller;
A needy, hollow eyed, sharp-looking wretch,
A living dead man.
WILLIAM SHAKESPEARE, *The comedy of Errors*, v. 1.238

It was Frankl's contention that unless a person can see meaning
and value in his continuing existence his morale will deteriorate,
his immunity will decrease, he will sicken more readily or even
commit suicide. On the basis of this and other observations
which suggest that feelings of hopelessness and helplessness may
predispose an individual towards disease, the psychologist Sidney
Jourard put forward his inspirational theory.

He proposed as a general definition that events, relationships
or transactions which give a person a sense of identity, worth,
hope and purpose in life are 'inspiriting', while those that make a
person feel unimportant, worthless, hopeless, low in self-esteem,
isolated, frustrated, and that existence is absurd and meaningless
are 'dispiriting'. He hypothesised that inspiriting events mobilise
the forces of wellness latent in all organisms bringing about an
optimal mode of organisation which both sustains wellness and
maximises effective functioning and behaviour. By contrast, dispiriting events render an organism vulnerable to the ever-present
forces of illness by weakening its optimal mode of organisation,
enabling illness to flourish. He therefore proposed that everyday
life should be scrutinised for 'dispiriting events' in order to
identify the psychological factors that predispose towards illness
and reduced effectiveness in living, and that there should be

serious study of faith, confidence, prayer, placebos and other processes which inspire health and well-being, and mobilise man's self-healing powers.

It was Jourard's view that there must be something about the normal or usual way of life that is periodically dispiriting to account for the regularity with which people suffer ailments such as headaches, colds, flu, diarrhoea, constipation or more serious illness. He observed that people who seldom become sick are those who have found ways of life that yield purpose, meaning, hope and interest; and satisfy needs for affection, love, sex, status and achievement. He suggested that when healthier people find their ways of life dull, frustrating or tedious they pay attention to these signals that all is not well and change what they are doing, including their ways of behaving with others. He acknowledged that 'it is difficult and anxiety-provoking to change what one is doing, to change or reinvent one's way of interacting with others; powerful forces from within and without tend to restrain change, and so most of us keep up the way of life that has been slowly "doing us in". Therefore, we become sick, and it is usually with some measure of surprise' (p. 77).

Jourard viewed sickness as a way in which people express protest against 'sickening ways of life' that will not support wellness and a temporary respite from the dispiriting conditions of life that existed prior to the onset of the illness. He suspected that people who are often physically ill are 'victims of their sense of duty' and commit 'altruistic suicide' by slowly destroying their bodies in order to preserve the social roles and systems in which they regularly participate; while those who become psychiatrically ill are 'rebels without courage or effectiveness' (p. 77). This being the case, it follows that 'if it seems to the patient that his usual life, the one that made him sick, cannot be changed, he may never get well. Why should he? Or if he does recover but then resumes his normal life, he'll be sick again before long' (p. 78).

According to Jourard, scientific medicine with its emphasis on neutralising illness by way of surgery and drugs, overlooks these factors, and the importance of the healing powers of altered behaviour, surroundings and rest. He advocated intensive investigation of the psychophysiological mechanisms involved in health and illness in order to identify what he called the 'healing reflexes', and to determine the conditions in which they can be brought under the control of either a therapist or the sick person himself. To this end he took a fresh look at the concept of 'spirit' by beginning to identify what can be observed and described when people refer to its presence in themselves or others by way of phrases such as 'he is a spirited lad', 'her spirit is broken', 'his spirits fell' and so on.

Jourard observed that when a person is said to have high spirits, to be inspirited or inspired, he might also be described as active, expressive, effective in his behaviour and high in morale. He speculated that when a person says he is in high spirits or feeling good there are probably physical, chemical and neural concomitants to that state (a speculation since borne out by research), and that there are external, describable conditions that are necessary and sufficient to produce a 'high-spirit' response – for example, being told that some significant other loves you or being engaged in effort towards personally worthwhile goals with high expectation of success.

In his analysis of the 'high-spirited' mode of being he employed a number of new and not so new concepts and terms, one of which, the 'spirit titre' can be thought of in much the same way as a 'spirit level'.

APPLYING THE SPIRIT LEVEL

Jourard saw the spirit titre or level as varying between 0 and 100, observing that at 0 death and dissolution of the body have 100 per cent probability, whereas the other extreme, which might be regarded as ultimate vitality, can only be reached with difficulty and only sustained momentarily, as in the ecstatic peak experiences described by Maslow. So by reaching either end of the scale a person can be regarded as being 'out of the body' in the normal sense. Jourard considered that most 'normal' people, who live a modal, respectable, socially patterned life, could probably be characterised as possessing a spirit level somewhere in the 30–60 range, with a mode of 45. At this level, he claimed, the body is poorly organised and not overly resistant to germs, viruses or effects of stress 'that are the inexorable consequence of the very way of life that is called respectability' (p. 82). Hence 'normal behaviour,' which conforms with the usual age, sex and occupational roles, regularly results in illness.

When spirit level falls below a wellness-sustaining level – which Jourard notionally located at around 20–30 per cent – the result, he claimed, is low spirits, depression, boredom, diffuse anxiety or 'kindred dysphoric psychological states', together with a diminished elegance, precision and zeal in the person's behavioural output. Over time this low spirit level permits 'illness' to become established, microbes or viruses to multiply, stress by-products to proliferate and latent illnesses to become manifest or 'galloping'. This being the case, how does one raise a person's spirits and inspire health?

RAISING SPIRIT LEVEL

Jourard addressed this question initially in relation to the very sick or dying. He observed that such people are usually removed from the dispiriting surroundings that gave rise to their illness and so the change of environment in itself may have inspiriting consequences. They are also likely to have placed themselves in the hands of a medical specialist – a process he regarded as 'notoriously inspiriting' and probably will have been 'looked at, poked, probed, punctured, diagnosed, dosed, and cut open' (p. 83), all of which has a general inspiriting effect because it sets in motion what he termed a 'general hope syndrome'. This can be characterised as a gradual rise in spirit level which in turn decreases the disorganisation of the body system and so brings about a higher level of wellness. As the spirit level rises to normal the body 'throws off' symptoms for a time. However, if and when the dispiriting forces recur the spirit level drops and the symptoms return. This, he suggested, is why new treatments and even placebos have only temporary effectiveness.

Jourard noted that a dismal prognosis is indicated when a patient has no hope and nothing to live for because his spirits fall to a low ebb. He is in danger of 'giving up the ghost' – losing his spirit completely and dying. Nevertheless, as Jourard observed, the history of medicine is replete with 'miraculous' recoveries from fatal illness and tissue destruction where the miracle consisted in a recovery by the patient of a will to live, the discovery that life is worth living and that people care. Similarly, less seriously ill people have had symptoms remitted by placebos in which they have faith and confidence. He therefore suggested that all healing is fundamentally faith healing in the sense that the patient has faith in what is being done to heal him. This triggers off an increase in spirit level which is the signal that healing is occurring.

GIVING UP THE GHOST

When a person dies he is often said to have 'given up the ghost', reflecting the commonly held belief that his spirit has departed. Jourard considered that there are many ways whereby the normal spirits of a person can be lowered, even to the point of death. He identified hexes as one such means, observing that they probably diminish spirit level to a very low ebb, permitting entropy to maximise within the organism. He suggested that there is also a class of dispiriting people who maintain their own spirit level by functioning among others to demoralise them by undermining their faith and confidence in themselves; and that social environments may be so devoid of opportunities for inspiring satisfaction of needs for love, security, esteem, sexual and other fulfilments that they too are demoralising or dispiriting.

Jourard claimed that a person's spirit can also be killed off in other ways, notably when he reaches the age at which he is expected to die, having been assessed as obsolete by others:

> We kill our citizens . . . by encouraging them to believe there is
> only one identity, one role, one way for them to be, one value
> for them to fulfil, rather than a host of possible 'incarnations'
> to be lived in a lifetime. When this one ground for his existence
> is outgrown, or lost, a person may begin to die, or he may kill
> himself more quickly – rather than reinvent himself anew.
>
> JOURARD, 1971, p. 95

In Jourard's terms, therefore, people frequently kill themselves following the loss of money, employment, status, beauty, sexuality, a loved one or their illusions because they cannot imagine or invent new purposes, identities or lives when the old ones have run their course.

> In fact, I believe that most of what we call mental and physical illness is evidence that the way in which the person had been living up to the point of his collapse has truly been outgrown and that it is time for him to stop that way of life and invent a new way which is more compatible with wellness. But members of our healing and helping professions construe the signals that a way of life has been outlived as an *illness to be cured, rather than a call to stop, reflect and meditate, dream and invent a new self.* The helping professions do not so much help a person to live as they help him to perpetuate a way of living that has been outgrown.
>
> 1971, p. 98–9

Therefore, in his view,

> We need to learn how to invite people to explore and try more of their possibilities than modal upbringing seems to foster, so the invitation to live and grow is as fascinating as is the invitation to die. In fact, we need a new specialist – one who helps people find new projects when their old ones, the ones which made life liveable, have lost meaning.
>
> 1971, pp. 98–9

To this end he advocated the study of the spirit, claiming that 'when we begin seriously to study spirit as a natural phenomenon, we will not only increase our grasp of nature's laws, but we will radically alter our personal lives' (p. 90).

Regrettably, Jourard's study of the spirit was terminated by his death shortly after the above comments were published. He did not live to see scientific research confirm or support many of his speculative claims. However, research in the field of psycho-neuroimmunology appears to do just that, by demonstrating that mood changes brought about by minor but negatively per-ceived life events alter susceptibility to colds, flu and infections, whereas positive mood changes and positive events are associated with improved immune function (Hucklebridge, 1993). Numerous studies have found that suppressed immune function is linked with depression, feelings of hopelessness, loneliness, marital disruption, unemployment, loss of a spouse and bereavement (Tuormaa, 1992); and many have reported spontaneous regressions from cancer following markedly favourable psychological or psychosocial changes (Weinstock, 1984). Specific life events identified as preceding cancer regression have included religious conversion, sudden marriage, death of a long-hated husband, reconciliation with a long-hated mother, positive career change and commencing/completing a long-standing project.

Furthermore, as a result of the work of pioneers such as Carl and Stephanie Simonton, Bernie Siegel, Norman Cousins (1981) and Lawrence LeShan there is a growing recognition within orthodox medicine of the need to inspire rather than dispirit patients and of the therapeutic importance of positive emotions, attitudes and hope.

As indicated in the previous chapter, the importance to health and well-being of spirituality is increasingly being recognised and investigated. Nevertheless, the investigation of spirit as a natural phenomenon, as advocated by Jourard, has not been widely pursued within the scientific community and has tended to be dismissed as 'unscientific' where it has occurred.

Within the field of healing there have been numerous attempts to investigate the spirit or life force which have used 'energetic' concepts very similar to those coined by Jourard. Indeed traditional approaches to healing throughout the world since antiquity share a belief in the existence of subtle energies, the mobilisation and balancing of which are considered fundamental to health. In the West most concepts of energy, such as Mesmer's magnetic energy, Bergson's *élan vital*, Freud's libido, Reich's orgone or bio-energy, von Reichenbach's odic force and the Theosophists' ether (which have variously informed the development of hypnosis, psychotherapy, bio-energetic therapies and spiritual healing) were formulated when Western science was conceived in exclusively objective, mechanistic terms. Accordingly the life force is viewed as some kind of substance which flows through the organism and is quantifiable in much the same way as conceived by Jourard.

However, in the East concepts of energy, variously referred to as chi, ki, prana, Kundalini or Shakti, are markedly different, being akin to those of pre-scientific Western civilisations such as Ancient Greece and Egypt, most notably Aristotle's concept of *entelekhia* or *entelechy* – the vital force which directs the life of an individual. Here energy is conceived not as 'anything' substantive but as continuous movement or change. This concept underpins Eastern traditions of medicine such as Ayurveda and Unami in India and Pakistan, and the practices of traditional Chinese and Japanese medicine such as acupuncture, acupressure, shiatsu, reiki, and modifications of these approaches such as reflexology. In recent times the concept of *entelechy* was revived by the German embryologist Driesch, who adopted this term to describe the impetus which impels the organism to self-fulfilment. A similar concept of vital force is the basis of homoeopathy, which was described by its originator, Samuel Hahnemann in much the same terms as the self-actualising tendency of Maslow, Rogers and Perls. However, the most striking similarities with ancient and Eastern concepts of energy are found in the ideas of Jung, who indicated that psychic or spiritual energy and physical energy are two aspects of one and the same reality, the world of matter appearing as a mirror image of the world of the psyche and vice versa.

Common to all these views is the fundamental conception of all matter, including the human body, the psyche and all phenomena, as comprising energy in a particular state of vibration, and having both physical and psychic aspects. Such a view is fully consistent with that of present-day physics (see Graham, 1986, 1990 for fuller discussion). 'Energy medicine' therefore utilises various vibrational forms such as light, heat, colour, sound, thought and imagery, to restore energy imbalances within the whole person, influencing the organism at a more fundamental 'spiritual' level than the physical or psychological symptoms of illness.

> When we realise in the final analysis our bodies are in fact made up of nothing but energy in constant transformation it is easier to understand how subtle non-physical energetic influences such as emotions and thoughts can have a direct influence on our physical functioning, just as our physical

functioning can have a direct influence on our emotional and mental experiences.

SCHWARZ, 1980, p. 21

Unfortunately insufficient people do realise this and even within the scientific community many find it difficult to accept the implications of scientific discovery, much less accept that these have been mapped out with striking similarity throughout the world since antiquity. Yet this clearly is the case.

Common to these approaches is the fundamental premise 'that the "energy" level of the human being, meaning the inner emotional and spiritual world, precedes, and in fact determines, all that is experienced at the physical level of life' (Shealy & Myss, 1988, p. 17). Such a view challenges the conventional medical view of the relationship of energy and matter, mind and body. Therefore the response of the orthodox medical community towards the emergence of a holistic model of health care has generally been to discredit and disregard its validity.

There are, however, a growing number of medical practitioners, like surgeon Bernie Siegel, who recognise that 'a rebirth of the techniques of healing or perhaps a relearning of what our ancestors already knew is required. If there is to be a twenty-first century, it will need to reflect a new level of spiritual wisdom and intuitive insight' (Siegel, 1988, p. xvii). He notes that he and other pioneers in medicine have struggled endlessly to gain acceptance of the fact that the health of the psyche and spirit are manifested on a cellular level, as physical health or disease; and that the human 'spirit' is the soil in which disease can take root. Like Jourard he views illness as a message to change one's life pattern. It is 'a reset button . . . a redirector of one's life' (1988, p. xviii). Therefore, just as the message to change and grow comes from within so also does all the information required in order for the person to become whole or healthy. Siegel considers listening to that inner voice or intuition as fundamental to health and healing, and he advocates the incorporation into medicine of intuition – that of both the patient and the health care professionals.

189

INTUITIVE MEDICINE

The integration of traditional medicine and intuitive wisdom is for neurosurgeon Norman Shealy the basis of the creation of health, the title of an innovative book co-authored with the intuitive diagnostician Caroline Myss about their research together in this field. Myss has developed her capacity to perceive a person's energy or life force to such a degree that she can intuit the nature and precise location of physical disease within a person's body. This insightful diagnosis, which forms the basis of their co-authored work and much of Shealy's clinical practice, has proved to be 93 per cent accurate. According to Shealy this achievement is 'truly awesome':

> Although we physicians are generally about 80% accurate in
> our primary diagnostic attempts, we are frustrated in
> determining the exact diagnoses for a variety of illnesses.
> Furthermore, many of the diagnostic tests carry a significant
> risk of damage to the patient'
>
> 1988, p. 67

Myss's accomplishment is astonishing not simply because she has no medical training or background, but also because all that she requires in order to provide the diagnosis is the patient's name and date of birth, which ordinarily are relayed to her over the telephone. She needs no physical contact with the patient, who may be hundreds of miles distant. Myss, however, is by no means unique in her abilities. As Shealy observes the use of intuitive diagnosis is probably as old as medicine and it almost certainly goes back to the days of Hippocrates, an intuitive physician who is widely regarded as the founder of Western medicine. Formal studies of intuitive diagnosis are, however, relatively recent, the first known to Shealy being that of John Elliotson, who, some 130 years ago, investigated mesmerism. Edgar Cayce is possibly the best-known and most widely researched intuitive diagnostician of all time, but perhaps the most influential to date is the Harley Street physician Dr Edward Bach, whose intuitively derived flower remedies are widely and increasingly used to good effect within holistic health care.

Shealy has conducted diagnostic research on several intuitives and claims to have found a 'significant rate of accuracy as determined by computerised evaluation' of results in detecting the nature and primary cause of illness in patients. He concludes that intuitive diagnosis is not only possible but also highly successful. One of the most outstanding intuitives of those studied was the internist, Dr Robert Leichtman, who was found to be 96 per cent accurate in his evaluations of 'patients'. Many doctors acknowledge that there is a strong element of intuition in all medical diagnoses and so might be more persuaded by the claims made in respect of Dr Leichtman than those made by intuitives with no medical training. However, Leichtman demonstrated his diagnostic accuracy using only photographs, the patients' names and birthdates. His medical knowledge or training played little or no part in the diagnoses. Given that medical knowledge or training does not necessarily inform accurate intuitive medical diagnoses, the question arises as to how medical knowledge and training might be informed by intuition.

The answer seems to lie in the soul, intuitives generally taking the view that the key to understanding processes of health and illness is an awareness of the human spirit or energy system. Indeed, according to Myss, intuition *is* awareness of the spirit or energy system; it is 'sensing information' in and around the body, and an awareness each individual possesses. She insists that intuition is not a gift, 'It is a natural internal skill that automatically gets developed within a person as that individual grows in self-respect and self-esteem. Logically, if you don't respect yourself, you are not going to honour the information your intuitive system is transmitting to you' (1991, p. 7). The 'secret' to clear intuition is therefore healthy self-esteem. According to Myss most people have unhealthy self-esteem in that they rely on others for approval rather than themselves. Consequently they doubt themselves, and their own wisdom and authority in favour of the authority of others. They don't take notice of the information provided by their own senses and so effectively block their intuition.

The first step in training intuition is therefore to form a healthy self-esteem, a sense of personal self-worth. This means taking back personal power or authority from those it has been given away to, which involves an examination of where and how power is lost, those to whom it has been given and the reasons why. Myss suggests that a person can establish how much their relationships, past history, current roles and lifestyle cost them in power by plotting this in percentage terms along a horizontal axis, in much the same way that Jourard conceived the notion of a spirit level or titre. In this way a person can make some crude assessment of how much of their energy is bound up with seeking the approval of others, and thus how much is available to them at any point in time.

I have used this simple measure many times and have found no one who cannot easily provide an assessment of his current energy level and an indication of those features of living that 'tax the spirit'. Almost all self-assessments of this kind fall well below the level Jourard identified as healthy. For example, among groups of undergraduate students ranging in age from 18–24 the average energy level was found to be around 35 per cent. Individually clients in therapy appear to range from 15–60 per cent and in both groups some individuals have identified their energy level as near 0. Many of these people have identified their efforts to live up to parental expectations or those associated with their various social roles as a major drain on their energies. None of them had previously considered these factors in energetic terms, but having done so were able to appreciate why they felt lacking in energy, fatigued, depressed and generally 'down' or 'low'. With all their energy effectively taken up elsewhere there is little left to fuel their activities in the here-and-now. Not surprisingly these individuals are at risk from complete breakdown and they invariably lack 'presence'.

Many of the 'dispiriting' features of people's lives are a consequence of the 'scripts' which have been written for them by others. These are relied on as guides to personal behaviour, attitudes, values and to provide meaning in life. However, at various stages in life such as adolescence, middle and old age, and at other times when there is a change or loss of role these 'scripts' fail; they let the person down, by giving advice that does not answer the person's questions and therefore no longer provide meaning as they have done formerly. Such crises frequently give rise to disappointment and pain. Like Eric Berne and Sidney Jourard, Myss views such crises as indications of the need to reappraise and reassess these scripts, and the roles and ways of being they relate to; to let go of these where necessary; and so take back the energy bound up in them. Myss insists that disorientation is necessary because if people do not become disappointed by the outside voices of their lives they will not let go of them. They will hang on to what is familiar in their world, even though it doesn't work for them any more, and creates depression, low spirits and poor health.

> The reason why this is so detrimental to your health is that keeping the past alive requires energy. Instead of using your daily allotment of energy as it is meant to be used, that is, to keep regenerating healthy cell tissue, you are directing this precious life force to keep alive old memories rather than your present body.
>
> 1991, p. 10

Myss claims that letting go of voices from the past removes obstacles to intuition and releases the energy bound up in these blockages. Taking back energy from the past effectively shifts the epicentre of power, maximising the energy available to the individual in the here-and-now. The person therefore has the ability to listen to his own wisdom and the capacity to act upon it. Hence, in Jourard's terms, the shift of personal power is highly inspiriting and health promoting.

However, many people do not use such crises, or the pain and suffering they give rise to as messages to reappraise and let go of those aspects of their life that are no longer meaningful or of value to them. They continue to live their lives according to outdated scripts acquired in the past which have no relevance to the present. They also continue to hold on to outmoded roles, behaviour, attitudes, beliefs, feelings dictated by these scripts, and the pain and hurt generated by them. In so doing they are like jugglers trying to keep too many different balls in the air at any one time and doing so badly.

JUGGLING WITH HEALTH

Juggling is an apt metaphor for living. Consider the proficient juggler on stage, juggling a number of items of varying shape, size and colour. This is a skilled performance which has become almost automatic as a consequence of a great deal of practice.

Some very subtle and sophisticated physical and psychological adjustments are required to achieve a flowing harmonious sequence so that the various items appear almost as one entity. Indeed, the performance involves the person's whole being. At the physical level it requires balance, precision movements, muscular coordination and control, integrated with highly complex and sophisticated psychological processes like perception, attention, concentration and motivation. It appears simple and easy because it is well rehearsed and practised.

Even when it has been learned, various other requirements must be met if the person is to juggle successfully and sustain the performance. If the juggler has not fulfilled basic physical needs or attended to certain physical functions – if he is hungry, thirsty or tired, or has a full bladder, is too hot or cold, or is in pain – he will not be able to perform effectively. Juggling may divert attention away from physical sensations, initially at least, but as tensions and pain develop, they will become more and more difficult to ignore, and will distract the juggler from his performance. These signals of unmet needs will continue to compete for the juggler's attention until they are acted upon. If unattended to the person may become so weak that he is no longer capable of performing. In one way or another, therefore, the act will break down.

Similarly, psychological needs also have to be met. If the juggler is worried about his overdraft or his agent, anxious about what others are thinking about him, or how well he is performing, is unhappy, depressed, angry; or overconfident and blasé, his concentration may be reduced and breakdown of the performance is more likely to occur. Spiritual needs also have to be taken into consideration. The juggler who begins to ask himself 'What am I doing this for?'; 'What's the point of all this?', is unlikely to continue unless he comes up with a satisfactory answer. Thus perceived lack of meaning or purpose in the activity will eventually lead to breakdown in its performance. So physical, psychological and spiritual needs must all be met if a person is to succeed as a juggler.

When these needs are met, however, a juggler may be able to sustain a performance for a considerable period of time with little or no detriment to himself or the act. Nevertheless, events might occur which interfere with the performance. Someone might bump into the juggler and knock him off balance; he might sneeze or be stung by an insect. These occurrences might lead to a 'hiccup' in the performance and the possibility of one or more items being dropped. A skilful juggler may be able to regain his composure and sustain the performance, although it may take a little time before he has fully restored control. Even having done so he may feel the need to pay careful attention for some time in order to be assured of this.

There may be instances where, despite all his efforts to adjust following a crisis of this kind, it is not possible to hold the act together. When one or more items fall from the array it may still be possible to continue with the performance, although the nature of this will have changed and adjustment will be required accordingly. However, the implications of the loss of one or more items may have devastating implications for others so that all of them come crashing down around the juggler resulting in a total breakdown of the performance.

In order for the juggler to get his act together following a trauma of this kind he must be able to locate the items which have fallen and perhaps scattered. For the juggler who knows the number, shape and colour of the items this may not be too difficult, but it will take time and effort to search and recover them. He might not bother to do so, preferring to take another set of items and begin to juggle with them. Irrespective of whether he picks up the pieces of his former act or begins afresh with new items he still requires the energy, interest, concentration and motivation to recommence his performance, and to sustain it.

As in juggling so in life. Each individual is like a juggler engaged in juggling a number of different roles, not all of which are fully visible at all times, some being partially or temporarily concealed and each being quite distinct, but which appear to come together as one entity.

When life goes smoothly you will move easily from one role and situation to another, and will give relatively little thought to the performances demanded in each because they have become automatic over time and with practice. You do not have to ponder over them but simply 'get on' with them, almost automatically. Certain events may unsettle, unbalance or disturb you, however, and require adjustments that demand time, energy and attention. Some crises can be successfully overcome so your activities can continue as they did formerly, but in some instances your act falls apart, resulting in a total breakdown. When this occurs you may be urged by others to 'get your act together', which in life is not always as easy as in juggling because you are, to a great extent, unaware or unconscious of the components of your former performance.

If juggling is a model for life it might be expected that with patience, persistence, and self-analysis complex physical, emotional and psychological issues can be simplified and life made more orderly, and that this can be achieved through a similar process of reducing these complexes to their smallest components and piecing them together again.

In Western culture, since its origins in Ancient Greek civilisation, complex life issues have been addressed in precisely this way, that is, intellectually by way of verbal, rational thought which characteristically is reductionist and analytic. A high value is placed on this mode of thinking in the West, and with good reason because, as scientific and technological advances show, tremendous progress in knowledge and understanding comes about from addressing issues in this way. However, all issues are not amenable to logical or rational analysis. Processes which by their nature are non-verbal, that is most physical, emotional and psychological processes, are not easily accessible by way of verbal language. Moreover, processes of which a person is largely unconscious or unaware cannot easily be addressed in this way.

Juggling is such a process, being both non-verbal and, once mastered, largely automatic so that the juggler is unaware to a great extent of its components. If you try to describe, much less explain, the act of juggling you will find that this cannot be achieved solely through logical analysis. You will find that it is virtually impossible to embark on the task without first of all seeing or evisaging the activity in the mind's eye, or attempting the activity yourself. Similarly it is difficult to describe or explain what is involved in a waltz or quick step. What these acts share in common is that they are all primarily non-verbal and need to be represented non-verbally before they can be represented verbally. These two different modes of representation, the verbal and non-verbal, are in fact complementary and often necessary features of problem solving. It is simply not sufficient to have only one way of representing issues, either logical or otherwise, because many complex issues are by their very nature not amenable to one or other approach. Therefore if juggling is to be of any value as a model for life you must either engage in it or imagine doing so.

As indicated above, most people appear to be engaged in a process of juggling various life issues, so asking them to picture in the mind's eye, through imagery, what they are juggling and how well, can provide them with a new perspective or insight into the issues in their lives and the ways they are handling them. One of the great advantages of doing so is that juggling is intrinsically absorbing and therefore relaxing. It is a present-centred activity which keeps the person in the here-and-now and 'out of the mind' in the usual sense of rational thinking. It sweeps the mind clear of tensions, and brings a sense of peace and order. In so doing it also allows the more intuitive features of mind to surface. As such juggling can be thought of in much the same way as meditation.

EXERCISE 7

Imagine that you are juggling. Observe the situation in which you are juggling in as much detail as possible, whether you are performing for yourself or for an audience and whether for some purpose; your own or the audience's amusement, or some other reason. Notice what you are wearing, how you look and how you feel about your appearance. Then focus on what you are juggling with. Notice the size, shape, colour and distinguishing features of these items and your feelings and thoughts about them. Assess how well you are juggling, noting any items, which are difficult to handle and the reasons for this.

Observe your reactions as you are juggling, identifying as you do so, what, if anything, is needed in order for you to improve your performance. Having done so allow the items you are juggling to fall, noting how you feel as they do so.

Now take some time to record your experiences during this exercise and to assess what you have learned or could learn from it.

Commentary

The setting

The situations in which people imagine themselves juggling are many and various, and invariably provide some indication of the way a person views the 'stage' on which their everyday performances take place. Many imagine they are on a stage or platform of some sort, in a theatre, hall or auditorium. Very commonly people imagine themselves in circuses, which may suggest that the performance is more transient or temporary than those that occur in more permanent establishments. Others are rather more exposed, performing in vast outdoor amphitheatres or arenas, or, less dramatically, on their own doorstep. Some are performing under spotlights, while the performances of others are only dimly illuminated. Most performances take place centre stage, although in some cases the person describes being both on stage and in the wings observing the performance simultaneously. One woman imagined herself aged three on stage in what she described as an 'Andy Pandy all-in-one striped play suit' with a prickly net collar scratching her neck and a red plastic comic nose pinching her face. This child was unable to juggle, and having only one ball resorted to rolling over and over with it in her hands, to peals of laughter from a huge audience. Her alter ego looking on in the wings wanted to rush out, grab her and take her off stage – but didn't, allowing the child to continue puppet-like in its performance, just as she allows a similar situation to continue in her everyday life.

Many people report juggling in domestic situations, usually their own home or that of their parents or other family members. These performances may be illuminated or in the dark. Some people describe juggling on their own. This may be on a stage or in an arena, a closed room or outdoors. In some instances 'high performance' is suggested by the setting, such as when it takes place on the top of a mountain range.

The audience

Many people imagine performing for a large or huge audience. In some cases they can see this audience, in others they cannot but are aware of its presence. One man, a market gardener, described a vast audience of people with featureless faces but many eyes, like potatoes. Some people are unaware of the audience until they react in some way. The audience may be quite specific, being composed entirely of children or professional colleagues. A young male student teacher on his first teaching practice imagined himself juggling in front of the class he had been teaching earlier that day. He described several of the children 'trying to knock away my balls and ruin my act; trying to make me lose my grip on things', while others enjoyed seeing him taunted; and thinking, 'This is meaningless. What am I doing this for?' In many cases the audience is specific but small, a family group, or one or more significant others. There may be no audience, only the solitary performer.

Costume

The juggler's appearance may or may not be salient but in either event is usually significant. A person who has difficulty imagining or detailing the juggler may, on closer analysis, be found to have difficulties in relation to their self-identity or self-awareness, perhaps being unclear about who they are, although not necessarily unclear about the issues in life which they are juggling or the audience for whom they are performing.

Shoes feature quite strongly in the reports of many people, suggesting perhaps the importance to them of having both feet firmly on the ground and feeling balanced or simply 'down to earth'. Many people describe themselves attired like clowns with huge shoes and apparently huge feet. Relatively few people describe themselves as barefoot, but where they do it is usually in a context which suggests naturalness and a sense of freedom from conventional restraints.

The possibility that many people regard themselves as somewhat clumsy, foolish or comic in their performances is suggested by the number who imagine themselves attired as clowns, jesters or comedians. One woman was very concerned by her appearance, because the yellow banana suit and three-point jester's hat with bells, black socks and white boots she described 'didn't go together', making her feel foolish and awful. She implied that this would not have been the case had the articles of clothing matched or harmonised.

Another woman described juggling in a competition for which she had been preparing for a long time. She had put a great deal of time and effort into her costume, arriving at the contest with one 'designed to knock everyone for six', which would attract all crowds to her act and away from rival competitors as soon as she put it on. As she explained, they would expect a great performance from her and wouldn't go elsewhere because the costume would say to them that she was absolutely terrific at what she was doing. Certainly when she arrived at the competition and donned this dazzling costume it did precisely that and attracted a huge audience. It was only then that she realised that she had put all her efforts into the costume and had given no thought to her performance. Not only did she not know how to juggle but she had no idea what she was going to juggle with and the only items she had with her were pink marshmallows. By the time she realised that she couldn't juggle these she had lost all credibility with the audience, which had wandered off. At this point a person she didn't know came along and began to juggle several conventional items in colours she disliked, and which she described as 'marshmallow pink' and those of the sweaters favoured by a leading national high street chain of stores. The unknown woman performed quite well, as she, by now all alone, looked on, feeling nothing much as these objects moved independently of her and beyond her control, and nothing at all when the act ended.

This fascinating account highlights the dilemma of someone who is unable to live up to appearances and yet is unable to take pleasure or interest in more commonplace and less colourful accomplishments. More significantly perhaps, although rather more obliquely, the cancer the woman is juggling with in everyday life reflects the 'off colour' performance of the imagery. It may even have a more tangential significance inasmuch that as a cancer patient this woman may know that the cancer specialist Carl Simonton advocates juggling as a means of relaxation for his patients, and has encouraged those attending his lectures and workshops in Britain to juggle with pink and white marshmallows.

The significance of the juggler's appearance is also highlighted in the account of another woman who described herself, alone in a white room which lacked definition of any kind, wearing colourless and featureless clothes, juggling colourless balls in the air above her head solely through the power of her mind and without any physical contact whatever. She was relieved when the exercise stopped because she found it boring. Indeed she admitted that she found her entire life colourless and boring, and that she analyses everything intellectually, 'on a head level', and is not really in touch with her feelings.

The juggler's array

Another woman imagined juggling bricks which turned into un-known heads and then back into bricks. When she dropped these bricks they formed a wall cutting her off from her audience, leaving her feeling trapped and depressed behind it. Thus in this instance 'heady' concerns block or get in the way of a person's relations with others.

Although heads feature quite frequently, most commonly people imagine juggling balls or the skittles favoured by professional jugglers. These items may be all of one colour, red and orange being particularly common, and yellow slightly less so. Frequently the items being juggled will be of two different colours, so that some are, say, red and others yellow.

Between three and five to seven items are most common but there is tremendous variation from one item to thousands. Some people realise that they are juggling too many items and might make a better job of it if they had fewer items, so discard some. Initially one man could not identify the items he was juggling, but when upon closer inspection he found they included heavy bulky items such as a car and a word processor he discarded them as too much of a burden. Similarly, some people change the items they are trying to juggle to those of more manageable shape. This may not always be possible however. A woman who imagined herself juggling with difficulty a heavy brick, a bell and a ball tried to change them for a set of balls she could juggle more easily. Eventually she realised that she could not change these items and must juggle with them. So she stood on the brick, put the bell on her nose and picked up some bean bags to juggle with the ball she was able to keep in the air. She reported that by 'getting on top' of the problem brick – the main difficulty in her act – she had gained stature and 'grown' – appearing bigger as a person, and that she had added more music to it by putting the bell on her nose, as a result of which she had freed herself to take up more items. Subsequently she was to apply this strategy to her real life. By 'getting on top' of a difficult relationship she was able to change her life and free herself to pursue a totally new career, and cope effectively with her new circumstances and independence.

Some people successfully change the nature of the objects they are juggling initially. Being unable to cope with the many oranges with which she was bombarded while various friends stood laughing, one woman changed them for a few red balls she could manage. Afterwards she indicated that the oranges represented the emotional difficulties she was struggling with at the time. This association between colour and emotion is not, coincidental. Colour is invariably highly significant, for reasons which are examined in Chapters 9 and 10, and should be noted carefully where it occurs in imagery. In the exercise under consideration here, oranges commonly symbolise a person's emotions or feelings. So a woman who reported juggling with three oranges, completely uniform in size and dullness of colour, considered these to represent accurately the dullness and smallness of her present life.

By contrast a woman described herself as juggling 'wonderfully' seven equal-sized balls, each a different colour of the rainbow. When it was suggested that she drop them she did so but picked them up again easily and continued juggling until the end of the exercise when they all followed each other 'rainbow-fashion' into the palm of her left hand. For the reasons examined in Chapters 9 and 10, this colour imagery is suggestive of flowing balanced energies and health. However, these features are by no means common in the juggling imagery. Indeed most people report some difficulty in handling the array of items they imagine.

One young woman imagined juggling a 50 pence piece, a St Christopher medal she had bought for a boyfriend (that he had never worn) and her nurse's cap, which she found particularly difficult to deal with and dropped. As she did so an audience she had previously been unaware of began to laugh unpleasantly, reflecting perhaps her anxiety about failing as a student nurse. Another woman described juggling a lettuce, a fish head, a piece of cheese, a light chequebook and a very heavy briefcase which was particularly difficult to handle, and so was the first item to fall from the array, although she tried to hold on to it. Identifying these items as representing the major concerns of her life, namely her home, work and money, she concluded that she needed to distribute her energies more evenly and balance her diet. Acting positively she started to imagine a heavier chequebook and a lighter briefcase, and was astonished to find that when she next lifted the latter it felt considerably less heavy than when she had put it down.

Syringes, knives and other sharp objects capable of inflicting pain if not handled with care commonly feature among the items people imagine themselves juggling. Nurses may include syringes among the items they imagine juggling, suggesting perhaps the possibility of pain or difficulty in relation to work that is not conveyed to the same extent by the catheter bags and dressings described by others. While some people are unaware of the possibly painful items they are juggling until it is pointed out to them, others realise that certain items in their array are potentially damaging or dangerous and often report a certain pride that they are able to handle these difficult items, often quite literally, as in the case of the woman who always grasped a hypodermic syringe by the handle so she was unhurt.

One young man reported feeling good because he was juggling a knife, plate and orange, each of which required handling in different ways, and doing so very well – so much so that success 'went to his head', the items turning into hats which he tipped on and off his head as part of the act. Other people do not find the task so easy. One man reported not wanting to handle, and almost dropping because of their sharp edges, tin toys in the shape of a house and a car, which for him were symbols of conventionality. Others surprise themselves by coping well with potentially hurtful items. Indeed they may manage these better than those which appear more benign. Thus one woman was surprised to find that the cubes she was juggling always fell flat into the palm of her hand, rather than on their edges or corners and therefore felt 'good' rather than sharp as she expected. However, she reported being unhappy about some of the cubes, which she described as feeling unpleasantly 'squishy' and some-what unpredictable, being similar in appearance to the others.

These items that 'went soft on her' clearly reduced her enjoyment of a performance with which she was otherwise quite satisfied.

Just as some items which appear unlikely to pose difficulties for the juggler are experienced as problematic, so other items that might be expected to be problematic prove not to be. Hence a woman who imagined juggling numerous items including several teapots, indicated that these were, somewhat unexpectedly, the easiest to grab because of their spouts.

Getting a grip on things

Getting a grip on items is a major difficulty for a significant number of people. One woman realised she needed to get a grip on her life when she imagined bunches of bananas swirling around her head totally out of her control while she 'went through the motions' ineffectually and without making contact with them. Once again colour is significant (see Chapters 9 and 10), reflecting this woman's tendency to deal with the issues of her life intellectually, on a 'head level', and to be out of touch with her feelings.

Another woman imagined numerous balls flying round in front of her which were animated externally and completely beyond her control. Eventually, out of a great sense of frustration at not being able to influence them in any way, she made a terrific effort and reached forward to grab one of the balls, feeling a great sense of elation when she 'pulled it off'. In so doing she realised that she was being held back by the lower part of her body which felt quite rigid and metallic, and prevented her moving, and that it was only by enormous effort and reaching out with the more mobile upper part of her body that she managed to grasp the ball. She interpreted this as an indication that many things in her life were out of control and that she needed to make a great effort to get a grip on things and get on with her act. Similarly, another woman described 'masses and masses' of small silvery balls floating around her out of reach, which she couldn't influence or affect in any way. While some imagine their performance to be totally out of their control, others describe losing control of it. This experience was very disturbing for a man who reported juggling five white plates, which he knew represented the major issues in his life, quite successfully for a time until one plate would 'go out of sync and ruin everything'. He saw this as an accurate reflection of his life and his belief that it would go smoothly for him if he could 'sort out' this one problem.

Sorting out the problem can be quite difficult however. One young woman reported being very concerned by her inability to pick up one of three very large red balls which she had dropped. She could not work out how to do this because she had one ball in each hand, and it took her a considerable time before she realised that she could sandwich the third ball between the other two and lift it. While this seems an enterprising solution it is by no means the only one. She could, for example, have tucked one or other ball under her arm while she lifted the third. Clearly it was important to her that she didn't let go of these balls, although she didn't know what they represented.

Many people have to make a considerable effort in order to juggle successfully. One woman described herself as concentrating very hard upon juggling five balls in her determination to 'do it right', and realised that this concern about performing correctly is a major source of her anxiety and tension in everyday life. Other people are not prepared to make the effort to perform well. One woman had, in reality, bought three yellow tennis balls because she had read about the benefits of juggling, but, on finding that it was difficult and couldn't be accomplished immediately, put them away in a drawer. In attempting the present exercise she imagined taking them out of the drawer and, as before, being unable to juggle them, and making no effort to do so. As she said, she 'couldn't be bothered'. This reaction is typical of this woman who wants to do many things that are seen as healthy and beneficial but does not work at any of them and soon gives up. She rationalised her lack of persistence at a previously attempted programme of physical exercises as follows: 'It looked easy, and would be good for me if I could do it, but I couldn't, and it was rather silly anyway'. She generally feels that people who succeed at an activity do so because it is easy for them rather than because they work at it, and admits both to envying them and worrying as to whether there is something wrong with her that prevents her succeeding as they do. She considers herself unlucky rather than lazy. Unsurprisingly, she envied other workshop members whom she perceived as being able to relax and visualise more easily than she could, while admitting that she hadn't really attempted to do either in the hope that a relaxation tape would make it easier for her!

Similarly a much younger woman claimed that she was shocked to be asked to do something active and 'simply could not', so allowed herself to go to sleep. She later confessed that this reluctance to attempt anything on her own behalf reflects her fear of failure and lack of belief in her competence.

A certain amount of luck, rather than skill or effort, seems to be involved in the performance of some people, such as the young man who imagined juggling two skittles and two black cats. However, for another young man cats had a very different significance. After juggling in the dark for a time before a spotlight was turned on him, he discovered he was juggling with his two pet cats that had been put to sleep by his mother some 18 months before without consulting him. He experienced great sadness and a fear of losing the cats altogether if he let go of them when instructed to do so. Indeed following the exercise he was overwhelmed with tremendous grief which continued for several days. As he subsequently explained, in the course of the exercise he realised that he felt more sad about the loss of the cats than any other event in his life, including the attempted suicide of his mother and her institutionalisation a few weeks later. As a result of the exercise he became aware of his feelings towards his family and how much emotion he had 'locked away' in trying to cope with a mentally ill mother as he grew up. He identified strongly with the cats, feeling he had been manipulated by others and without control in the situation as they had been. Also, he realised that in juggling them he was juggling with death: theirs, which he had to face and deal with, but also that of his mother, the threat of which had been an ever-present feature of his life and with which he still had to cope. As in this case, long-hidden issues and related feelings often 'come to light' in this exercise, awareness of them coming in sudden flashes or glimpses as though a spotlight has been turned on them, which is how these insights are often described.

Keeping a grip on things

As in the above example, letting go of the items they are juggling with is for many people difficult and even traumatic. One woman identified her difficulty in juggling as being unable to let go of those items in her left hand with the result that she couldn't keep anything in motion. Initially she was unable to find any significance in this imagery, but when asked what she tended to hold on to in life she indicated that she had been very disturbed by her inability to let go of what she described as an 'outmoded emotional entanglement'. Although she knew this was no longer viable she clung to it, fearing that this might be her last chance for such a relationship. Unable to let go of the past, she was unable to live in the present and this has given rise to a great deal of upset and depression, which she admitted was her reason for attending the workshop in the first place.

Another woman described 'feeling great' swirling eight identical white skittles easily and well, but found herself looking around to see if there was anything more interesting to juggle with. Finding there wasn't she continued and when instructed to let the items fall she dropped only one of them and carried on with the others. Puzzled by this and her apparent dissatisfaction 'with her lot', she pondered this imagery for some days before realising that her white skittles were the cigarettes she had struggled to give up for many years. Although she had made gestures towards giving up smoking she had never succeeded. However, she repeated the juggling exercise until she could imagine letting go of all the items, by which time she had quite effortlessly given up smoking.

It is interesting to compare her experience with that of another woman who had allowed herself to be pursuaded to undergo hypnosis in an attempt to give up smoking. This proved successful but for months afterwards she felt unaccountably depressed until she began smoking again. Some time later she decided that she wanted to give up smoking and did so with little difficulty, realising in so doing that her earlier depression had arisen because what she described as an important 'prop' had been taken away from her rather than given up by choice. As the juggling imagery reveals, it is very difficult to let go of or give up those things which a person wants to, or needs to keep hold of.

One woman described herself as she had been ten years ago, just before her marriage, juggling innumerable small white objects for her parents in the living room of the home where she lived with them, and finding it an immense stuggle to continue to put on a good performance, but essential that she did so. Although her audience appeared quite indifferent to her performance, which was quite predictable and expected, she could not let the objects fall to the floor where they would be spoiled by contact with the ground. She therefore felt completely trapped by the situation and obligated, craving privacy away from the audience and the relief of the act ending. Initially unable to identify what she was juggling, and why she felt obliged to continue doing so, she repeated the exercise several times in the following weeks during which time she also gained insight from various memories and dreams. She remembered having 'second thoughts' prior to her wedding but not voicing them because of the upset it would cause. She therefore went ahead with the marriage, which provided security and love – the soft, glowing, beautiful items she was juggling in her imagery – just as her parents had done and, although she didn't want to let go of these, she did so, obtaining a divorce after five years in order to become independent and 'do her own thing'. Describing her feelings subsequently it was clear that she was still troubled by doubt and guilt, which, one might speculate, are the possible consequences of 'spoiling' the ideals of others by bringing them down to earth.

Another person reluctant to let go was a young man who imagined himself juggling four eggs, which he recognised as the issues in his present life about which he was anxious. He reported feeling that he would have to juggle them for ever because in order to stop he would have to catch two eggs in one hand and he worried that he would break them. The anxieties people juggle and often have difficulty letting go of are reflected in the account of a man who found himself juggling miniature bank managers. He couldn't drop them, and so kept moving lower and lower to the ground so that he could put them down gently. He indicated that his difficulty in letting go of these figures reflected the fact that he had to treat them with care at a time when his business was in difficulties. The possibility that by doing so he was in some way 'lowering himself' is also suggested by his imagery.

For some people letting go of the items is something of a 'put down'. The man whose performance 'went to his head' felt really annoyed when instructed to let go of the items and thinking 'Sod it' walked off stage without bowing to his audience. A woman explained that she 'didn't care' when told to let go of the items because she had never started to juggle, being unable to lift a large brick-like object and indicating that, until then, when she realised she couldn't get her act together, she had not appreciated how low her self-esteem is. She simply couldn't let herself down further.

Having let go of the items they are juggling, some people find they are unable to pick them up again for a variety of reasons. A woman who imagined herself juggling thousands of things thought she was 'doing wonderfully', coordinating and balancing these items until she let them go, and they fell into a metal crate in front of her, filling it up. She felt an enormous sense of relief not to be juggling any more and on attempting to lift the crate found that she could not because of its weight. She therefore bowed to the audience and turned to walk off stage only to discover that she couldn't find a door or way out, which she interpreted as an indication of all the things in her life she wants to be able to walk away from and can't. Another woman tried to contain the items she dropped by directing them into a plastic bucket, but whereas the lavender bottles she had been juggling went into it, she lost a number of oranges and was unable to find them. Some people do not want to risk losing items, as in the case of a woman who avoided losing any of the large, fluffy pom-poms she had been juggling by dropping them into the cavernous pocket of her clown's trousers.

One man who at the outset imagined himself dressed as a clown and confidently juggling fruit for his family, began to see that he was juggling a rainbow from one hand to another, but as he watched this it began to change into a Donald Duck figure and hundreds and hundreds of Smarties. The problem of juggling all these sweets was solved when Donald swallowed them, and then proceeded to do forward and back flips from one hand to another, effectively taking over the act and performing himself. When the man attempted to put him down Donald became belligerent, arguing, complaining, criticising and then stealing the limelight completely by performing on his own so that all attention was focused on him, leaving the man angry and resentful at having lost the attention and the spotlight. Having given a good deal of thought to this complex imagery the man later identified a number of transitions within it that correspond with various phases in his actual life, and which he explained in terms of an idyllic, colourful and magical situation that produced children in whose goodness and smartness he was initially reflected before they gobbled up all the colour and sweetness in life, taking all the attention away from him, and moved on, leaving him resentful in the background.

Transitions or life changes of some kind are often indicated by a sudden change in imagery. Thus a woman who initially perceived herself on a longboat moored at the side of a canal suddenly found that this was moving quite smoothly and quickly along in the opposite direction, while she juggled coloured balls at the prow. As she passed through familiar scenery she was able to continue juggling easily, creating a pleasingly balanced harmonious pattern, but as the boat moved into less familiar waters she began to feel uneasy and considered putting the balls down as it moved into an unknown area which drew her attention away from her performance. Although at the time the significance of this imagery seemed unclear to her she realised the following day that it was a very accurate reflection of her present life in which, up until recently, she had felt herself to be restricted and getting nowhere, only to find herself suddenly progressing along quickly, smoothly and purposefully in a quite different direction, and moving into a quite novel situation.

Similarly, a man who initially imagined himself juggling competently as a character taller than his actual self, composed of his heroes, idols and role models, suddenly saw himself as a small, somewhat absurd jester standing on a street corner clumsily juggling a number of items he didn't want to handle while laughing mockingly at his audience. Eventually giving up this performance, he sat down feeling sad and dejected, but after a while he began to smile and chat to passers by, idly picking up a ball and beginning to play with it as he did so. These changes represented what he described as a series of changes in his identity and world view. The first is that of an idealised, albeit immature self, falsely trying to be someone he isn't and failing. The second figure reflects himself at a later stage, bitter, cynical, disillusioned but at the same time tired of mocking conventionality, who eventually lets go of these features of his past, and after an initial period of sadness and depression, discovers a genuine warmth in his new friendliness, rather than his former superficiality, and a new interest in life.

This imagery indicates that it may be necessary to let go of certain attitudes, values, thoughts, beliefs, convictions, emotions and habits before other significant changes in performance can take place. Another man realised from his imagery that he tended to be rigid and that to be able to change the pattern of his juggling as part of the performance as he wanted to, he needed to be more flexible and to take on the views of others. Moreover, he recognised that in order to do this he had to play to an audience rather than remain closed away and isolated from others, as was the case in his imagery and in his recent life. Other changes may be necessary or desirable if performance is to be improved. A man who decided that his act would be livened up by more colour remedied the situation by imagining himself in a very brightly coloured and ornate cape.

When asked what they need to improve their performance many women specify greater appreciation, support, encouragement or applause. Invariably they describe themselves as juggling domestic items such as washing-up bowls, pots, pans, cutlery, plates and, for some reason, sticks of celery. (It has recently been suggested to me that 'celery' could well be a word-play on 'salary' – a 'tricky' issue for many of these women.) One woman spoke of wanting applause because she was happy and enjoying herself, and wanted to be able to smile and show it. She interpreted this as showing the extent to which she tends to be influenced by others, even in the expression of her inner feelings. Another woman, who imagined herself resplendent as a clown in green boots, bright red trousers and a highly-spangled sparkling top, juggling successfully and enjoyably among other things her husband and children, a computer and a number of shiny stars, immediately responded to the question of what would improve her performance with the thought 'spotlights, of course!'

Another women considered that she could perform better with greater confidence. Imagining herself juggling three balls and realising that she was better at this activity than she had expected to be, she came to the conclusion that she perhaps has more ability than she thinks, which gave her more confidence, not merely within the context of this exercise but more generally. A variant on this was provided by another woman who insisted that her performance would improve if she were taller, as in this way she would have greater stature!

However, as a result of the exercise most people acknowledge that in order to improve their performance as a juggler they need to make changes and that this usually means letting go of something. They therefore come to appreciate Perls's observation that 'the ability to resign, to let go of obsolete responses, of exhausted relationships, and tasks beyond one's potential is an essential part of the wisdom of living'.

❧ CHAPTER EIGHT ❧

Healthy Priorities

Space flights are merely an escape, a fleeing away from oneself, because it is easier to go to Mars or to the moon than it is to penetrate one's own being.

C.G. JUNG

The cancer specialist Carl Simonton (1983) has declared that in contemporary Western society cancer is the most effective problem solver apart from death in that it provides a socially acceptable way of getting out of an intolerable situation, and that all illness serves a similar function. He observes that people are not educated in how to live their lives but are taught primarily rational strategies for dealing with problems, and become ill when these fail because they cannot solve their problems in any other way. If they could do so, he claims, they would not become ill. Nevertheless in his view illness is not a conscious strategy, but an unconscious one because by his definition illness arises only when a person is *unaware* of any solution.

Accordingly illness is not a conscious creation but an unconscious expression of a personal dilemma. It is, according to Jung, a means by which the soul expresses an important message. Moreover, if as he claimed, the physical disorder appears as a direct mimetic expression of the psychic situation, this message is fairly exact. He insisted that the development of neurotic symptoms should not be regarded as merely the onset of illness but as a signal for self-examination and re-evaluation in order to attain a new and better adaptation. He therefore considered symptoms as having the positive function of compelling a person to look inwards and engage in some soul-searching. However, this view of illness as symptomatic of a suffering soul or literal *psychopathology*, which forms the basis of all traditional approaches to healing, has become obscured, and the exclusive focus of scientific medicine on the mechanics of disease has led to its message being overlooked. This is a very serious oversight if, as Siegel (1990, p. 39) claims, 'our bodies mean what they say' and that by listening to them we can begin to use our diseases to redirect our lives. Like Simonton and Jung, he urges people to regard illness as an opportunity to pause and consider what is occurring in their lives, claiming that those who do so invariably recognise their illness as a message to change.

A person who can attest to these claims is New York therapist Niro Asistent who in November 1985 tested positive for human immune deficiency virus (HIV) and was diagnosed as having the AIDS-related complex (ARC), yet was symptom-free, in full remission from ARC, and confirmed as HIV negative by May 1986, and has remained so since. By listening to her intuition she discovered the source of imbalance that lead to her dis-ease and also what she needed to do in order to support her own healing:

> My intuition also told me that this condition was my 'wake-up call'. I could have chosen either to respond to the message or to roll over and go back to sleep. I chose to wake up. Every crisis, whether it be an illness, the consequences of addiction, or the loss of a loved one, offers us an opportunity to wake up. It is like an earthquake. What I mean is this. Life punched me in the face so forcefully that I was unable to escape the shocking reality. My reactions ranged from numbness to anger to despair and finally to soul-searching questioning. As I questioned my life, I realised that I had spent the majority of it asleep. I had forgotten who I am and why I am here. I was moving through life unconsciously, like a sophisticated robot. My diagnosis served as a wonderful tool to assist me in examining the limitations of my conditioning.
>
> I had never taken time to question my early conditioning and the personality I had created based on it. It was time to examine these things honestly, keeping what served me and discarding what was no longer appropriate. I began to take

responsibility for my life from that new state of awareness, moving from the indulgence of the victim to the integrity of the master.

1991, pp. 5–6

There are many people like Niro Asistent who accept the invitation offered by illness to change their lives and who subsequently acknowledge it as the best thing that ever happened to them. However, as she points out, faced with a similar crisis many people do not respond to the wake-up call their body is sending them; all they want is for the symptoms to disappear, and they are willing to endure the most extreme and expensive treatments to this end.

It is often very difficult for people to make changes, even when they want to, because of pressures from others. An example which is commonly reported by cancer patients is the resistance they encounter from family and friends to recommended dietary changes, which are usually very low on the scale of life changes they might need to make. Changing jobs, personal relationships or habits of a lifetime generally meets with much more strenuous opposition. Niro Asistent discovered that when she began to live her life according to her own needs instead of constantly trying to please others as she had been conditioned to do, many of her friends and relatives could not understand her 'strange behaviour'. As a result some friendships disappeared, but others deepened; 'The things that were important, like loving relationships with my family and friends, stayed, and what was superfluous, like social acquaintances, fell away' (p. 58).

Some people, while acknowledging the message communicated by their illness, succumb to the pressures applied by others and do not act accordingly. Many people prefer to continue with sickening and often potentially deadly ways of life or remain ill rather than face up to the need for change in their lives. Indeed, as Carl Simonton observes, in his experience many people would prefer to die rather than divorce. Similarly surgeon Bernie Siegel has indicated that given a choice between an operation for a serious illness and a change in lifestyle, 80 per cent of people will opt for the former because it demands no action on their part, transfers responsibility elsewhere, and maintains the status quo. Hence, even after

215

'successful' surgery people often do not get well, much to the dismay of transplant surgeons whose patients often succumb to a recurrence of heart disease, sometimes within a few months, or develop cancers at an alarming rate (Gillman & Gillman, 1993). Moreover, as Caroline Myss observes, there are those who remain ill despite having tried every known treatment, conventional and alternative, who report that their cancers have returned, or never-ending battles with various other chronic dysfunctions, and symptoms of exhaustion and depression. Indeed, the habitual relapse into illness is not confined to the physical domain, as any psychotherapist or psychiatrist knows only too well. The question arises, therefore, as to why it is that some people do not heal.

PAINFUL RELATIONSHIPS

In an attempt to provide an answer Myss has identified what she terms the intimate language of wounds. This, she claims, is perhaps the first spoken form of intimacy learned by an individual. She observes that as people get to know each other their first act of trust is usually to reveal something about themselves. The material that is shared in this initial bridge to intimacy is, as a general rule, a wound – a memory of a past or more recent injury, the expected response being that the other person will match this disclosure with some memory of equal and intimate proportion. This expectation is justified, for as research reveals (Jourard, 1971), self-disclosure is a reciprocal phenomenon based upon the shared assumption that whatever is presented to the other is disclosed in privacy and will not be betrayed to others who are not present.

> Following this unofficial ceremony of bonding, the automatic assumption on the part of both the individuals is that the contents of the wounds shared will remain private and moreover, from that moment on, each of the individuals will respect the boundaries and requirements of those wounds. For example, if I shared with you that I was completely traumatised during my childhood by large dogs, your job would be to lock up your dog when I came to visit. That act would prove to me

that you respected me by respecting the demands of my wound. And if you told me that you associated your discomfort with heights with a parent's suicide, my job would be to never take you to high places. While this type of behaviour appears to be respectful and loving, it is simultaneously extremely anti-healing as it keeps our wounds alive and well and prevents us from letting go and getting on with our lives.

MYSS, 1992, p. 8

Indeed, as Myss indicates, 'the intimate language of wounds is powerful glue. It binds us not only to our past, but to each other in ways that may appear to be healthy but are, in fact, risky because wounds set a tone and a purpose in a relationship that eventually becomes the strongest pattern for being together. Many marriages and intimate relationships have come together over dinner and wounds' (1992, pp. 8–9). She explains the reason for this deep connection in terms of people's need to have their wounds validated; to have someone acknowledge that they have been through an experience that has harmed and scarred them. This, she claims, is necessary for healing to take place. Perls has similarly observed that you have to know you are hurt in order to heal.

However, there is a fine dividing line between validating a person's wound and supporting it. The challenge, both for the sufferer and others, is to recognise the very subtle difference between needing to talk about wounds in order to heal them and doing so in order to control other people or as an excuse for certain behaviours. The distinction here is between a person genuinely wanting to heal, and wanting to keep their wounds for personal and social motives; that is, as a means of establishing intimate social contact with others, or of providing an excuse to avoid saying or doing things that need attention. However, becoming aware of the functional significance of wounds and relinquishing them is far from simple for many people. As Myss observes this is 'tricky business' because 'the idea of releasing wounds permanently and getting on with one's life is extremely threatening, odd as this may seem' (p. 9). Some people would have little or nothing else to talk about; and no basis for their closest relationships. Moreover, the issue is further confounded by the problem of forgiveness.

217

Myss observes that while genuine forgiveness demands that wounds are relinquished, most people forgive mentally while holding on to the resentment they feel towards those who inflicted them. They say 'I realise that he or she had problems BUT . . .' and proceed to follow this with a statement of why they still feel hurt by them. Emotionally, therefore, people are attached to their wounds, longing for the opportunity to face their aggressors with their rage, hurt and anger, and for them to acknowledge the injuries they have inflicted. Despite what their minds tell them, their hearts cling to this desire. It is therefore very difficult to exorcise the individual's idea of himself as an innocent victim.

> Forgiveness exorcises the victim in us and it is extremely
> difficult to release the victim because along with releasing our
> victim consciousness goes all of the excuses of the victim. In
> letting go of our past, we are, in fact, letting go of an entire
> life-style and much about our present life has to change as a
> consequence, and the reality is most people are terrified of that
> type of life-style change. Clinging to the past, however difficult,
> is nevertheless 'the devil we know'.
>
> MYSS, 1992, p. 10

Moreover, releasing the victim means that there is no one to blame and with no one to blame there is no alternative but to take responsibility for one's own life, which is precisely what many people wish to avoid.

For Myss, what she describes as the 'healing journey', involves not simply the discovery and processing of the wounded past, but its eventual release. She insists that without this essential release stage nothing is healed; wounds are merely reopened that never stop bleeding. Her advice to others is thus:

> Take the courageous step of not allowing your wounds to do
> the speaking for you. Observe your fears and motivations and
> study yourself to learn why you find yourself speaking
> 'wound-ology' – and then force yourself not to. Force yourself
> to give up the power of your wounds and to create patterns of
> human interaction that are based upon your strengths and not

your wounded history. Force is a strong word to use, but force is exactly what it takes to liberate yourself and free your spirit from yesterday's nightmare. It's worth the effort. I've never met a free and liberated person who prefers living in the past once they've made it to present-time.

1992, p. 11

HEALING THE HUMAN CONDITION

Original as Myss's observations may appear, there is in fact nothing new in her analysis, it being precisely that offered by the Indian master Siddartha Gautama, the Buddha, in his teachings over 2000 years ago. One of Buddha's most penetrating insights was his understanding of the role of suffering in human experience. He recognised that suffering is a consequence of living in process and is experienced because of change or impermanence. Man therefore suffers through his awareness of physical, mental and emotional change and its consequences – illness, ageing, death, loss, changing relationships and separation. He also recognised that the human needs for security and permanence, which imply a resistance to change, are also a manifestion of suffering; as is the deep-seated fear of losing identity or the sense of self. Change creates anxiety and fear by creating instability and uncertainty, and is only tolerated if it does not compromise identity. However, irrespective of man's intolerance of it, change is an ever-present condition of human life. Existence itself is therefore the cause of all human sorrow and as such is not what people want it to be. They therefore defend themselves against change by clinging to the familiar and the habitual, which gives rise to a false sense of security and a frail sense of identity.

Buddha, however, saw possibility for transformation through acceptance of change. He advocated the development of self-awareness or insight, primarily by way of meditation and adherence to a code of conduct, which, simply stated, is as follows:

· first you must see clearly what is wrong;
· next decide to be cured;
· then you must act;

- you must speak to aim at being cured;
- your livelihood must not conflict with your therapy;
- therapy must go forward at the 'staying speed', the critical velocity that can be sustained;
- you must think about it incessantly;
- and learn how to contemplate with the deep mind.

WILSON-ROSS, 1973

The same procedure for cure can also be stated more succinctly in a simple list of steps:

- right seeing;
- right purpose;
- right conduct;
- right speech;
- right lifestyle;
- right effort;
- right kind of awareness;
- right concentration.

In each case what is *right* is that which is perceived as such by the individual concerned rather than laid down by any dogma or social prescriptions, and arrived at by way of a process of self-questioning or soul-searching.

Myss's prescription for healing is similar in that she urges people to let go of past resentments and live in the present; 'Remaining in a condition of resentment creates a phenomenon that I think of as a time warp. Your body is in present time but the emotional energy of the spirit remains in the past'. It is therefore necessary to pull these energies back from yesterday's traumas and into today.
This involves:

- forgiving the past;
- letting go of resentment;
- prioritising one's needs in the present;
- acting upon them;
- living fully in the present;
- and in gratitude.

The efficacy of so doing is confirmed by Niro Asistent. She describes how, on becoming ill, a quiet, almost imperceptible voice reminded her 'to learn from what is happening now' and to explore what she knew in her soul. She realised that in order to do so she had to look into her past.

> As the days passed, I became more and more frustrated about
> how unfair life seemed to be. I was ready to give up. I was
> living in that dangerous place of 'either-or'. Somewhere in my
> conscious mind I held the belief that no matter what I did it
> would not produce the promised results so what was the point
> of continuing? In search of an answer I examined my childhood
> to see what decision this belief may be based on. Then I
> remembered.
>
> 1991, p. 38

What she remembered was feeling cheated and betrayed following an incident in which her parents failed to fulfil a promise to her when she was ten years old. From that moment on she lost trust in them and became a 'victim', believing that she could trust no one and that life would not give her what she deserved, and pledging never to tell the truth or to love in order to avoid being hurt again. Upon acknowledging that it was finally time to let go of the resentment and blame she had been holding on to for over 30 years, and the beliefs generated by these feelings, she realised that they were the filters through which she perceived 'reality' and no longer appropriate to her life as an adult.

She had quite literally believed that she needed the love and approval of others in order to survive, and because she had never questioned the validity of this belief she had entered into a succession of unhealthy relationships. She began to realise that this belief, more than any other, was making her sick; draining most of her energy and making her feel hopeless, miserable and trapped. Moreover, she was doing everything she could to keep these old beliefs alive:

> Even though intellectually I knew it was time to examine each
> belief 'voice' within my head, I was afraid of letting go of my
> old conditioning. I was afraid I would 'disappear' if I were to

really examine who I thought I was and be willing to let go of my 'identity' in the process.

p. 41

This release finally occurred as she was counting on a calendar the 492 days of life which remained to her, if she was lucky. Suddenly she understood that each moment was precious and could not be wasted and this totally transformed the way she responded to life. It was then that she realised that although she knew a good deal about her past and the personality she had created in order to survive, and was intimate with her mistakes, regrets, dreams, fantasies and habitual reactions, she knew very little about herself and wanted to discover who she was before she died.

Accordingly she gave up the superficial social activities that consumed much of her time and her concerns about 'doing the right thing'. Indeed she began to appreciate for the first time that she was living a life that went mostly against her own nature, while pretending that this was the way she wanted to live. By starting to live life according to her own needs and what was 'right' for her instead of trying to please others as she had always done, she experienced what it felt like to make herself the first priority. She began to stand up for herself and her needs in spite of the fact that this did not meet with the approval of others. As she explains, 'I was finally learning how to establish my boundaries ... In fact my inability to establish boundaries had been a major emotional factor contributing to my disease ... So as part of my search for my maximum potential I needed to discover what my personal boundaries were in relation to the people in my life' (p. 58).

Previously she had believed that if she gave a certain amount to someone then she would receive a certain amount back from them. However, having put herself 'at the top of the list' she found that giving to others became a reflection of giving to herself and that as she stopped trying to please everyone she was giving from the heart. She realised that only by being selfish in this way could she be truly selfless. Niro therefore began to express her feelings and to change her ways of relating to others as she became self-motivated rather than by 'shoulds' imposed by others, and as she became more confident in her own authority and authentic wisdom she began to make changes in her lifestyle. During meditation, of a kind she had previously practised regularly, 'something very strange happened. Somehow I could see inside of my body; I literally saw my liver, my stomach, my intestines, and my other internal organs, and they looked a putrid shade of yellowish-green. It lasted for only a few moments, but the impact of this experience was so strong that I had to sit and integrate what I had seen. Shocked by what I saw I intuitively began to use mental imagery to purify and rejuvenate my internal organs' (p. 65).

She also changed to a healthier diet to cleanse her body of toxins, began to exercise, and to meditate regularly, and it was subsequently during a meditative walk on the seashore that she experienced the healing power of a 'peak experience'. In this state of total awareness she felt a sense of becoming one with everything around her and of utter completeness, and such gratitude to have experienced 'the gift of total merging' that her life could have ended at that moment and it would not have mattered to her. Shortly afterwards, acting on intuition, she asked for another blood test, and was found to be negative for HIV antibodies. Intuitively she knew that her healing was the physiological consequence of living in total alignment with the essence of life itself, and that she had discovered what enlightened masters have taught since the beginning of time, which is that 'when we are truly committed to live in the present, in acceptance of both ourselves and our surroundings, miracles can happen' (p. 75).

Siegel attests to the truth of this claim, observing that exceptional patients such as Niro who make 'miraculous' recoveries and greatly outlive medical prognoses, are all people who have become authentic: 'They do not reach the point of death only to find that they've never really lived. Sometimes they only "really live" for a few moments before they die. But they have lived and they are ready to go, as their choice. They know who they are, where they've been and why' (1990, p. 246).

Feeling that such an experience is not personal but part of the 'collective experiment of the universe', Niro Asistent was determined to share what she had learned with others. However, although people were curious about her personal healing experience, she found that they were unwilling to commit themselves to a similar process, preferring to take symptom-suppressing drugs rather than experience the discomfort of examining their lives in order to discover the source of their illness or change their attitudes and behaviour. Nevertheless she insists that healing involves acceptance of all of who we are, including the disowned parts of ourselves; those we are afraid to look at, including illness, addiction, anger, sadness, fear and denial. Therefore, 'on the healing journey we must travel through the darkness to return to the light' (p. 111).

This is the theme of the following exercise.

EXERCISE 8

Take some time to relax in whatever way you find most effective. Having done so, imagine that you have been chosen for an exploratory mission to the end of the universe. How do you react to this news? How do you prepare for the trip? What business do you attend to? What phone calls do you make? What letters do you write? What messages do you leave? How do you spend your last days and hours on earth?

Once aboard the spacecraft you discover that its advanced equipment not only records and relays information about outer space by way of numerous monitors but also about your inner space or internal processes; your thoughts, feelings, memories, and imaginings. How do you feel as you leave the earth? How do you occupy yourself during the long space flight? What are your thoughts and feelings?

Eventually you see a small light on one of the monitors and beneath it a caption which indicates that this is the end of the universe. As you approach it the light becomes larger and larger until the spacecraft enters into it. As the spacecraft comes to rest you are met by a figure. Clearly you have been expected and are welcomed. Noting its features and your thoughts and feelings towards it, you ask the figure where you are. Telepathically it communicates that you are on the planet Now. It asks your purpose in coming to the planet and you explain that you are on an exploratory mission to the end of the universe. You are then told simply that there is nothing beyond Now; that Now is all there is and that this is the message you must take back to earth. You are then courteously shown back to your spacecraft and directed to return to earth.

You have plenty of time to ponder this message and your feelings as you return to earth. Having done so record your experiences and what you might have learned from them.

Commentary

Initial reactions to the prospect of journeying to the end of the universe vary enormously. Many people welcome the opportunity gleefully, with great enthusiasm and excitement, describing feelings of exhilaration, delight, curiosity and a sense of great possibilities unfolding. Fairly typical of this kind of reaction is that of a woman who reported being thrilled to be given an opportunity that would never occur in real life. Others, however, are distraught at the prospect, fearful and apprehensive, some with tears visibly pouring down their cheeks. Generally these people are distressed by the awareness of what they are leaving behind rather than by the prospect of the flight itself, although one woman reported being so terrified of the flight that she would not embark upon the journey. Once again this illustrates the way in which fears and anxieties restrict experience, even at the fantasy level.

As might be expected from their initial attitude towards the journey, people differ considerably in their feelings about leaving earth. Some who are otherwise quite excited by the prospect of adventure, nevertheless express sadness and concern about others. Typically these are women whose caretaker role involves them in looking after elderly parents and who worry about arrangements for them during their absence. Many people are reluctant to leave parents, some because they fear that they might die while they are away and others because they feel guilty about leaving those who have invested so much in rearing them. Some people are reluctant to leave children because they will miss them growing up. One man reported feeling saddened by the prospect of not seeing his godchild again because by losing her he felt he was losing something of his own childhood, which he didn't want to leave behind. Many people are concerned about leaving pets, especially dogs.

While the attitude of most of these people is perhaps best described as excitement tinged with sadness, there are many for whom there is no excitement whatever, only dread. One woman was very distressed at the prospect of leaving her two dogs, insisting that she could not leave them even for one day, much less for the duration of a mission into space. In my own case I was quite overwhelmed by the prospect of leaving *everything*, not simply my family and animals. I wanted to see the spring flowers and to be with my sick dog, to know whether he recovered or to be with him when he died. I wanted to be able to breed more puppies and watch them grow, and the prospect of not seeing my niece grow up was devastating. I didn't even want to leave my job! I felt despair because I had so much to see through, and so much that I didn't want to miss and the prospect of not being around was like being given a terminal diagnosis. Indeed, I lived each moment of the remaining time on earth as if I were dying.

In contrast many others were dying to get away! Some people expressed relief at being able to leave their problems and difficulties behind them. Several were pleased to be relieved of pressures in their lives, one man reporting that he was glad to be leaving 'a lot of pressure from women', and a number of women expressing their pleasure at being able to leave their husbands and children. Others were keen to leave their job, and without exception all the students who shared their experiences reported being happy to get away from their courses and to have no regrets about leaving their colleges.

One man found himself thinking that as there is no edge to the universe he could not go to a place which rationally does not exist. However, upon realising that he was intellectualising the issue he acknowledged that he needed to leave his rational, intellectual approach to life behind him and successfully did so. The limits that the rational mind imposes upon experience are highlighted, however, by a young woman who was proceeding quite happily with the exercise until she began to think about it. She explained: 'As there are no known habitable planets within our solar system one would have to travel very great distances to find another planet. The distances would be vast and any space

various ways, with almost everyone commenting on the colour of the monitor screens, which are usually red, orange and pink or, occasionally, blue. Some people describe turning to different monitors every time an unhappy or disturbing memory appeared, or engaging in other diversionary strategies, such as allowing themselves to fall asleep. A woman who imagined herself as resigned and waiting for death, and who did not want to upset herself by recalling the past, described leaving the memory monitors blank and walking around the spacecraft. One man diverted himself from unhappy memories by attempting to improve the gadgetry in the spaceship and a woman who did not want to look inside herself distracted herself from looking at any of the monitors by looking out of the windows.

One man who tried this found he was looking in on himself from outside the spacecraft. This didn't mean a great deal to him until a week or so later when he felt rejected by his family at a wedding and 'like an outsider looking in'. Only then did he realise the extent of his alienation from his family, and began to look more closely at some of the problems and hurts he suffered in his relationships with them. Indeed many people subsequently report that during this phase of the exercise they have became aware of issues, both positive and negative, which they had not previously recognised as important for them. One young woman, for instance, whose spacecraft had a built-in safety device that enabled her return to earth at the push of a button, became aware of her tendency to distance herself and escape from difficult issues.

For many people the importance of the exercise lies in the opportunity it affords for reassessing and prioritising issues in life. One woman reported that it had enabled her to realise the importance of her family and close relationships; and also that she had a problem about time, tending to be anxious about the future and guilty about the past, as a result of which she failed to live in the present and tried to fix and control time rather than 'go with the flow'. Unsurprisingly, I experienced abject misery during the trip and imagined passing the time looking through photographs and reminiscing. I regretted what I had not done with my life and those things I had not made the best of; what I had not said and done to show my full appreciation and affection to those I loved and cared for. I wished I had taken more time 'to watch the grass grow' and less time over things which didn't really matter. I wished I had lived life more fully.

Always rather slow to master any technological apparatus, it was only after some time that I realised I could not only review memories by way of the monitors but could also interact with people through the mental images I projected on to the screens. This 'virtual reality' made me more depressed, however, and it was only the discovery that I could talk to spirit guides in this way that kept me 'sane'. It was therefore with great relief that I saw the light on the monitor signifying, as I thought, the end of everything. This, in itself, is quite an intriguing commentary on the power of imagery. It should be remembered that I was engaging in an imaginary exercise which I had dreamed up in the first instance, so knew what was to follow. Yet despite this I was totally absorbed in the immediate 'reality' of the experience. So too were those people who described approaching and entering the light in awe. One woman imagined that she was in heaven, and was therefore most upset when she was told to return to earth.

Few people appear to consider the figure who greets them as particularly salient in this exercise. Most describe vaguely humanoid forms or white lights, although gremlins have been described and 'Lowry-like stick figures'. It may well be in this case that the medium is the message. Certainly most people appear to be affected by it, sometimes powerfully, although they may not understand why. One woman admitted to feeling that she had learned something important from it, but didn't know what exactly. In much the same way a young man described it as like a zen koan and, as such, very perplexing. Indeed Fritz Perls described this message, which he viewed as the essence of his gestalt therapy and of most oriental healing traditions, as like a koan:

> The koan is: Nothing exists except the here and now. The now is present, is the phenomenon, is what you are aware of, is the moment in which you carry your so-called memories, and your so-called anticipations with you. Whether you remember or anticipate, you do it now. The past is no more.

The future is not yet, When I say 'I was', that's not now, that's the past. When I say, 'I want to', that's the future, it's not yet. Nothing can possibly exist except the now.

1976, p. 44

Many people find themselves wrestling with this koan-like riddle long after the exercise is finished. One young woman found to her astonishment that 'everything stopped' for her, having been 'cancelled out' by the message in that her mind went completely blank when she heard it. This continued to puzzle her until some days later she realised that she was so future-oriented in striving towards a career that she felt unable to enjoy the present, which seemed not to exist for her. Her inability to live in the present explained why in the exercise she had been unable to progress and had come to a dead-end when the future was eliminated. This awareness gave rise to feelings of resentment as she realised how much of her life was being sacrificed to the promise of the future.

Another woman was confused by the message because she didn't know how to discriminate the past from the future, and had no idea what it meant to live in the present. Attempting the exercise again some time later she was met on the planet Now by a businessman who said he was the president of the 'Here and Now Club'. When she asked how to join, he said that joining the club is not the problem but remaining in it; that everyone begins as a member of the club but quickly drops out of it. He took her to meet other members of the club and as a result she appreciated for the first time the difference between living in the present rather than the past or future.

Many people are disappointed by the message, some because they have been anticipating a better future and others because they 'couldn't see anything in it'. One woman who expressed this view declared her disappointment at being sent back to earth 'empty-handed' and with 'nothing', suggesting perhaps that she places more value on material possessions and 'things' rather than abstract knowledge and wisdom. Some people appeared disappointed by the simplicity of the message. Some reported thinking 'Well, that makes sense' or 'That's obviously a simple truth'. One man declared that while he felt the sentiment of the message was 'good' it was too simplistic and that as we are all determined by our past so we cannot ignore it. However, this would appear to confuse awareness of the past with being dominated by it. For while the past cannot be changed the effect it has on the present can. One woman reported feeling angry because she saw her past as too important to be forgotten, being the reason for how she is in the present. However on considering this further she acknowledged that her present life was not happy because of her attachment to the past and she must cut the ties that bound her to it, however painful that might be.

Other people feel angry when given the message. One man was annoyed because it was not new knowledge. He felt that he had been tricked and was wasting his time. Another man was angry about having to travel so far to find out what he already knew until he realised that though he knew it he didn't act on it, having not regarded it as important. I too experienced very intense anger at having lost all I cared about in order to find out something I already knew, but more so about being sent back to a world which would not be the same. I realised that everything would have changed and so it would not be a case of picking up where I had left off but of starting again totally – a prospect I found dreadful. Anger gave way to feelings of loneliness, isolation and sadness for my lost years. However, I tried to relate the wisdom I had gained from the message to these feelings and insights, and decided that from then on I would live each day as it came along, in the now and make the best of it. Subsequently I realised that the whole experience had affected me very profoundly, influencing my approach to life and the events and people in it. However, looking back on that first space trip, I realise with regret that I lost much that I gained from the experience, having reverted back to taking life for granted. It is indeed only too easy to drop out of the 'Here and Now Club'.

Another woman, who initially felt silly upon being sent back to earth after anguishing over leaving it, nevertheless felt totally enlightened by the message. 'This came as a complete revelation', she later wrote, when she realised that up until then she had not appreciated the present, taking it for granted and using it as a safe base in which to dwell on the past and speculate on the future. Since then she tells herself everyday that there is only here and now, and that 'life is not just a one-way ticket to death. It has a purpose. I can be secure and happy in the knowledge of this'.

One woman, however, who had experienced 'heaven' well away from the realities of her everyday life and did not want to return, was angry at being told to do so. Her anger gave way to resentment which dominated the return trip as she realised just how much she wanted to get away from every aspect of her life, which she saw as a trap. She recognised this as the source of her disease and admitted that by going back to it she would make herself more seriously ill. However she regarded change as impossible and could see no alternative to what she considered to be an inevitable fate. Thus, while she could acknowledge her sickening way of life she could not see that she was choosing to keep it that way by holding on to those things in it that she despised. Several other people assured her that they had felt exactly that way about their lives until they had been compelled by serious illness to make changes and live in the present. One of these, a young woman, who had consciously and successfully tried to put her past behind her and ignore the future so as to enjoy living in the present following the diagnosis of a brain tumour, questioned the benefits of living in the present for those are depressed by it.

Closer examination will invariably reveal that depressed people are not actually living their present but are being 'pulled down' by past events, regrets and guilts, or future anxieties, fears and concerns. Many of them vacillate between ruminating over the past and agonising about the future, and never 'touch down' in the present. Like some of those referred to above, such people have no concept of 'now' and therefore do not understand what is meant by living in the present or by 'presence' . The message of the present exercise is therefore 'lost' on them. Given that they cannot be shifted into the present intellectually it is necessary to try and get them to experience more of the present. One means of facilitating this process is the 'gold-prospecting' exercise included in Appendix II. This exercise, which develops a procedure recommended by Brian Roet (1988), is also very useful for attempting to change attitudes from negative to positive. However, it is recommended as an auxiliary to the present exercise primarily because it focuses attention on now, it not being possible for a gold prospector to sieve a stream for gold anywhere other than where he now is. It therefore reinforces the message of the present exercise by providing insight into how to live more fully in the present and highlights the wise counsel of Oscar Wilde:

> Don't squander the gold of your days listening to the tedious, trying to improve the hopeless failure or giving away your life to the common and vulgar. These are the sickly aims, the false ideals of our age. Live! Live the wonderful life that is within you.
>
> A PICTURE OF DORIAN GRAY

CHAPTER NINE

Healing Forces

How can a man's life keep its course
If he will not let it flow?
Those who flow as life flows
Know they need no other force:
They feel no wear, they feel no fear,
They need no mending, no repair.

LAO TZU, *The Way of Life*

The ability to forgive the past and cease blaming or feeling resentment towards people and events, is necessary if a person is to live fully in the present.

Forgiveness is the act of pulling back your spirit from yesterday's traumas. What remains after a genuine act of forgiveness is that you are able to have the memory of an event, but the memory is empty. It no longer has 'power' over your present day emotional, psychological or physical self. Your spirit returns to present time and your body responds with a feeling of an electrical charge of energy and liberation.

MYSS, 1992, p. 10

According to Myss, therefore, when you give, you also receive. Forgiving or letting go of the past is essential to the healing process because it releases energy into the present. The question arises, however, as to what is meant by energy in this or indeed any other context.

ENERGETIC IDEAS

In Western scientific thinking from the seventeenth century to the early twentieth century energy was equated with work; a concept usually illustrated with reference to levers and applied to machines. This concept of energy was also applied to the human body, which the philosopher Descartes (1643–1727) viewed as a machine governed by mechanical principles. Accordingly, the movement of bones, muscles, blood and other bodily fluids could be understood in terms of various forces.

It follows from this mechanistic model that energy or work is required to tighten muscles and that the greater the tension the more energy is expended. As many muscle tensions result from mental processes – from anxiety, worry, persistent thoughts, determination and so on, thinking can be seen to drain energy. This may be compounded because tense, anxious people 'with a lot on their mind' often cannot relax enough to sleep and report that their 'mind will not stop working'. A result of the inevitable fatigue is that subsequent activities require greater effort and further energy expenditure, which is why activities seem to be much harder work when we are tired. In this way a tension/fatigue spiral is generated which is the insomniac's dilemma. Such people often describe feeling totally 'drained', which is not unjustified because tense people use more of the neurotransmitter involved in nerve action. In effect they are 'heavy on fuel'. It follows that tensions created by past events and unresolved issues in which a person's thoughts and feelings remain bound up, whether consciously or unconsciously, impose a constant demand on energy, reducing that available for everyday activities. Within this formulation of energy it can be seen that letting go of anything being held on to releases the energy involved. So letting go of the past will relieve the tension held there and provide an energy boost.

This mechanistic view of energy still dominates everyday thinking. However, the modern understanding of the universe ushered in by Einstein and other physicists early this century overturned the older notion of energy. According to this new physical view all phenomena are dynamic patterns of activity, movement or change, to be understood in terms of vibrations, pulsations, flow, rhythm, synchrony, resonance and as relative to time. Indeed, modern physicists and ancient mystics describe the universe in remarkably similar ways, as an energy dance, and all phenomena as a manifestation of this activity. All traditional approaches to healing rest upon this mystical conception of reality (hence the Greek *energeia*: activity), health being viewed as a balanced harmonious flow of energy and illness as the result of stagnation or disruption of energy patterns. Niro Asistent interprets this conception of health and disease as follows:

> Energy is the miracle of being alive, right now, this second, and we can use that energy in any direction we like. We can direct it into anger, or we can channel it into love. It is the same energy; we can use it however we like. It is our choice. When we use our energy to resist, our entire life falls into a pattern of resistance, and our energy does not flow. Because the energy is contained, it eventually forms a stagnant, rotting swamp. Again, we choose this unhappy state, usually unconsciously; no one is doing it to us. The way we control our energy is by saying no to life. When we are willing to say, our energy can be free, and in order to say yes we need to wake up.
>
> 1991, p. 103

Within this formulation holding on to the past constitutes a refusal to live fully in the present. This resistance takes up energy which consequently is not available for everyday living and therefore depletes vitality. Relaxing or letting go is therefore necessary to restore the natural flow of energy, much as in the more mechanical view. However, the dynamics of this process are conceived very differently within the two approaches.

Common to the mystical traditions of the ancient world is the concept of energy distribution through the human body by way of several major power centres or vortices located along the length of its spine. These centres are described as three-dimensional pulsating wheels which rotate rhythmically from the midpoint outwards, rather like catherine wheels, in a way which appears to seers or clairvoyants like cones, trumpets or convolvulus flowers, and according to the direction of the spin, either draw energy in or direct it out of the body, vitalising or enervating it.

The Hindus located seven major wheels or chakras at the base of the spine, gonads, solar plexus, heart, throat, between the eyebrows and the crown of the head, and a number of minor chakras elsewhere on the surface of a finer or more subtle body by way of which energy is drawn into its physical counterpart. Known in various traditions as the vital body, the astral, etheric body or double, the Ka, doppelganger, linga sharirah or perispirit, this is generally seen as synonymous with the spirit, and as surviving physical death.

THE CHAKRA SYSTEM

According to ancient wisdom, energy in the form of light is drawn into the physical body by way of its immaterial counterpart, which acts like a prism breaking it down into seven streams corresponding with the frequency bands of the energy spectrum, each of which is drawn by the principle of resonance to a different chakra whose vibrations are of the same frequency. These vibrations become progressively dense, heavy and lower in frequency along the length of the spine to its base where they merge with earth energies, represented in Indian thought as a coiled serpent, or Kundalini, and in Chinese thought by a dragon. The upward spiral motion of these energies around the central axis of the spine is represented in the caduceus, the traditional symbol of the healing arts and the emblem of modern Western medicine.

The chakras, which may be conceived as transmitters or transformers of energy, are believed to vibrate at a characteristic frequency as they distribute energy throughout the body. The energy patterns around each chakra, although continually changing, are therefore predominantly of a certain colour whose vibrations correspond with its basic frequency and these base colours rarely change. The prevailing colour of a chakra indicates how well its energies are being transformed and transmitted at a given time, and therefore reflect current experience.

Each chakra is also associated with a musical note, a symbolic form and certain elements of the same characteristic vibrational frequency. Certain traditions also assign planets to the chakras, thereby suggesting that each is sensitive to planetary influence and providing a physical rationale for astrology. More recently however the chakras have been identified with the location and functioning of the major nerve plexuses of the body, each of which is connected to one of the glands of the endocrine system, namely the gonads, liver, adrenals, thymus, thyroid, pineal and pituitary. Accordingly, the slightest imbalance of energy in any chakra is thought to influence the corresponding gland giving rise to fluctuations in hormones which are secreted directly into the bloodstream, creating immediate changes in mood, appearance, tension, respiration, digestion, intuition and intelligence, thereby affecting the entire organism. However, the correct and balanced action of these seven spinal chakras is expressed in absolute perfect health on all levels of the individual.

According to this system man has a seven-fold nature. The first and second chakras which are principally concerned with receiving and distributing physical energies combine to give the individual physical potency, vitality and the will to live. The third, fourth and fifth chakras are concerned with psychological energies and thus with personality rather than physicality, and the sixth and seventh chakras with spiritual energies which are an expression of an individual's relationship to his spirit or soul. Moreover, the chakras function as an integrated system, rather than in isolation. If one begins to dysfunction, so will others, as they attempt to compensate for reduced energy transmission in one centre by working overtime. Being concerned thus with physical, psychological and spiritual well-being, and with the integrity of body, mind and spirit, the chakra system provides the impetus for the regulated, balanced flow of energy throughout the whole organism which is equivalent with health.

The aura

The flow of energy is however not confined within the body as this is normally conceived. In the ancient view the body emits a radiant energy which relates specifically to the location and intensity of energy within it, and therefore reveals something of its state of functioning. This hazy emanation, which is widely referred to as the 'aura', represents the sum total of the energy emitted by the chakras and extends around the body for some distance beyond its surface. Normally invisible but discernible by seers and clairvoyants who, since earliest times, have described it as a large, shimmering oval, comprising a mass of fine luminescent fibres or rays, arranged in seven bands each corresponding with the functioning of a chakra, the aura reveals the physical, psychological and spiritual well-being of the individual it envelops. When the chakras are functioning normally each will 'open' by spinning clockwise and drawing energy in from the universal energy field for distribution throughout the body. When the transmission of energy has occurred the colour emanating from each chakra should be very pale. However, when the chakra spins anti-clockwise it remains closed to incoming energies, which consequently are not distributed within the body and manifest as darker, more dense patches or blotches of colour in the aura. The space between the body and the first colour emanation of the aura is referred to as the ovum. It is not 'empty' as such, being the most dense and therefore most easily visible part of the energy field but is colourless, or a dull white/gold, and thus appears blank.

The first layer of the aura, the health band, emanates from the base chakra and reflects the overall vitality of the physical body. It is traditionally described in the metaphysical literature as red. *The second layer of the aura*, known as the emotional or astral band, emanates from the second chakra, reflects physical and sexual activity, and 'gut feelings', and is orange in colour. *The third layer of the aura*, the mental band, emanates from the solar plexus chakra and reflects mental functions based on the intellect, and personal power. It is yellow and shiny or brilliant in a mentally alive person. *The fourth layer of the aura*, or heart band, emanates from the heart chakra, is green, and reflects inspiration in all forms. *The fifth layer of the aura*, or causal band emanates from the throat chakra, is blue, and reflects self-expression and the karma of the soul – its progress through successive incarnations. *The dark blue sixth layer*, or spiritual band, of the aura emanates from the sixth chakra, reflecting the spiritual development and intuitive awareness of the individual; and *the seventh layer*, or cosmic band of the aura reflects the soul principle or cosmic consciousness of the person. It is purple in colour.

Each band radiates different colours of varying intensity that reveal to those who can discern them the individual's state of health, character, emotional disposition and tendencies, abilities, attitudes, past problems and spiritual development. The aura can therefore be used for diagnosis and throughout history seers or sensitives have reported using it as the basis for healing. Furthermore, a study of orthodox Western physicians (Karagulla, 1967) has revealed that many diagnose illness through the energy field they perceive around their patients or energy vortices connected with the endocrine system, and one of those who does, John Pierrakos, has conducted extensive research on the phenomenon.

However, while the vital force of the aura is self-evident to many healers it has eluded modern scientific research until relatively recently. Researcher Michael Watson (1988) claims that this is because its subtle energies are found only in living matter and can react only with, and be detected by living organisms. When the matter is living and the vital force finds its counterpart a reaction ensues, which is detected by the human being. This reaction forms the basis of healing diagnoses, dowsing and water divining. However, no detection can occur without a reaction and, as Watson observes, if a force cannot be detected by physical instruments in the orthodox scientific world it is deemed as having no physical reality.

The aura-chakra system and health

In the USA there has been extensive investigation of clairvoyants and healers such as Jack Schwarz and Rosalind Bruyere, who perceive chakra and aura energies and utilise them in diagnosis and treatment. This research appears to confirm the observations of the ancients. Hence disturbances in the energy distribution of the base chakra are found to correspond with lack of physical energy and general 'sickliness', chronic lower back pain, sciatica, varicose veins and rectal problems, including tumours and cancerous growths. Energy blockages in the second chakra or 'hara' generally result in reduced physical and sexual activity because the pelvic area is the major source of vitality in the body. Energy imbalances in this chakra commonly result in female dysfunctions such as menstrual difficulties, infertility, vaginal infections, ovarian cysts, endometriosis, tumours and cancers of the female organs; and male disorders such as impotency and prostate problems. In both males and females pelvic and lower back pain, sexual difficulties and disease, slipped discs, bladder and urinary problems and infections, and frequent loss of sexual fluids commonly occur when this chakra is unstable.

The most common physical dysfunctions arising from disturbances in the energy flow of the third or solar plexus chakra include arthritis, ulcers and related stomach problems, poor digestion, chronic or acute indigestion, eating disorders such as anorexia and bulimia nervosa, nausea, abnormal appetite, colon and intestinal problems including cancer, pancreatitis and pancreatic cancer, diabetes, kidney and liver problems, hepatitis, gall bladder and adrenal gland dysfunctions, and influenza. When the fourth or heart chakra is unstable there may be cardiac or circulatory abnormalities which commonly result in heart attack, enlarged heart, congestive heart failure, blocked arteries, asthma, allergies, lung problems including cancer, bronchial difficulties, pneumonia, poor circulation, upper back and shoulder problems.

People with imbalances in the fifth or throat chakra have a tendency towards skin problems and allergies as a result of poor detoxification within the body, thyroid conditions, throat infections, sore throat, loss of voice, laryngitis, tonsillitis, cancers of the throat and mouth, problems with the teeth and gums, misalignment of the jaw, curved spine, stiff neck, tension headaches arising from the base of the neck, and swollen glands. The sixth chakra or 'third eye' has a strong influence on the balanced functioning of the endocrine system, visual functioning, sleep, clarity of mental functions and general energy levels. Instability in this chakra is reflected in fatigue and tiredness, migraine and tension headache, irritability, anxiety, nervousness and depression, nervous breakdown, psychotic illness including schizophrenia, sleep irregularities, coma, neurological disorders including blindness and deafness, epilepsy and seizures, learning difficulties, brain tumours, stroke and blood clots to the brain. Instability in the seventh or crown chakra can result in disorders of the nervous system, paralysis, bone problems and debilitating illnesses such as multiple schlerosis.

Taken together therefore the chakra and aura systems provide a comprehensive and consistent account of the distribution and functioning of subtle energies within and around the body, and an integrative framework for what can be thought of as subtle energy therapies, such as those traditionally practised in India, Tibet, China, Japan, among Native American Indians, Aboriginals and the Kahunas of Hawaii, including acupuncture, acupressure or shiatsu; and more recent practises such as reflexology, craniosacral therapy, radionics and polarity therapy (detailed further in Graham, 1990).

Homoeopathy, which was developed during the last century by the physician Samuel Hahnemann, also has a similar conceptual basis to these approaches. He considered there were certain basic vibrational patterns of dis-ease or imbalance, which he termed miasms, originating in the aura and influencing all the subtle energies of an organism. In attempting to restore balance the organism produces the symptoms and signs of illness, which are not the disease *per se*, merely an indication of the extent of the fundamental imbalance and of how profoundly the organism is affected by it. These signs and symptoms can therefore be used to determine treatments appropriate to restoring balance and health. Homoeopathy employs the principle of resonance, applying treatments which subject the organism to a periodic disturbance of the same frequency as that of the body, at which frequency the body displays an enhanced oscillation or vibration. It therefore restores the balance of subtle energy fields of the organism by matching various natural remedies of different vibrational characters with the disharmonies of the body.

A similar therapeutic approach was developed in the 1930s by the distinguished British bacteriologist and Harley Street physician Edward Bach, who identified a number of plants which, he claimed, activate all the layers of the human aura and can be used to treat incipient illness before it manifests in the body. Such a view was not new, but a feature of many traditional healing systems, including that of Tibet. Like Hahnemann, he viewed illness as merely symptomatic of a more fundamental disease. He insisted:

> Disease will never be cured or eradicated by present materialistic methods, for the simple reason that disease in its origin is not material. What we know as disease is an ultimate result produced by the body, the end product of deep and long acting forces, and even if material treatment alone is apparently successful this is nothing more than a temporary relief unless the real cause has been removed.
>
> 1931, p. 6

Bach considered the 'real' cause of disease to be psychological conflict between the soul or spirit and the mind which manifests in a distortion of wavelength in the energy field of the body, slowing its vibrations and bringing about negative 'soul states'. He claimed that these soul states correspond with 38 flower remedies, each of which has the same vibrational frequency as the soul quality or psychological traits concerned, but at the natural rhythm and without distortion. Each Bach flower remedy therefore has an affinity with a particular soul quality, and is able to influence and restore harmony to it by way of its own harmonious vibrations. The remedies, operating at subtle energy levels through the principle of resonance, thus act as a catalyst for reintegration or healing. In each case Bach chose the mental outlook of the patient as a guide to the necessary remedies because he believed that the mind shows the onset and cause of disease more definitely than the body.

Indeed in all traditional systems of healing disease is viewed as fundamentally spiritual in origin, as an imbalance or disharmony in the energy of the soul, which manifests as a conflict or problem at the psychological level and only finally presents as symptoms of physical illness in the body. These approaches to healing therefore address the disease primarily at the spiritual and psychological level, and diagnosis tends to emphasise these energies rather than the physical.

Auric diagnosis is especially helpful in this regard because as the physicist and healer Barbara Brennan observes, 'the aura is really the "missing link" between biology and physical medicine and psychotherapy. It is the "place" where all emotions, thoughts, memories and behaviour patterns are located' (1988, p. 89) and reflects the activity of the chakras which represent the psychological patterns evolving in an individual's life throughout development.

She observes that most people react to unpleasant experiences by blocking their feelings. This affects the chakras by restricting a great deal of their energy flow and inhibits fully balanced psychological functioning. Thus if a child is rejected many times when he tries to give love to others he will probably stop trying to do so and will therefore block or repress the inner feelings of love on which his former actions were based. In order to do this he has to stop or slow down the energy flow through the heart chakra, which will affect its functioning. It may become 'blocked' with stagnant energy, spin irregularly or anti-clockwise, become disfigured or distorted and eventually result in the development of a physical problem. This same process applies to all chakras.

Moreover, this process not only generates illness but the individual's reality.

Since chakras are not only metabolizers of energy, but also devices that sense energy, they serve to tell us about the world around us. If we 'close' chakras, we do not let information come in. *Thus, when we make our chakras flow counterclockwise, we send our energy out into the world, sense what the energy is that we send out and say that it is the world. This is called projection in psychology*
1988, p. 72. ITALICS AS IN ORIGINAL TEXT

Furthermore Brennan claims that since the imagined reality projected on to the world by the individual is related to an 'image' of the world based on childhood experience and thinking, his overall long-term and current life issues can be determined by examination of chakra functioning.

Chakra dysfunction and psychological disorder

Brennan and John Pierrakos have related chakra dysfunction to psychological disorder and claim to be able to diagnose a person's psychological needs in this way. Their analysis generally accords with traditional and more contemporary accounts, the common points of which are summarised below.

When the base chakra is functioning normally the person is well grounded in the here and now of physical reality, and has power and vitality, or 'presence', and a strong will to live. Such a person feels secure and 'grounded'. When this chakra is blocked the person lacks physical vitality and strength, and fails to make a strong impression in the physical world. Such a person lacks 'presence', feels insecure in and threatened by the world, may not feel 'at home' anywhere or have a sense of belonging, and feels alone and unsupported. Motoyama's research (cited by Young, 1990) reveals that a predominance of energy in this chakra can lead to violent aggression and that accidents causing sudden injury to the coccyx, the spinal energy pump, can cause an uncontrolled release of energy which may contribute to certain types of psychosis.

Normal functioning of the second or sacral chakra is related to giving and receiving of physical and sexual pleasure, the capacity for orgasm, and to strong 'gut feelings' and emotions. However if the centre is dysfunctional it will give rise to sexual difficulties, feelings of sexual inadequacy, impotency, lack of orgasm, feelings of low self-esteem and generalised anxiety. Myss also identifies this chakra with 'passion' for money and power, indicating that when dysfunctional a person's anxious concerns about money, material possessions and power may create imbalances in all forms of relationship with the material world. Motoyama has indicated that the opening of this chakra is associated with spontaneous intuition, uncontrolled psychokinetic phenomena, such as so-called poltergeist activity, the development of extra-sensory perception such as precognition and out of body experiences.

The third or solar plexus chakra normally functions to empower the person mentally and emotionally. When it is unstable the person may have rapid mood swings, a tendency towards depression and anger which results from being controlled by others, a tendency to victimise and be highly critical of others, and to fear failure. Energy dysfunction in this chakra often results in stress disorders characterised by excessive adrenalin production, ulcers, nervous disorders or chronic fatigue. When blocked, feeling and thinking will not be very clear, decision making will be poor, and the person may fear taking responsibility for his or her life, thoughts, feelings, attitudes and personal actions. Such a person may fear intimidation and criticism. According to Motoyama, clairvoyance and mental telepathy may accompany the opening of this chakra.

The more open the fourth or heart chakra the greater is a person's capacity to love. When functioning effectively the person feels self-love, and love for family, friends, children, animals nature, and all creatures on earth. When the chakra is dysfunctional the person may be over-excitable and extrovert and ambitious for fame. When it is blocked other people may be seen as obstacles to accomplishments and fulfilment of the heart's desires, and resentment or bitterness may arise towards others who are seen to receive more love and attention. A 'broken heart' may result from excessive grief and sorrow. The opening of this chakra is often associated with the development of healing abilities.

The fifth or throat chakra normally functions to facilitate personal expression or individuality, will-power and creativity. When the chakra is open the person can communicate thoughts, feelings, needs, attitudes and opinions, but if this centre is dysfunctional self-expression is adversely affected and creates interpersonal difficulties. As Myss (1988, p. 110) observes, 'the inability to communicate your feelings, your ideas, your sorrow, your anger or your joy is like pouring concrete around your heart and into your throat. This blockage aborts the growth process and causes destructive behavioural patterns . . . that are guaranteed to contaminate every intimate relationship'. Dishonesty and lying may also result from inadequate self-expression and other negative behavioural patterns may develop such as fear of self-assertion, allowing oneself to become victimised by others and gossiping. Motoyama has identified clairaudience and awareness of the past, present and future with the opening of this chakra.

The normal functions of the sixth chakra or 'third eye' are associated with clear thinking and imagery, insight and intuition. Anti-clockwise movement of this chakra is associated with confused or negative mental concepts and images about reality. If the centre is blocked creativity is poor because imagination is restricted and problem-solving capacity is similarly limited. Other behavioural patterns associated with blocked energy in this chakra include resistance to looking inwards or introspection and self-examination; suppression of intuitive abilities, rigid thinking, lack of openness to new ideas or those of others; unwillingness to learn from life experiences and lack of self-awareness. Opening of this chakra, according to Motoyama, enables perception of non-physical reality and spirit entities.

When activated the crown chakra heightens physical and mental senses, and promotes wholesome being or health. It provides clear focus and awareness, and when open the person experiences a state of being which transcends the physical world, creating a sense of wholeness, peace, faith and a sense of meaning or purpose to existence. However, when it is blocked a person is closed to spiritual experience and has little or no understanding of the spiritual experiences of others. Such a person is likely to find life meaningless, to experience negative feelings and thoughts, to lack faith in himself, to fear self-development and knowledge.

According to traditional systems and contemporary intuitives such as Schwarz, chakra functioning can be assessed and influenced by way of mental imagery. The following exercise facilitates such a process.

EXERCISE 9

Imagine a bright, moonlit night and that you are sitting with your back against an upright post fixed into the ground. The top of the post is level with the top of your head and the point where it enters the ground is level with the base of your spine. Positioned along the length of the post at points corresponding with the top of your head, the centre of your eyebrows, the centre of your throat, the middle of your breast bone, just above and below your navel, and the centre of your pubic bone, there are seven catherine wheels connected to each other by fuse paper. Imagine that the fuse paper just above your head is ignited, activating the catherine wheel there. Watch how quickly and effectively it moves into action, the direction and character of its movement, and its predominant colour. Observe the emissions from it, their character and pattern of distribution.

Having done so, observe the entire sequence of wheels, noting particularly the direction and character of their movement, their predominant colours, and the character and distribution of their emissions. Examine the pool formed upon the ground by the emissions from all the wheels, noting its features, especially its extent and colour(s).

Having done so, allow the image to fade and record your observations of this experience.

Commentary

A very similar exercise is included in my book *The Magic Shop* (Graham, 1992) where I indicated that I normally provide no introduction to this exercise in workshops in order to avoid expectation effects. The majority of the people participating in the exercise have little or no prior knowledge of chakras and the aura, and even those who do are generally not sufficiently familiar with their details and subtleties to correlate their own imagery with the physical, psychological and spiritual characteristics attributed to them in traditional theory. Nevertheless, the correspondence between them is striking and consistent, and usually sufficient to persuade those who might otherwise be sceptical as to their validity.

Few people have difficulty in visualising the wheels, which they invariably perceive within their body rather than external to it, and many physically sense them, reporting feelings of heat, tingling, vibrations and pulsation in the relevant body areas. One man experienced such heat that by the end of the exercise he was hot and perspiring. Very commonly people find themselves moving synchronously with the wheels and circular or swaying movements are perceptible to observers. In one instance, however, a man reported that the base wheel was not attached to its post and was therefore not in alignment with the others, but lying on the floor beside him. Accordingly it was not integrated into his body or with 'the overall scheme of things'. Upon further examination it proved to be a roulette wheel, and irrespective of what he did to try and influence it, the ball continued going round and round. He associated this image with gambling, chance, risk, unpredictability and unreliability which he related to his lack of security and sense of belonging. Certainly such an interpretation appears consistent with his life experience, given that he had previously identified the emotional trauma of being reared by a mentally ill and suicidal mother.

Frequently, however, people imagine that one or more of the wheels are missing, or hard to picture in detail. Women frequently report that the throat wheel is missing completely. One woman indicated that she was feeling 'choked' by some of the insights derived from previous imagery exercises and also suffering from tonsillitis. A man who reported seeing no throat wheel on first attempting this exercise imagined a very sluggish wheel at his next attempt three months later. During the intervening period he had suffered glandular fever, severe laryngitis, various throat problems including intermittent loss of voice, and a loss of confidence. He continued to be anxious about his throat and his voice in particular, which would suddenly disappear or become very quiet, to the irritation of others and his embarrassment. He also indicated that more generally he was anxious about his inability to 'speak up' for himself.

Sometimes the heart wheel is missing, as was the case for a woman who explained that she had 'lost heart' since the death of her husband a year previously; and a 'heart-less' woman who described herself as unable to give or receive love identified this as a major factor in the development of her current serious illness, a metastasised breast cancer. A doctor in general practice who had difficulty imagining this wheel later admitted to not having her heart in her job, while a man who was unable to visualise the heart wheel, attributed this to the fact that he had smoked cigarettes for over 30 years.

More usually the wheels are all present but some are dysfunctional. Frequently the base wheel is described as wobbly, insecure or 'unsteady on its pins'. A woman who described hers as wobbling so much that it almost fell off its pin subsequently identified problems of insecurity and infertility. The top wheel is also prone to wobble, although erratic, or eccentric movement is commonly found in all the wheels, but most especially the throat, suggesting that many people have difficulties in expressing themselves authentically.

Wheel size and movement

Most people find that their wheels differ in size and velocity, with each wheel becoming progressively larger and slower in movement. This is quite intriguing because according to the traditional wisdom the vibrations of each chakra become progressively more dense, heavy and lower in frequency down the length of the spine. However, some wheels are imagined as moving very slowly, sluggishly or not at all, irrespective of their location. One man described his wheels as varying from football to ping-pong ball size, with half the base wheel stuck in the ground. By contrast, one or more wheels may appear to be moving very rapidly. Usually this is the solar plexus wheel, the one above the navel, and this tends to be associated with high levels of stress. Very frequently people describe this wheel as 'burning itself out' or burning up and consider it to be a very appropriate metaphor of their lifestyle. One woman whose solar plexus wheel burnt itself out described herself as very anxious, hypertense, and receiving long standing treatment for hypertension and high cholesterol. Another woman who described sparks falling from this wheel and those below it creating a circle of fire on the ground below reported that until recently she had plenty of mental and physical energy, when she had begun to feel that these energies were becoming burnt out. One woman described her wheels progressively 'running out of steam' and her entire system as running down.

The direction and quality of movement tends to vary appreciably from person to person and within a person from one wheel to another. In some cases all the wheels are moving harmoniously in the same direction. More typically one or more wheels are moving anti-clockwise. This is consistent with Barbara Brennan's observations that most people have three or four chakras spinning counter-clockwise at any one time. Again the throat wheel features strongly in this category. Fairly typically those with anti-clockwise movement in the solar plexus wheel feel out of control to some degree. One man who described a particularly strong movement of this kind later indicated that he had recently achieved the maximum score on a stress test and been advised that his stress levels were dangerously high. By contrast, a woman with a less than robust anti-clockwise movement in the heart wheel indicated that she had both a breast cancer and an immuno-suppression problem. In some cases the movement of the wheels is chaotic, each moving in different directions and 'with sparks flying everywhere'. Sparks may well fly when the wheels in question are those which relate to strong passions and emotions. This is particularly true of the base wheel, whose overactivity may be associated with cruelty, violence, sadism and sexual deviance. Overcharge in the hara is associated with hyperactivity, hyper-reactivity, overeating and digestive problems. Where overactivity occurs in the solar plexus wheel the mind is constantly 'on the go', resulting in stress. This may also result from an overactive heart wheel and can prove deadly; whereas overactivity in the throat wheel may manifest in thyroid problems.

Wheel colour

The emissions from the wheels are very variable. Most people describe sparks of coloured light and in most cases this corresponds with the colours traditionally assigned to the chakras, although in many cases colour will be displaced so, for example, yellow may appear in the brow wheel, as it did for a woman who admitted to intellectualising everything, or the man with 'anger in his heart' and red 'fire' in his heart wheel. Where red appears out of context it usually indicates aggression or irritation, so if red appears in the hara wheel it may indicate heated passions and stomach problems. When it occurs in the solar plexus wheel the person may 'see red' and be angry or aggressive, while in the heart wheel it may indicate passionate love or deep hurt – a bleeding heart. Red in the throat wheel may indicate feelings of irritation or swollen glands and mental illness where it appears in the brow wheel.

Orange indicates activity and rarely occurs other than in the hara and the lower wheels. Hence orange in the base wheel is suggestive of an active sex life and a lively mind is indicated when it occurs in the solar plexus wheel. Yellow energy indicates rationality and in some instances it displaces all other colours. Where this occurs it indicates the tendency to be analytic about everything. Hence where it appears in the base wheel sexuality tends to be governed by the mind, and in the hara it suggests that the 'gut' feelings and passions are under rational control and intuition is repressed. Similarly, where it occurs in the heart wheel it indicates intellectual control of emotions – the head ruling the heart. Yellow appearing in the throat wheel is often a sign of the need to constantly demonstrate cleverness, whereas in the brow wheel it indicates balance between intuitive and intellectual energies, and thus insightful understanding. One woman who visualised yellow in each of her wheels later admitted to powerful, wilful, intellectual control of her emotions and sexuality which had 'wreaked havoc' in her interpersonal relationships.

Many people lack green in the heart centre, indicating that they are not 'hearty' enough. Often this is because of oversensitivity and indicates a defensive reaction to emotional pain. Dark green in this wheel indicates possessiveness and envy, as the well-known phrase suggests. Where green occurs in other wheels it denotes sensitivity. Hence where it appears in the base wheel it suggests that a person's heart is in their sex life. Green in the hara indicates emotional vulnerability and also a sensitive digestion. If green does not appear in the solar plexus wheel this indicates an unemotional, detached and analytic approach to life. Similarly some green in the throat wheel is desirable, otherwise the person communicates little warmth or kindness. However, excessive green in this wheel is suggestive of too much kindness and the possibility of being exploited by others. Green in the brow wheel indicates generosity of spirit.

Sky blue is suggestive of coolness wherever it appears. Thus blue in the base wheel indicates a cool attitude to sex, and in the hara is a sign of poor health and appetite. Blue in the solar plexus wheel indicates a clear, cool head and intellectual detachment, whereas in the heart wheel it indicates emotional detachment and difficulty in forming relationships. Where blue appears in the brow wheel it is a sign of healing ability. Dark blue or indigo is an indication of impartiality wherever it appears and violet reflects an artistic or aesthetic quality. Clear 'fluid' light emissions appear to be associated with well-functioning wheels, and gold and silver emissions from each wheel appear to be a feature of a harmoniously balanced system. All the wheels may vibrate so harmoniously together that a pure, bright white light is observed. One young man who imagined all his wheels moving harmoniously in the same direction and throwing out golden-white light which formed a pool extending outwards some 6 ft on all sides of the base wheel, was astonished when this 'shot' to the top of his head and out into infinity so that he 'became' a column of light.

Generally the colours noted in the pool around the base wheel tend to correspond with anomalies in the relevant wheels, which reflects the correspondence between chakra functioning and the appearance of the aura. Hence a person who reports imagining a bright blue pool of light typically describes 'problems' in relation to the throat wheel, while a person who describes significant amounts of red within it usually reports difficulties with the base wheel.

Sometimes people report that certain wheels are unlit, or splutter and go out, and because they do not distribute light, these are usually described as black. One woman who imagined her base wheel as black reported that she had no vitality whatever. Indeed any suggestion of dark colours, especially black, in relation to the wheels is a fairly reliable indication of blocked energy and dysfunction. Brown indicates stagnant, stale energy and black or grey, depressed energy and negativity. Brown commonly appears in relation to the base wheel and may indicate lack of sexual fulfilment. In the hara it suggests sluggish digestion, lack of physical and emotional vitality. Brown in the solar plexus may be a sign of mental withdrawal from others and depression, and where it appears in the heart wheel it is often a sign of grief, bereavement and susceptibility to heart disease. Brown in the throat wheel indicates the tendency to withdraw from communicating with others and throat problems, and in the brow wheel it signifies a tendency to withdraw from the outside world.

Thick, dense and sticky substances such as tar, glue, mud or sludge are very commonly described, as is dense smoke and steam, and wheels that produce 'blobs' of black oil that fall into the pool surrounding the base wheel, forming blotches and patches. The immobilisation resulting from stagnant energy is very aptly conveyed by people who describe themselves as 'stuck in the mud' surrounding the base wheel. Many people describe oil or grease seeping out the wheels, especially the base wheel, which characteristically in these instances is very sluggish and is seen to produce a black greasy pool around it. In one instance a woman described the rainbow-like reflections of an oil-slick as the only colours visible in this pool. When it was suggested that her energies might be taken up in reflecting the needs and expectations of others she acknowledged this to be very true of herself. Like many others who imagine their wheels emitting black noxious substances she didn't want to contaminate others or 'clog' them up with what she considered to be her 'negativity'.

A most graphic example of 'negativity' was provided by a woman who was very depressed following the diagnosis of extensive cancer. She visualised her top three wheels as totally inert and black, the heart wheel missing, and the bottom three wheels unlit but giving off voluminous black choking smoke and tar so that she experienced herself sitting in a black tar-like pool surrounded by litter and cigarette ends. She described feeling guilty about the contaminating effect of her 'effluent', and admitted that her negativity and depression had seriously jeopardised her marriage and family relationships which, like her, were 'in a bad way'. She regarded the missing heart wheel as an indication of her long-standing difficulty in either giving or receiving love from others, and the choking smoke as a sign that she was being consumed by negative thoughts, attitudes and feelings.

This woman acknowledged that her imagery accurately reflected both her physical and psychological state. Indeed, there is usually very substantial agreement between a person's self-report of their mental and physical condition, and that which can be intuited by way of their imagery, given knowledge of the traditional teaching on subtle energy. When presented with information about the latter people are generally very impressed by the extent to which the images they have produced in this exercise coincide with the characteristics traditionally attributed to the chakras and aura, and their own physical and psychological functioning.

This prompts the question of how useful it is for people to be able to access information about themselves in this way; a case in point being the woman referred to above, whose awareness of her desperate state might arguably have given rise to more profound depression and despair. Certainly such a response can occur.

Ultimately it is a matter of choice as to whether a person accepts the validity of their intuition and whether or not they act upon it. It is possible to influence mental and bodily processes by way of imagery (see Chapter 10). Indeed many traditional practices are directed towards influencing chakra function in this way, and there are indications that modifications of imagery, such as slowing or speeding certain wheels, changing the colour or direction of movement and effecting repairs in this instance, have beneficial effects. Those who do so invariably report positive changes in their imagery and in their corresponding mental and physical condition.

For example, a young woman who realised that her wheels were all very sluggish and discoordinated the first time she attempted the exercise, subsequently discovered on repeating the exercise after practising yoga daily for a short period that all her wheels were moving harmoniously and fairly forcefully in the same direction, and emitting gold and white light. A man who noted a change in the direction of movement in the brow wheel over a three-month period attributed this to the increased insight he had gained as a result of using imagery in the development of self-awareness. Similarly a man described a change of direction and ease of movement in the throat wheel after focusing his attention on it during imaginative exercises, and noted a corresponding improvement in a serious throat condition and also his self-confidence. These are fairly typical examples of the health changes that can be brought about by cultivating positive imagery. Thus it would appear that, as John Lennon observed, a great deal can be gained simply by 'sitting watching the wheels go round and round'.

Energetic Treatment

When the cloud is scattered the rainbow's glory is shed.
SHELLEY

The psychological approaches to healing most obviously consistent with the notions of health and illness advanced in the traditional 'energy' model derive from the work of the Austrian psychoanalyst Wilhelm Reich who developed various devices for concentrating energy and techniques for removing obstacles to its natural flow that have become known as bio-energetics.

PSYCHOSOMATIC MEDICINE

Reich was a student of Freud and as a young man made significant contributions to the development of psychoanalysis. All his ideas have their foundation in Freud's theory of psychic energy, which Reich conceived as the life force that sustains being. He claimed that this is what moves when a person is 'moved'. Its motion is therefore e-motion, which constantly builds up as muscular or electrical tension and is naturally released in various forms as fluid, sound, movement, sensation or feeling. However, if its expression is inhibited neurotic responses are produced that are indicated physically in characteristic patterns of muscular expressions and postures, or 'muscle armouring', which over time set up a chronic imbalance in tissues and organs allowing infection or functional disorder to become established. It was Reich's view, therefore, that character itself is a disorder – a hardening of fluid human reality into a fixed, limiting pattern of behaviour, both mental and physical, with the body merely expressing the mind's rigidity, and developing character armour as a defence against the fearful uncertainties of life and painful feelings. He regarded the neurotic as a literally rigid, tense and inhibited person who defends against the spontaneous expression of emotion by holding on to it, thereby creating tensions in various parts of the body which predispose it to breakdown. Accordingly, in order for neurosis to be eliminated and physical dis-ease avoided, the natural flow of energy needs to be re-established. Reich advocated the use of physical methods, claiming that as emotional problems have physical manifestations they could be approached by way of the body. In his view manipulation of the parts of the body where the energy is blocked releases the emotion held there. Accordingly the relaxation of bound-up energy in any part of the body is often accompanied by recall of the trauma which had led to the contraction or neurotic symptom in the first place. Therefore neurotic symptoms could be addressed at the same time in both their psychic and somatic manifestations. By recognising that emotional and psychological reactions are reflected in the body and vice versa, Reich laid the foundations for a somatic psychology, and for psychosomatic treatments, which quite literally address the psyche, mind or soul, by way of the body.

Reichian therapy is therefore directed to 'character analysis' or identification of the characteristic patterns of muscular tension in the body, and the normalisation of physical and psychological functioning by release of the bound-up energy and re-establishment of its normal flow. Reich achieved this by manually pressing, pinching or stretching tight muscles which hold back emotional expression, particularly the breathing muscles which he viewed as essential in maintaining an even flow of energy. He insisted that the first step in overcoming nervous tension is to learn to breathe deeply using the stomach and solar plexus as well as the chest, and thus instituted deep breathing exercises as part of therapy. In addition to breathing exercises Reich also manipulated muscles in a process that was often painful for the recipient. He therefore attacked the muscular armouring or attitudes of the patient physically by provoking a sharp contraction of the musculature in order to make the patient aware of contractions which had become chronic.

He found that through deep breathing many of his patients felt vital and alive, and experienced a mystical sense of oneness or harmony with nature, which some personified as God. He therefore came to believe that he had discovered the active force that pervades the universe and is responsible for the human longing for orgiastic or mystical union with God. He conceived of this life force – which he termed orgone energy – not simply as a biological energy or bio-energy – but energy endowed with a spiritual quality.

Although Reich abhorred mystical or metaphysical descriptions of reality the system he developed may be regarded as mystical and as bearing a striking resemblance to the chakra system. Reich describes seven rings of tension or character structure resulting from muscle armouring at right angles to the main axis of the body and divided into sections as follows:

Armour segments	*Character structure*
eyes, forehead, scalp	ocular
mouth, chin, jaw	oral
neck, shoulders	cervical
thorax, heart, lungs, arms	thoracic
diaphragm	diaphragmatic
abdomen, pelvis, lower back	abdominal
pelvis, sex organs, legs	pelvic

These seven rings correspond closely with the traditional chakra areas and various commentators, including John Pierrakos, Barbara Brennan and psychotherapist David Boadella, have interpreted the principal character structures of Reich's theory as primary functional disturbances of these energy centres.

Many different forms of bio-energetic therapy or 'bodywork' have grown up in the Reichian tradition with the common aim of relaxing the body and releasing the energy held in various tensions, and Reich's insights have formed the basis of many other psychotherapies, notably gestalt therapy. Similar principles and practices underpin *bioenergetic analysis*, developed by Alexander Lowen, a pupil of Reich, as a means of integrating physical and psychological functions. It emphasises breathing, relaxation of character structures and grounding, placing emphasis on a particular stance which promotes the harmonious flow of energies through establishing positive contact with the ground, thereby enabling, both literally and metaphorically, contact with reality and the development of a sense of individual identity.

Numerous other therapies, such as biodynamic therapy and structural integration; methods which aim to improve functioning by increasing awareness of postural attitudes, notably those developed by F.M. Alexander and Moshe Feldenkrais; and systems of exercise such as Hatha yoga, t'ai chi and aikido are all clearly physical attempts to promote the flow of energies within a person. A less obvious but none the less physical means of doing so is by way of light and colour.

ENLIGHTENED TREATMENT

According to traditional wisdom, energy in the form of light sustains life, and all the functions and processes of the human organism. En-lightenment is therefore synonymous with wholeness, holiness and health, and the effective distribution of light by the chakras essential for healthy functioning. The brow chakra or third eye is traditionally considered to be of particular importance in the regulation of light energy. This intuitive understanding of its functions within the ancient world may underpin Christ's teaching that 'if your eye is sound, your whole body will be filled with light' (Matthew, 6.22). Until very recently the orthodox view of Western science was that the function of light relates primarily to vision. Indeed it was not until the early 1970s that the non-visual functions of light were recognised, when it was established that light entering the eyes reaches not simply the occipital cortex by way of the optic nerve but affects the whole brain and the entire body. It does so by influencing the hypothalamus, which is a major control centre in the brain responsible for most life-sustaining functions, the autonomic nervous system and the endocrine glands. It also initiates the body's stress response and directly affects the immune system. However the functioning of the hypothalamus crucially depends on the pineal gland in the centre of the brain, a tiny pea-sized structure shaped like a pine cone which functions as the body's light meter. Regulated by changes in environmental light and in the earth's electromagnetic field relayed by way of the eyes and the hypothalamus, it integrates and relays information about the length of daylight to every cell in the body by way of the hormone melatonin, enabling the orchestration of internal functions, synchronisation with nature, and the maintenance of the body's biological clock on a daily, seasonal and yearly basis. It would therefore appear that the pineal, working with the hypothalamus, 'lays the foundation for . . . harmony between the inside and outside of our being' (Liberman, 1992, p. 22).

It is also the foundation for the newly rediscovered field of phototherapy, which uses light in the treatment of disease. As one of the leading researchers in this field photobiologist John Ott (1991) observes, ancient peoples and even entire civilisations worshipped the sun for its healing powers, using its full spectrum of light to treat physical and mental problems. This practice, known as 'heliotherapy', is now claimed as hazardous to health by modern medical research and has been replaced by many artificial approaches such as radio and chemotherapy. However, bright white full-spectrum light is now being used in the treatment of cancers, seasonal affective disorder (SAD) or so-called 'winter depression', general depression, anorexia and bulimia nervosa, insomnia, jet lag, shift-working, alcohol and drug dependency, and to reduce overall levels of medication (Liberman, 1992). White light has also replaced blood transfusions as the treatment for babies born with potentially fatal neonatal jaundice. Nevertheless, although there is a growing use of bright white light in treatment coloured lights are being found to be more effective (Oren, Brainard et al., 1991). This is not altogether surprising: 'Since light plays such a major role in the stimulation and regulation of the body's physiological processes, and since color is merely our perception of light of different wavelengths, is it not logical that different colors might then create different physiological as well as psychological effects on us?' (Liberman, 1991, p. 41).

The colour red, which has the longest wavelength, and therefore the heaviest and slowest vibratory rate, is traditionally associated with the functioning of the base chakra. Accordingly it is a warm, dynamic and sexy vibration, associated with heat, both physical heat such as fire and also 'heated' emotions, and expressed by inflammations and fever. It is regarded as a stimulant of the blood and nervous system. Orange and yellow are also stimulating colours. Orange stimulates all appetites and physical activity, and is anti-depressant in effect, whereas yellow stimulates mental activity. The former can assist the assimilation and digestion of food and the fluid balance of the body, whereas the latter may improve brain function, vision and arthritic conditions.

Green is associated with the heart, and is traditionally regarded as the colour of balance and love. It can be used to stimulate the immune system or to regulate it in the case of auto-immune conditions, notably rheumatoid arthritis. Blue is traditionally associated with communication and sound, with calmness and coolness. It is therefore considered to have a sedative and anti-inflammatory effect, and to be applicable in cases of fever, infections, inflammation, irritation, skin complaints and burns. Violet, which combines red and blue in perfect balance, is traditionally the colour of spirituality. It is believed to strengthen the nervous system, and to soothe tensions in the head and throat.

Modern research supports these intuitive notions about the therapeutic uses of colour, by showing it has marked physical effects. Various studies have confirmed experimentally that red excites the central nervous system, raises blood pressure, increases respiration, pulse rate and heartbeat. Red light increases physical strength and the electrical activity in the arm muscles, and may be utilised to improve athletic performance (Liberman, 1991). Bubble-gum pink has also been demonstrated in studies by the clinical psychologist Alexander Schauss to exert a physical effect, relaxing the muscles, which reduces the incidence of violent and aggressive behaviour, and as a result is used in many correctional institutions, adolescent units, family therapy centres and business settings. By contrast, there are indications that yellow should be avoided in such contexts as it has a highly stimulating effect, and a correlation has been noted between the incidence of violent street crime and the use of sodium yellow street-lighting. Nevertheless the more stimulating colours also have demonstrable therapeutic properties. Red light is very effective in the treatment of migraine headaches and cancer (Liberman, 1991, 2), and yellow can improve the performance of those with learning difficulties. Even more recently, research has shown that colour-tinted spectacles can be highly effective in the treatment of learning difficulties, notably dyslexia, and also epilepsy and migraine. The effectiveness of tinted lenses as a reading aid was first discovered by an American psychologist Helen Irlen but was regarded with scepticism until investigations by the British Medical Research Council confirmed her claims. In June 1993 a new optician's device, the Intuitive Colorimeter, was made available to British opticians to enable them to measure which tint – bright pink, yellow, green or blue – best helps individuals who normally see text as swirling, wobbling or with letters appearing in the wrong order. Literacy expert John Bald has described the use of tinted lenses as 'the single most important advance in the treatment of reading difficulties' (Brace, 1993, p. 10).

Another new technique which has been developed in the US as a result of pioneering research over the past two decades is photodynamic therapy or PDT, based on the discovery that certain intravenously injected photosensitive chemicals not only accumulate in cancer cells but selectively identify these cells under ultra-violet light and then exclusively destroy them when activated by red light, whose longer wavelength allows it to penetrate tissue more deeply than light of other colours. Accordingly, PDT can be used for both diagnosis and treatment. Dr Thomas Dougherty who developed PDT reports (1989, 1990) that in a worldwide experiment more than 3000 people, with a wide variety of malignant tumours, have been successfully treated with this technique, which currently is being evaluated and compared in relation to conventional cancer treatments.

Blue light has even more marked healing qualities and numerous applications within orthodox medicine. It is now extensively used in healing injured tissue and preventing the formation of scar tissue, and in the treatment of cancers, non-malignant tumours, skin and lung conditions. It has proved more effective than white light in the treatment of neonatal jaundice and has been successfully used for reducing the pain of rheumatoid arthritis (McDonald, 1982). In 1990 scientists also reported to the annual conference of the American Association of the Advancement of Science on the successful use of blue light in the treatment of a wide variety of psychological conditions, including addictions, eating disorders, impotence and depression.

Indeed studies confirm ancient wisdom on the effects of colour on the emotions and psychological functions. Understanding of these effects has come about by relatively recent research into the hormones melatonin and serotonin, both of which are produced by the pineal gland. The former is known to be the crucial chemical pathway by which animals respond to light and synchronise their bodily functioning with diurnal, lunar and seasonal variations; and the latter is a very important neurotransmitter in the brain whose action has been linked with mental disturbance, notably schizophrenia and hallucinogenic states.

Serotonin is produced by day and has a stimulatory effect, whereas melatonin output increases when it is dark, and has a generally depressive effect which is reversed when it is light and its production drops. It is linked with sleep and possibly dreams. As Roney-Dougal (1989) indicates, its main site of action appears to be the hypothalamus which is that part of the brain involved in mediating the effects of various hormones and regulating emotions. However, fluctuations in the output of melatonin in response to light influence every cell of the body, notably the reproductive processes which are particularly sensitive to such variations. Very high levels of melatonin have been found in women with ovulation problems and anorexia nervosa – a characteristic feature of which is amenorrhoea or absence of menstruation; in men with a low sperm count; and people suffering from Seasonal Affective Disorder, which usually occurs during winter. Indeed depression in general appears to be closely linked with melatonin levels and to show rapid improvement in response to natural sunlight or light therapy using full spectrum lamps.

COLOUR THERAPY

These discoveries lend support to the theories of Rudolph Steiner, who advocated the use of colour in treatment of various conditions, and Dr Max Luscher, a former professor of psychology at Basle University, who claimed that colour preferences are indicative of both glandular imbalance and states of mind, and can be used as the basis for physical and psychological diagnosis. His theory, which forms the basis of the Luscher Colour Test, is that the significance of colour for human beings originates in their early history when their behaviour was governed by night and day. He claimed that the dark blue and yellow light of these periods is associated with differences in metabolic rate and glandular secretions necessary for night-time sleep and rest, and daytime foraging and hunting, and that other autonomic responses are associated with different colours. His thinking is quite consistent with the chakra system and with the principles of energy medicine which derive from it. Indeed, as Liberman observes, the profound effect of colour on life was probably first recognised by humans whose existence was dictated by day and night, light or darkness. All living things are vitalised by the bright reds, oranges and yellows of daytime and calmed and rejuvenated by the blues, indigos and violets of the night, and this observation was probably the basis of the use of colour in the treatment of physical and psychological ailments.

COLOUR CONSCIOUSNESS

Awareness of the subtle effects of colour, and its uses in self-healing and the promotion of personal growth, has been termed colour consciousness. Its aim, according to Bek and Holden (1989) is to create a rainbow of colours, each as strong, clear, ethereal and radiant as the other. 'This rainbow or spectrum attunement vitalises the chakras and "exhorts" them to a healthy level' (White, 1989, p. 14). During healing the colours of the chakras alter as they become more balanced in their functioning, and these changes are reflected in imagery.

Colour therapy is based upon understanding of these principles. Colour therapists may work with the aura, sensing imbalance clairvoyantly or intuitively, or by passing the hands over the body and noting changes in vibration associated with various parts of the body. Coloured light may then be projected to the relevant chakra by means of various lamps or filters, or the therapist may consciously direct certain colour vibrations to the relevant chakra by visualising colour. Imbalance in the chakras can also be detected by way of personal imagery and for this reason colour associated with imagery should always be noted, especially persistent colour which may be indicative of specific chakra dysfunction. Understanding of the significance of colour in imagery can thus be used for identifying and regulating imbalances in the chakras, and as such is an important means of self-healing.

One approach to self-healing by colour is colour breathing, whereby a person imagines inhaling breath of a certain colour and drawing it to a particular chakra. This is widely practised in many traditions, both ancient and modern. Another approach is colour imagery. Colour researcher and therapist, Theo Gimbel, a former student of Rudolph Steiner, advocates this approach, claiming that the power of images is increased by visualising colour and thus 'when image supports colour and colour supports the image' (cited by Branson, 1988, p. 10). However, Buddhist traditions emphasise the importance of identifying with the chakras by focusing awareness on them and thus sensing rather than thinking about them. Barbara Brennan also makes this distinction, observing that healing with colour is not a matter of thinking a colour, but of experiencing it and therefore directing the sensations rather than the thought of colour to a chakra. This is because in energetic terms thought is a yellow vibration, so irrespective of what colour you think of you will create yellow. Therefore 'to make blue you must "be" blue, whatever that means to you. So you need to experiment for yourself what it is like to be in a state of blue' (1988, p. 237). This involves becoming aware of how you feel when you wear blue or sit in a blue light, and of what blue means to you, how it looks, feels and sounds. In order to develop colour consciousness it is necessary to explore your relationship to each colour in this way. The following exercise is directed towards facilitating colour consciousness and enabling individuals to find and express their 'true colours'.

EXERCISE 10

There are several variations of this exercise, and it is
recommended that you attempt them in the following order.

10a Sitting or lying comfortably with eyes closed, focus your
attention on your pubic bone. Allow yourself some time to
become aware of the sensations in this area. As you do so
allow the image of a hat to form. Don't try to force or censor
the image, simply allow it to emerge. Notice its colour and
details and your reactions to it. Then imagine putting it on,
noting your reactions as you do so and wearing it. Observe
how you behave, feel and think while wearing this hat. Having
done so, proceed to do likewise for each of the following
areas: below the navel; above the navel; the centre of the
breast bone; centre of the throat; centre of the forehead; crown
of the head.

10b Focus your attention on the pubic bone and the
sensations in that area. As you do so, allow yourself to form
the image of a red hat as vividly as possible and note your
reactions to it. Try it on and wear it. Observe where you go
and what you do while wearing it, and your feelings and
thoughts as you do so.

Having done so, focus your attention on the area some 2 in
below your navel, becoming aware of the sensations there, and
as you do so allow the image of an orange hat to form, noting
your reactions as previously.

Then, following the same procedure, imagine a yellow hat
forming in association with the area some 2 in above the navel,
a green hat forming in association with the centre of the breast
bone, a sky blue hat forming in association with the centre of
the throat, a dark blue hat forming in association with the
centre of the eyebrows and a purple hat forming in association
with the crown of the head. Imagine trying on each hat,
wearing it, and noting your behaviour, feelings and thoughts
as you do so.

10c Imagine seven hats, each a different colour of the
rainbow, red, orange, yellow, green, sky blue, dark blue or
indigo, and purple. Note their specific features and which of
them you are most attracted to. In order of preference, try on
each hat, noting your reactions as you do so. Then imagine

wearing the hat somewhere, observing your behaviour, feelings and thoughts.

After each exercise record your experiences.

Commentary

The focus of each of the above exercises is slightly different. 10(a) highlights the way in which the chakras are functioning currently and therefore what energies are being expressed in relation to each centre. 10(b) highlights personal features which might be expressed if the energies in each of the chakra areas were to be used more appropriately and effectively. 10(c) identifies the energies being most strongly expressed at a given time and those which are being less actively expressed or blocked. These can be stimulated by 10(b).

In most cases the colour, style and function of the hats imagined in 10(a) corresponds with those traditionally associated with the chakras. The base chakra is typically associated with red hats which are described as sporty, sexy, smart or sophisticated. Frequently people imagine themselves wearing red hats when engaged in physical activities, especially when participating in or spectating at sporting events, and feeling lively, flamboyant or uplifted in so doing. Invariably 'red hat' activities are social and associated with status. Women often imagine themselves wearing red hats – sometimes described as being like those worn in the TV soap *Dynasty* – to 'society' weddings and functions, royal garden parties, Royal Ascot, cocktail parties and other 'classy' social gatherings. Red thus appears to be associated with status consciousness, which is indicated in its traditional use in ceremonial robes. More generally it tends to reflect what Myss refers to as the 'tribal' features of base chakra energies, by which the person relates to his racial, ethnic, national, cultural, social and familial origins or 'roots'. Security in these relationships may also be indicated, as in the case of a woman who described herself holding hands with a long line of friends while skating in a red hat. However, a certain coolness in this otherwise red hat/hot energy is suggested by those who describe ice skating, skiing, tobogganing and snowball-throwing. Indeed some people describe a desire to get away from the strongly physical red energy, which they experience as claustrophobic and oppressive.

Orange hats are generally associated with energetic activities, athleticism, play, fun, laughter and childhood, features which are commonly reflected in relation to children's parties and games, circuses, clowns, sporting activities and dance. One man imagined himself as a child in an orange cap jumping up and down on a pogo stick, and another imagined himself morris dancing. The 'fun' aspect of second chakra energy is reflected in the imagery of one woman who imagined herself with an orange attached to her head by elastic and of a man who described himself in a large floppy hat in which he felt he wanted to laugh hilariously, at nothing at all, until he fell over.

Yellow hats tend to be large and expansive with wide brims – sombreros, Napoleon-style and Chinese coolie hats. The intellectual aspect of this chakra is reflected in the significant number of both men and women who imagined themselves in mortarboards, while issues of power, control and steering are perhaps indicated in various 'driving' hats, notably that described by one man as 'like a set of handlebars' and in various hats worn while directing or controlling traffic. In this context the shrunken hat described by one woman does not appear to be a very positive asset.

Green hats tend to reflect the outdoor life. 'Robin Hood' style hats are very common, as are waxed waterproof country hats, pixie caps, riding hats, fishing headwear and boaters. Less common is the hat of leaves 'overlapping like fish scales', described by one woman. The functions at which green hats are worn also tend to reflect country living and pursuits. Hence more modish hats may be worn to open a village fete or country fair, to attend a garden party or spend a day at the races. Army berets are sometimes described, which perhaps suggests that the energy in the heart centre is somewhat controlled or regimented.

Pale or sky blue hats convey to those who imagine wearing them a sense of being 'cool' or 'toned down'. This is often associated with cool water, blue hats being worn while boating or punting on rivers; and with snow and ice, the ubiquitous 'bobble hat' featuring strongly in this context. One man who imagined that his head actually did 'bobble' up and down in jerky movements, as though he had hiccups, noted that this corresponded with the erratic movement of the throat wheel in the previous exercise. The same man also imagined himself jumping up and down on a pogo stick wearing an orange hat when he focused on the second chakra area, suggesting a correspondence between his mode of self-expression, and his deep feelings and passions. The normal expressive style of the chakra is often reflected in the style of the hat associated with it. Sombreros for keeping cool in the desert are commonly described, along with turbans. One man interpreted his turban as an indication of his tendency to keep himself 'under wraps', whereas a woman who saw herself in a turban felt that this enabled her to assert her more masculine qualities.

Certainly, wearing a blue hat can be a liberating experience for those people who normally do not express the energies of the throat centre, as in the rather extreme example provided by a young woman who imagined that she disappeared into a huge turquoise hat and became invisible. Many people are attracted to blue hats, such as the woman who reported being unaccountably drawn to one after having worn predominantly black and cream for the past 25 years and the rather inhibited young man who imagined being able to dance without restraint when wearing a blue hat in a disco. Similarly a very shy, inhibited and inarticulate man imagined himself behaving in 'cavalier' fashion, wearing a large blue tricorn Cavalier's hat.

When wearing blue hats many men express themselves in ways they often describe as 'silly', which is no doubt a reflection of the inhibiting effects of social pressure on men to be serious and sensible rather than frivolous. Interestingly the word 'silly' comes from an Old English word meaning 'happy'. Hence, it would seem, the male role conventionally precludes expressions of happiness – and much else. One man who imagined himself wearing a blue nurse's cap and carrying a stethoscope, described 'helping people and doing silly things like that'. However, blue hats may liberate other socially controlled male behaviours, as is illustrated by the man who imagined himself shouting rude and bawdy sexist remarks to women from the window of the bus he was driving. Women in blue hats may also be liberated from social stereotypes of appropriate feminine behaviour. Thus a woman who imagined herself in a blue mortarboard at an American-style graduation ceremony recognised this as an indication that normally she fails to express her intellectual energies fully. Another woman found that when wearing a blue hat she could be more assertive, and a young woman who described herself as normally serious, anxious and rather staid, imagined wearing a blue hat at a hilarious mad hatter's tea party, throwing buns and enjoying herself enormously.

Many people experience difficulty imagining themselves in a dark blue hat, which is perhaps quite strange given that many occupational groups routinely wear such hats as a feature of their uniforms – police officers, train and taxi drivers, chauffeurs, pilots, sailors, car park attendants, traffic wardens, firefighters and nurses are but a few that spring readily to mind. These groups share a common ethic in that they serve others, which is intriguing, if only because in many traditions awakening of the 'third eye' or brow chakra is associated with service, to God(s) and/or fellow human beings. However, these more commonplace hats do not appear to figure very greatly in response to the present exercises. Rather, the hats described tend to be very idiosyncratic. How else would one describe a hat in the form of a tiered Chinese pagoda growing ever upwards and more elaborate? One woman described herself wearing a floppy sultan's hat and flying off on a magic carpet to 'see what is going on elsewhere'. A similar far-sightedness is indicated in the imagery of a man who saw himself wearing a turban with a large central jewel that enabled him to see all kinds of distant and future happenings.

Purple hats tend to be tall and reach upwards, often in a triangular or conical fashion. Hence archbishops' mitres, wizards' and witches' hats, headwear such as that favoured by pharaohs and Egyptian queens such as Cleopatra and Nefertiti, the cornet caps of medieval times and mantillas worn over high combs in the hair in Spanish style, have all been described. Wearing these hats makes people feel taller and 'above things', as in the case of the woman who described herself 'like the Lady of Shallot' in a purple cornet cap and long mauve veils, looking down from a high tower on to a jousting contest below. Feelings of power, transcendence and raised consciousness are also sometimes reported, and spiritual qualities, which may be reflected by mitres, mantillas and other forms of clerical and monastic headwear. Some people have described feelings of ecstasy, notably a man who imagined himself as the pilot of a single-seater aeroplane and a woman who described herself floating in a hat with a huge, wavy brim.

In many cases the style of the hat appears to reflect the expressive style of the associated chakra. In some instances all the hats are of one type: top hats or bowlers, which are suggestive of formality and rigidity; softer but nevertheless somewhat controlled or regimented school caps and berets; more casual but none the less preformed or styled trilbys; even more sporty baseball or ski caps, which, although casual are usually associated with a certain discipline; softer and perhaps more childish or funny 'bobble' caps; functional work-a-day hats; and 'floppy', shapeless, flexible hats.

The size of the hat appears to reflect the effectiveness of the chakra. Thus wide-brimmed 'picture' hats tend towards display and greater expressiveness than small hats. 'Box' shaped hats are commonly described and these suggest that the associated energies are contained rather than expressed. The frequent reference to 'pill-box' hats also raises the question as to the healthy functioning of the relevant chakras. A tentative association appears to be indicated in this respect, but nothing more conclusive. Hats which are part of a uniform may also indicate controlled or restricted expression. One man whose hats were all parts of different uniforms admitted to 'acting out' a number of roles and being able to express himself only when disinhibited by alcohol. This was such a strong feature of his imagery that he described becoming 'drunk' on lemonade when 'play-acting' as a child at a party.

In some cases the colours traditionally associated with the chakras are displaced, indicating that energies which are not being utilised appropriately in one centre are, of necessity, expressed elsewhere. Hence a man who described a yellow and green striped cap in association with the base chakra felt very uncomfortable about wearing it among others in a bar. Repeating the exercise some time later, he found a dark blue cowboy hat where the striped cap had previously been. He wore this and entered a bar, where among many men in similar dark hats he encountered a 'colourful' character, obviously very relaxed and content, who advised him to 'keep alive; make yourself real'. Another man imagined a red bowler in association with his heart chakra and a green one in the base chakra. A young man who associated his solar plexus or third chakra with a blue hat felt himself floating and a strong fear that 'they' could easily drop him, letting him fall to his death. Subsequently he realised that 'they' were his parents, who would not always 'be there' for him, hence the feelings of insecurity and fear expressed by this centre, and that he needed to become independent of them in order to take control of his own life. A woman who imagined her hair blazing red fire in the heart centre, recognised the 'hot-headed' anger she felt towards significant people in her life.

In some cases the hats imagined are not standard colours of the rainbow but black, brown, grey or white. Where white appears it usually indicates healthy functioning of the chakra and positive activity, which may also be reflected in the accompanying imagery, such as dancing in a white top hat like Fred Astaire. By contrast black is suggestive of negativity and unexpressed energies. In focusing on his throat chakra one man imagined himself wearing a black trilby at a funeral and being unable to cry, despite wanting to. In so doing he realised that he had not expressed his grief about the death of a close relative many years previously and was still carrying it within him. Similarly a woman who associated this centre with a 'wraithlike' image of herself in a church congregation dressed in a long black dress realised that she was living in the past, still mourning the loss of an intimate relationship which she had been unable to let go of. A woman who, when focusing on the base chakra, formed an image of herself in a black bowler and dressed like Charlie Chaplin at a 'silly party', subsequently acknowledged that she tended to trivialise and deny the feelings associated with this chakra. Hats with black trim or detail may also be indicative of problems and may correlate with details of the butterfly imagery (see Chapter 1 and appendices). A woman reported that the black-tasselled red fez she associated with her base chakra prevented her 'going anywhere'. Another woman 'felt OK' wearing the black hat she associated with her base chakra in exercise 10(a) but very uncomfortable with and self-conscious and insecure about her sexuality when wearing the red hat she imagined in exercise 10(b).

Brown hats are an indication of 'stuck' or blocked energies, as is most graphically indicated in the imagery of a man who, while attending to his solar plexus chakra, visualised himself looking on as a group of people discussed an open sewer. He later reported himself as 'always going on about life being shitty and doing nothing about it'; and the realisation, prompted by this imagery, that by 'being open' and constantly talking about his 'shitty' past, he was actually holding on to it rather than closing this issue. Focusing on his second chakra some time afterwards, he imagined himself standing in a brown hat looking across some freshly-manured fields, which suggests that the 'shit' from his past was still being spread across his emotional life. Grey hats suggest that the associated chakra is not functioning as effectively as it should. Thus a woman who described a grey hat in relation to her second chakra reported problems with fluid retention, while a man who associated this chakra with an image of himself standing in a grey hat in the pouring rain reported the opposite difficulty.

In some instances a person will visualise only one hat or describe every hat as the same colour. When yellow predominates, as in the case of the woman who imagined only one huge Mexican sombrero, this may be an indication of eccentricity. Some people imagine trying on the hats but do not wear them anywhere, often because they lack confidence or are self-conscious. This is suggestive perhaps of people who are aware of or willing to explore their potentials but not to reveal them to others. Several women have expressed concern about the 'outfit' to wear with each hat, indicating anxiety about the roles or images they are expected to convey.

Some people refuse to put on hats which, in their judgement, do not suit them or which compromise their view of themselves. Thus some people will not try on hats, particularly of the 'bobble' variety, which they believe will make them look foolish. This overconcern with appearance is clearly repressive, preventing as it does exploration and expression even at the fantasy level. Others refuse to wear any hat. One woman did so despite being attracted to a blue hat on the grounds that it was a rebellion against school authority of 25 years before. This suggests that she was stuck with outmoded childish attitudes which adversely effect her self-expression in the present. Another young woman who admitted to finding the exercise difficult because she had never worn a hat once again indicates the way in which people resist new experiences even at the fantasy level. Similarly a woman who reported initial difficulty with the exercise because she 'would never dream f wearing a hat', thereby indicating a somewhat rigid self-concept, reluctance to change and a tendency to control fantasy, resolved the problem by 'allowing' her long hair to become various styles of head-dress.

Most people are intrigued by their different responses to the exercises and the insights they derive from them. Their usefulness in prompting self-awareness is perhaps best conveyed by one man who claimed that each hat had given him a totally new perspective on reality; and thus new ways of seeing and thinking about himself and his world. In this respect the exercises might be considered to have a similar function to those described by the psychologist Edward de Bono in his book *Six Thinking Hats* (1990), the aim of which, according to the author, is to allow people to *switch* their mode of thinking and change the way they operate or function so as to be more effective. In fact, the similarity between the exercises presented here and those of de Bono is quite coincidental. In developing my exercises I drew on the experience of a woman who found herself imagining hats as she focused attention on the chakra areas highlighted in a previous exercise. The valuable insights she derived from her imagery prompted me to develop it more systematically and to 'test' it on other people. The different variations on the same theme are the product of this experimentation. However, the woman whose spontaneous imagery initiated the exercises was very surprised to see de Bono's book in a library a week or so later, and even more astonished upon reading it to discover the similarity between her imagery and that prescribed within the book.

De Bono advocates imagery wearing six different hats to promote different styles of thinking:

- **a white hat** for neutral, objective, factual thinking;
- **a red hat** for thinking that allows the feelings, emotions, hunches and intuition of the thinker and others to be explored;
- **a black hat** for thinking that is specifically concerned with negative assessment – pointing out what is wrong, incorrect or in error, and identifying risks, dangers, disadvantages;
- **a yellow hat** for positive, constructive and optimistic thinking which probes and explores, and finds logical support for value

and benefit, producing concrete proposals and suggestions, and 'making things happen';

- **a green hat** for creative thinking which is adaptable and generates new concepts and perceptions; and
- **a blue hat** for controlled, organised, disciplined thinking of the kind expressed in summaries, overviews and conclusions.

It would seem therefore that the basic message to be gleaned from the exercises recommended by de Bono and the other exercises presented in this chapter can be paraphrased in terms of the well-known maxim: 'If the cap fits, wear it'.

CHAPTER ELEVEN

Healthy Solutions

As with any work of imagination, I discovered new
meanings every day in this strange tapestry.

BRIAN KEENAN, *An Evil Cradling*

The psycholinguist Gregory Bateson described his scientific investigations as a search for the 'pattern which connects'. The pattern
which connects the various components examined in the previous
chapters of this book into a unified whole or person has been
represented as a jigsaw puzzle, and termed a healing puzzle
because the formation of complete and comprehensive patterns
is the condition of wholeness or health. The progression towards health or wholeness constitutes growth. It is only by
connecting the pieces of a jigsaw puzzle that it grows and becomes complete. Any incomplete pattern represents an unfinished situation which if unattended to creates stagnation and
regression instead of growth, as you will know if you have ever
left a jigsaw incomplete. It remains a puzzle rather than a
solution.

Fritz Perls (1973) considered neurosis one of several symptoms
of growth stagnation. Others include the need to manipulate the
world, character distortion, reduction of human potential, lack of
'response-ability' and, 'most important of all, the production of
holes in a personality' (p. 9). He claimed that the neurotic
personality is characterised by a great number of these holes or
unfinished situations, which the person is either unaware of or
incapable of coping with. However, while these holes are the

main characteristic of the neurotic personality, Perls regarded no one as complete.

> I believe that every one of us has holes. Where something should be, there is nothing. Many people have no soul. Others have no genitals. Some have no heart; all their energy goes into computing, thinking. Others have no legs to stand on. Many people have no eyes. They project the eyes, and the eyes are to quite an extent in the outside world and they always live as if they are being looked at. A person feels that the eyes of the world are upon him. He becomes a mirror-person who always wants to know how he looks to others. He gives up his eyes and asks the world to do his seeing for him . . . Most of us have no ears. People expect the ears to be outside and they talk and expect someone to listen. But who listens?
> . . . the most important missing part is a center. Without a center, everything goes on in the periphery and there is no place from which to work, from which to cope with the world. Without a center, you are not alert.

1976, pp. 39–40

According to Perls these holes arise because of a demand on the individual to be what he or she is not; and thus to actualise an ideal rather than the self. When this happens, he claims, the individual becomes lopsided. Some of his or her potentials are alienated, repressed or projected. 'Other characteristics are put on as phoney behaviour, requiring strain without self-support, exhaustion without satisfaction' (1973, p. 10); and eventually this division between biological and social existence leads to more and more conflicts and more 'holes'. It may lead to complete vacuousness. Thus 'where some people have a self, most people have a void, because they are so busy projecting themselves as this or that. This is again the curse of the ideal. The curse that you should not be what you are' (Perls, 1976, p. 20).

Completing the pattern and becoming whole requires the holes in the personality to be filled. Perls (1977) insists that neither the importance nor difficulty of this task should be underestimated. There may be hundreds of 'holes' to be completed and, because these are in effect 'blind spots', the individual lacks awareness or is unconscious of what is missing, where the holes are and the ways in which they are normally avoided, although in the vicinity of these holes or voids a person tends to become confused or nervous. However, as Perls points out, these missing holes are always visible and may be obvious to others. Ordinarily they are projected on to the outside world but in psychotherapy they are projected on to the therapist, who, in principle at least, presents the person with the opportunity to discover the missing parts he has alienated and given up to the world, by frustrating him until he is face to face with the very features he is avoiding. In this way the person is obliged to reown the disowned parts of his personality, his possibilities and potentials. Therapy therefore provides the opportunity and situation in which to grow. Nevertheless, Perls emphasises that what a person expects from a therapist he can do just as well himself:

> Everything the person disowns can be recovered, and the means of recovery is understanding, playing, becoming these disowned parts . . . But the person has to discover this by seeing for himself, by listening for himself, by uncovering for himself, by grasping for himself, and by becoming ambidextrous instead of closed, and so on. And the main thing is listening. To listen, to understand, to be open, is one and the same.
>
> 1976, pp. 40–1

The exercises presented in the earlier chapters facilitate a step-by-step process whereby you may discover and complete the pattern which is uniquely yourself. This may be considered 'do-it-yourself' psychotherapy or self-healing, because as Myss (1991, p. 83) observes, 'Completion is the opportunity to understand and bring to a close – literally and figuratively – the open wounds of your life'. The process is analogous to completing a jigsaw puzzle.

THE HEALING PUZZLE: SELF-HEALING THROUGH SELF-AWARENESS

Whereas the picture provided on the box of a jigsaw is usually a reliable facsimile of the puzzle inside and hence a reliable guide to its completion, this is not the case for the human being. Instead, other people provide 'a sort of identity kit, whereby one can piece together a picture of *oneself*' (Laing, 1972, p. 87). This is the basis of one's self-image or concept, and of self-identity, 'the story one tells one's self of who one is' (Laing, 1972, p. 93). However, the image projected by others may be a poor guide to self-identity, bearing little or no relationship to the individual it purports to represent. Moreover, there may be as many identity kits as there are others to provide them. Hence they are often inconsistent or mutually exclusive, contradictory or paradoxical. Accordingly it may be highly misleading and confusing to rely upon definitions provided by others, as R.D. Laing (1977, pp. 26–7) has observed:

> For as early as I can remember I never took myself to be what people called me. That at least has remained crystal clear to me. That is, whatever, whoever I may be is not to be confused with the names people give *to* me, or how they *describe* me. I am not my name.
>
> Who or what I am as far as they are concerned, is not necessarily, or thereby, *me*, as far as I am concerned.
>
> I am presumably *what* they are describing, but not their description. I am the territory, what they say I am is their map of me.
>
> And what I call myself to myself is, presumably, my map of me. What, or where, is the territory?

The challenge offered by the healing puzzle is precisely that of finding the answer to this question *oneself*, for, as Laing has stated (1972, p. 95), 'the identity of the self can be self-defined'. This self-definition is not a matter of stating in words or describing in rational concepts but of determining by way of experience. It is self-knowledge or self-awareness which comes from exploration of the actual territory or ground rather than study of a map or image. Perls (1976, p. 17) has little doubt 'that awareness per se – by and of itself – can be curative', essentially because it opens the person to intuition, or the wisdom of the organism, which left to its own devices without external interference operates homeostatically to regulate the integrity and balance of the whole system, equivalent with health, in contrast to the pathology which results from interference with this subtle self-control. Self-awareness can therefore be likened to the process of attempting to complete a jigsaw puzzle without looking at the picture on the box. Most people are capable of looking at themselves, and assessing their state of physical and psychological health or wholeness. Whether or not they choose to is a different matter, just as it is a matter of choice or preference as to whether people attempt jigsaw puzzles and enjoy doing so or not. The latter will tend to determine the individual's ability to find solutions to the puzzles, more than any inherent capacity or lack of it, although perceptual deficits and lack of sensitivity will tend to limit effectiveness.

Closer attention to overt personal features will increase familiarity with 'the lie of the land'. It may also expose the 'blind spots' or holes which exist and their location in relation to known features may provide clues as to their nature. However, acknowledgement of those features of the self which are known to be 'in place' – features that one has 'in mind' and of which one is conscious – is in itself an insufficient basis for solution of the puzzle. It is necessary to 'open the box' which holds the missing pieces and identify the hidden contents of the unconscious. As the psychiatrist Roberto Assagioli observes (1991, p. 25), 'in order to know ourselves it is not enough to make an inventory of the elements that form our conscious being. An extensive exploration of the vast regions of our unconscious must also be undertaken'. Like Perls and Laing he believes that this search can be undertaken by oneself, but is a tremendous undertaking, long and arduous, which not everyone is ready for.

> But between the starting point in the lowlands of our ordinary consciousness and the shining peak of Self-realisation there are intermediate phases, plateaus at various altitudes on which a man may rest or even make his abode, if his lack of strength precludes or his will does not choose a further ascent.
>
> 1991, p. 128

Puzzling methods

However, while he acknowledges the process may be very slow he indicates that it can be considerably accelerated by deliberate conscious action and by the use of appropriate active techniques. As previously indicated, a rather desultory 'dipping into' the unconscious in much the same way as you might pick the jigsaw pieces from their box is unlikely to yield quick results. A more systematic and controlled approach is desirable. Assagioli recommends an objective and critical survey of all the contents of the unconscious. This means facing up to or confronting them, much as you might turn up all the jigsaw pieces removed from the box to reveal their hidden features. In this way numerous images of varying degrees of completeness and complexity appear, and it is by relating these items into meaningful wholes that the overall pattern or puzzle is resolved.

Engagement of active imagination by way of guided imagery exercises, such as those presented in the earlier chapters, serves to reveal formerly hidden features of the unconscious in much the same way. The imagination is the vehicle by which unconscious content becomes known. It can be thought of as a way of turning over in the mind various concepts and issues so as to gain a new perspective upon them. The means by which this is achieved is essentially non-rational in that it does not involve reasoning or thinking about issues logically, but relies upon the capacity for visualisation or 'seeing in the mind's eye'. By themselves these insights into the contents of the personal unconscious do not amount to much more than a fascinating kaleidoscope, like a dream. Indeed guided imagery can be likened to a waking dream, and dreams, according to Perls, provide excellent opportunities for the discovery of holes in the personality. However, logical or rational processes must be employed in order to impose some meaningful structure upon the dreamlike images, just as visual and logical processes must be combined in the solution of a jigsaw puzzle.

Not uncommonly various images arise together in association as complexes, in just the same way as pieces of a jigsaw often emerge from the box joined together. Although seemingly related and 'fitting', closer examination often reveals that this is not the case and that the pieces are merely 'stuck' together. These complexes need to be taken apart or resolved into their elements if they are to fit into the overall pattern appropriately, and to allow growth and development. The same is true of the healing puzzle.

Perls (1976, p. 42) observes that invariably people discover the areas where they appear to be stuck are not real but illusory. The problem for them is if they continue to believe in their reality and attempt to build their lives around them. Inevitably they will discover that they 'cannot go on' or progress. Many people, however, prefer such an impasse to awareness of how they are stuck, because it maintains the status quo and avoids change. Clearly, however, awareness is necessary if progress is to be made. Without it such people will function badly, carrying numerous unfinished situations that always demand completion.

Freud was primarily concerned with identifying these complexes, and their inhibiting effects on psychological growth and development. He indicated that the power of these complexes lies chiefly in the fact that they are unconscious and are therefore not seen for what they really are. It was his claim that when they are revealed, understood and resolved into their elements by way of psychoanalysis they cease to be problematic. Similarly, Assagioli (1991) advocates the disintegration of potentially harmful complexes by the methods of objectification, critical analysis and discrimination.

> That is to say, we must employ cold, impersonal observation as if they were mere natural phenomena, occurring outside ourselves. We should create a 'psychological distance' between ourselves and them, keeping these images or complexes at arm's length, so to speak, and then quietly consider their origin, their nature and – their stupidity!
>
> 1991, p. 127

In other words we should sort out these difficulties in a detached way, just as we would deal with the pieces of a jigsaw, thereby enabling the components to be utilised more appropriately. The same methods can then be applied to all the other emergent features, after which, Assagioli claims, the actual construction of the personality can begin.

While Assagioli is correct to emphasise the importance of being able to stand back and rationally and objectively assess the images which emerge from the unconscious, and to make logical connections and relations between them, sole reliance on these methods is unhealthy in that issues are not addressed by the whole person. Identification with the intellect and explanation excludes the body, and thus the total organism. Therefore while images may be reasonably understood they nevertheless relate to no-body. Moreover, intellectual approaches may be more destructive than constructive. Alvin Toffler (1984, p. xi) observes that dissection – the reduction of problems to their smallest possible components – is one of the most highly developed skills in contemporary Western civilisation: 'We are good at it. So good, we often forget to put the pieces back together again'.

Arguably, this criticism can be levelled at various approaches to psychotherapy, notably psychoanalysis. The gestalt therapy inspired by Perls differs from most other psychotherapies in that it does not focus on analysis *per se* but on both differentiation and integration. By itself differentiation leads to polarisation and division, whereas integration of opposite traits leads to completion. Perls's method of working with dreamlike imagery is therefore quite distinctive. It was Perls's contention that

> All the different parts of the dream are fragments of our
> personalities. Since our aim is to make everyone of us a
> wholesome person, which means a unified person without
> conflicts, what we have to do is to put the different fragments
> together. We have to re-own those projected, fragmented parts
> of our personality.
>
> 1976, p. 71–2

This reassimilation, or taking back features that have been projected outside of yourself, is achieved by projecting oneself completely into the images produced.

> Instead of analysing and further cutting up the dream, we
> want to bring it back to life. And the way to bring it back to
> life is to re-live the dream as if it were happening now. Instead
> of telling the dream as if it were a story in the past, act it out
> in the present, so that it becomes a part of yourself, so that
> you are really involved. If you understand what you can do
> with dreams, you can do a tremendous lot for yourself on your
> own.
>
> 1976, pp. 73–4

Perls recommended that when working on dream images oneself, the dream is first written down and all the details of the dream listed. Then each detail is worked on by *becoming* it.

> Get every person, every thing, every mood, and then work on these to *become* each one of them. Ham it up, and really transform yourself into each of the different items. Really *become* that thing . . . use your magic. Turn into that ugly frog or whatever is there – the dead thing, the live thing, the demon – and stop thinking. Lose your mind and come to your senses. Every little bit is a piece of the jigsaw puzzle, which together will make up a much larger whole – a much stronger, happier, more completely *real* personality
>
> 1976, p. 4

Becoming your images essentially involves identifying with them, describing them in the first person present tense and thus translating all the items or 'its' into 'I's'. This I-dentification with the features of imagery effectively reverses the tendency to project them outside of oneself and helps to promote ownership of and responsibility for them. Perls claims that if a person understands some aspect of his imagery each time he identifies with it in this way he increases in vitality and potential. This is because the energy which has been dissipated through projection is regained.

The understanding, however, is not simply an intellectual understanding. As Perls suggests, it does not come from thinking *about* the images but from sensing them; that is, from identifying the physical and emotional feelings, sensations, impressions and perceptions they evoke. Indeed, Perls suggests that each one of these different items, characters and parts should encounter the others, and that a dialogue should be allowed between opposing forces in order to enable an appreciation of differences and the integration of opposites. He claimed that every little bit of work attempted by the individual will result in 'the assimilation of something'.

ORDER OUT OF CHAOS

Assimilation of the projected features of the self by identifying with them progressively imposes order on the chaotic contents of the unconscious. Perls identified the organisational principle which creates order as the figure/ground formation. Just as a jigsaw puzzler attends first to those features of the overall pattern which stand out as the most easily identifiable shapes, forms or pictures so, according to Perls, the individual's interest and attention is drawn to features of the self which correspond with his or her most identifiable need. This need comes to the fore as the dominant reality. Hence the person's foremost need makes reality appear as it does.

> Bring the Sunday's *Herald Tribune* into a large family and watch the diversity of interests. Father seeks orientation in the business section, while mother skims the paper for basement bargains. Alec looks for instances of hardships of the suppressed classes, while Jack gets enthusiastic about a football match. Aunt Jenny indulges in the obituary columns, and the twins fight over the funnies.
>
> 1977, p. 51

Perls observes that the most important fact about the figure/background formation is that when a need is genuinely satisfied, the situation changes. The reality becomes different to that which existed when the situation was unfinished. Immediately one task is finished it recedes into the background, allowing the one which is currently the most important to come into the foreground. The situation which takes precedence over others is that which is most urgent at the time. This, he indicates, is the principle of organismic self-regulation, and it characterises healthy functioning. Health, or integration, therefore involves identifying with all vital functions in this way.

> If you understand the situation you are in, and let the situation you are in control your actions, then you learn how to cope with life.
>
> PERLS, 1976, p. 20

According to Perls, therefore, the fundamental principle of health is that 'you listen to the situation'.

Clearly the strategies outlined above are highly appropriate in the context of jigsaw puzzling and have an intuitive 'goodness of fit' when applied to everyday living. The question arises, however, as to whether this 'common sense' model finds more general support within scientific thinking. It does. In 1977 the Russian scientist Ilya Prigogine was awarded the Nobel Prize for his work on the thermodynamics of non-equilibrium systems. Not satisfied with the usual scientific endeavour of taking things apart, Prigogine was more concerned with putting the pieces back together again, and explaining how order and organisation can arise spontaneously out of apparent disorder and chaos. His transformation theory holds that all systems contain sub-systems that are continually fluctuating. Minor fluctuations have little effect on the structural integrity of the whole but a single fluctuation or combination of them may be sufficiently powerful to 'perturb' or shake up the pre-existing organisation of the system. At this point the elements of the old pattern may come into contact with each other in new ways and make new connections, so that the parts reorganise into a new whole or the system may totally disintegrate.

Accordingly nature has the potential to create new forms by allowing a shake-up of the old and it is this capacity which is the key to growth. The stability of the system is largely determined by its existing state of balance or equilibrium. If in or near equilibrium, minor fluctuations will be easily assimilated, with little effect or change in the system. In such systems very substantial fluctuations are needed to bring about any significant change. By contrast, far-from-equilibrium systems are very sensitive to external influences, and small inputs may produce substantial and dramatic results, as very small perturbations or fluctuations become amplified into structure-breaking waves. Prigogine's theory not only accounts for numerous physical processes at both the macro and micro levels but also 'sheds light on all sorts of "qualitative" or "revolutionary" change processes' (Toffler, 1984, p. xvii), including social, economic or political realities. It is relevant to processes of health and healing because within the framework of transformation theory dis-ease, whether physical or psychological, is clearly a perturbation of either major or minor magnitude. It is therefore a means whereby the system can, in Prigogine's terms, 'escape' to a higher level of organisation or integration, and thus to greater wholeness and health.

The tenets of transformation theory are already invoked in many complementary health care methodologies, notably subtle energy therapies such as homoeopathy and Bach flower remedies, and also in orthodox medicine. Immunisation, for example, involves inducing a mini-disease just sufficient to stimulate the body to produce protective antibodies, thereby 'producing an evolution toward biological complexity through intentionally perturbing the immune system' (Dossey, 1982, p. 89). Moreover, if perturbation of the body's integration never occurred it would be defenceless, because necessary protective mechanisms would not evolve. Clearly, therefore, perturbation or dis-ease and health are complementary. However, orthodox medicine frequently moves against perturbation rather than with it, opposing external threats to health with a vast array of medications. Unsurprisingly, from the perspective of transformation theory, antibiotic, antibacterial and anti-viral treatments often prove counterproductive, not only preventing development of the immune system by denying it the possibility of challenge, but also actually contributing to the development of super-resistant strains by perturbing viruses and bacteria.

The same criticism can be levelled at orthodox medicine in respect of its treatment of psychological disorder. Here again the emphasis is on avoidance of problems, either by use of anxiolytic and antidepressant drugs, or surgery which excises difficult memories, emotions or thought processes. Intriguingly, electro-convulsive therapy (ECT), which can prove effective in the treatment of some psychological conditions, for reasons as yet not understood by the medical profession, may be so because it provides a massive shock or perturbation to the brain, enabling it to become organised more coherently, rather than by eliminating thoughts, memories and feelings as has been widely speculated.

The central tenet of transformation theory, that order and organisation can arise spontaneously out of disorder and chaos through a process of self-organisation, lends support to the view advanced by Laing (1960) that mental illness or 'dis-order' frequently results in reintegration of the personal self, rather than disintegration. It also accounts for the effects claimed for psychotherapy. Ferguson (1982) proposes that reliving an incident in a state of highly focused inward attention perturbs the pattern of that specific memory and triggers reorganisation into a new pattern or structure. This may also explain the transformative power of processes such as relaxation, meditation and hypnosis, guided imagery, ancient and oriental healing systems, and psychological approaches which facilitate confrontation with problems as a means to their solution, rather than opposing them.

These different therapeutic approaches all have at their core the understanding that everything is in flux or process. Hence there is never any *one* solution, but a series; never one jigsaw to complete but a succession, each tending to become more complex, challenging, rich and rewarding. Hence, paradoxically, the final piece of the jigsaw is ultimately the most perturbing to the whole, because, after a brief interval the puzzle is likely to be totally dismantled and put away before another is embarked upon. Brian Keenan describes this process in the frontispiece to his book *An Evil Cradling*, as follows:

> I feel like a cross between Humpty Dumpty and Rip Van
> Winkle – I have fallen off the wall and suddenly awake I find
> all the pieces of me, before me.
> There are more parts than I began with.
> All the King's horses and all the King's men, cannot put
> Humpty together again.

And so it is in life. The following exercise provides an indication of 'work in progress' – the pieces of the current pattern which are in place, the connections established among them, and the gaps or unfinished areas which require further attention. It also provides, in relation to the exercises of the previous two chapters, an indication of whether or not the pattern is being worked in 'true colours'.

EXERCISE 11

Relax in whatever way suits you best and having done so imagine looking at the back of a tapestry that you are working on. Notice its size, scale and shape; the materials you are working with; their texture, quality and colours; and whether

the work is neat and tidy or knotted and tangled.

Observe the state of completeness of the tapestry; whether parts are complete or missing, or only odd bits have been attempted here and there; and whether any picture or pattern is discernible.

Note any feelings, sensations, impressions, memories or thoughts it gives rise to.

Now look at the other side of the tapestry, becoming aware as you do so that this represents your life. Note your reaction to this awareness. What is your first impression of the tapestry; and your overall assessment of it?

Observe the images, pictures and patterns. Are they as you imagined or intended?

What colours have been used and which predominate? How do you feel about them?

How much more of the tapestry needs to be completed? What features need to be completed and where; and with what materials and colours?

Is there anything you wish to change; any feature that you would like to unpick, remove or redo? How can you go about this? Do you have the appropriate tools at your disposal; or, if not, can you obtain them?

Do you know how you would like to complete the tapestry; or, if you don't wish to, what you would like to see in its place?

When you have addressed these issues return to ordinary awareness and record your experiences.

Commentary

Most people imagine very large tapestries that are much bigger than themselves. Sometimes they describe feeling overwhelmed by their size and scale. In one instance the tapestry was described as extending from ceiling to floor and wall to wall of a huge church, and vast, wall-sized tapestries are commonly imagined. Generally they are vertical, supported by frames, such as a shuttle or loom; hanging from wires or suspended in some other way. Some allow access on all sides whereas others are against or near to walls and are difficult for the person to work on. One woman described herself as feeling enclosed by her tapestry and others describe feeling trapped by it or claustrophobic. One young woman, who imagined it so close that it was pressing roughly against her face, smelling old and musty, and occupying all the space in front of her, felt agitated by it. Sometimes the tapestry is described lying horizontally across a loom or table. Hence one woman described herself looking down on a huge tapestry, which she initially thought was a carpet, until she realised that it was in fact a free standing wall-covering and did not have to lie down. She interpreted this as indicating that although she usually tends to look down on herself and 'to put herself down', she can be independent and stand up for herself.

Commonly the tapestries are delimited by frames or looms. One man reported thinking that his tapestry could have been larger had it not been restricted by a low stone ceiling. This comment is reminiscent of Paul Simon's observation that 'one man's ceiling is another man's floor' and perhaps suggests a low level of aspiration imposed either by himself or others. Some tapestries are not restricted by fixed boundaries. Many are described as circular, and some as able to grow and expand indefinitely. One man described a circular hologram which from both sides appeared as a vortex spiralling downwards into infinity, becoming ever more complex. Although multi-coloured its predominant colours were red and yellow, which were associated with hyperactivity in previous exercises where they had predominated, and black, which related to the 'blackspots' in his life.

The rear view of the tapestry is very variable. Some are very neat and tidy with threads carefully knotted and secure. Others may be neat and tidy but the threads may be too short to be knotted and may indicate insecurity or that the person is not tied down in any way. One man described the back of his carpet as 'organised chaos', carefully and deliberately crafted and 'workmanlike', whereas others describe it as a complete mess. The longer the strands of material being used the more likely they are to be tangled and untidy. One woman who visualised long straggling knotted pieces of thread at the back of her tapestry unknotted them because they looked untidy and imagined combing them so that they looked really neat. She liked the effect created and enjoyed doing it, but perhaps more significantly recognised that since embarking upon guided imagework she had begun to comb through her inner world to good effect also.

Frequently the back of the tapestry is very different from the front, which may surprise and even shock its creator. The back appears to represent the inner or private person; the person as they know themselves to be; while the front of the tapestry represents the public front, image or persona which is presented to the world. Very often appreciably more work has gone into the front than the back, so that it appears far more complete. However, such a front is superficial and tenuous, lacking substance and support 'behind the scenes'. One woman, despite having no very clear picture of what lay behind it, recognised the superficiality of her 'front' by the fact that the threads in it were too short to be tied to the underlying fabric and decided that she needed to change her outer self in order to bring it more into line with her inner self. She realised that the image she projected by her highly social and materialistic lifestyle gave no indication of her deeper, more spiritual interests, and provided little expression for them. Hence the imagery was a very appropriate representation of her current life situation.

In many cases, however, the work behind the scenes is reflected on the front of the tapestry and people are very aware of the relationship between the two areas. This is highlighted in the account of a man who indicated that he knew there was a horse on the other side of the tapestry because every time he drew a stitch through the material it reared up as though its reins were being pulled. This imagery clearly suggests awareness that what appears in public is influenced, although not necessarily controlled, by strings behind the scenes. Indeed when this man viewed the front of the tapestry he saw that a number of golden thoroughbred (and presumably highly strung) horses were galloping across it, apparently out of control, and could not be contained within its frame. Initially he denied that this frenetic scene was his creation but then conceded that every stitch he attempted caused chaos. This same man had, in a previous exercise, become aware only with hindsight that his attempts to 'keep others in stitches' through what he regarded as hilarious or impulsive behaviour had in fact been highly disturbing to them. Closer examination of the tapestry revealed that the apparent wildness of the horses was because they were running away in panic from indistinct scenes of carnage depicted in red to the right of the picture. Pondering this imagery later he remembered that in previous exercises the colour red was usually associated with females and the feminine, and that this feminine red energy was a persistent theme of his imagery. The tapestry and his almost stereotypically masculine profession suggest the possibility that he might be running away from his feminine side, giving full rein to his headstrong rational and intellectual features, perhaps to the extent of producing uncontrolled, apparently 'wild' ideas and the reckless, impulsive behaviour which appeared to characterise his childhood and youth. Certainly his consistently 'wild' and wonderful imagery has proved endlessly fascinating, highly stimulating and memorable to others in those groups of which he has been a member.

Many people realise from the outset that the task upon which they are engaged represents life's rich tapestry, but others do not and attempt to change it when they realise what it reveals about them, without success. In some instances people appear embarrassed by their own 'effrontery' in giving themselves more positive attributes and potentials than they ordinarily recognise or own up to. Thus one man wanted to change the half-completed picture of a medieval crowned king surrounded by deer in a forest and a woman wanted to change a huge golden dragon.

Some people find it difficult to live up to the image they project. One woman saw a lovely glass vase filled with deep blue delphiniums. Although she really liked the picture it made her anxious because she didn't know how to complete the vase realistically, so that it appeared as a transparent container and did not detract from the colours of the flowers within it, and the more she pondered the problem the more overwhelmed by anxiety she became. The concern with appearances in this instance suggests someone who wants the true colours of her inner self to be visible to others but finds this difficult to achieve. Another woman was somewhat surprised to discover that the black profile of Queen Victoria she had been working on in a corner at the back of the tapestry appeared on the front as a colourful, full-face centre piece, and gave no indication of the tense, edgy and sometimes severely depressed person she knows herself to be. Yet lengthy acquaintance with this woman does little to dispel the relaxed, cheerful and light-hearted impression she habitually displays to others.

Some people are disappointed by the front they portray. One woman admitted feeling very disappointed because the rich, deep colours and textures she was working with 'behind the scenes', appeared dull and lacking in vibrancy when viewed from the front, and the overall picture looked flat and 'in need of relief'. She acknowledged the tapestry as an accurate representation of her failure to show her true colours, and an indication that she needs to relieve her front or image by becoming more light, bright and vibrant. Another woman, who had no clear idea of any picture while working individually on quite unconnected blocks of red, maroon and cream, described herself as 'absolutely shocked' to see on the front of her tapestry a picture of a huge, old-fashioned, empty and driverless bus with bright chrome wheels. Although she claimed initially that it was quite meaningless for her, she subsequently acknowledged that it was fully consistent with her previous imagery in suggesting great but unused energy and someone needed in the driving seat.

However, people may be delighted with the image on the front of their tapestry. This was true of a young woman who imagined herself working on a tapestry of a Spanish dancing girl of which she had completed only the uppermost part of the head and the bottom of the skirt. This is intriguing in itself because it corresponds very accurately, not only with her previous imagery in relation to the chakras, but also the physical effects of a long-standing pituitary dysfunction. She was therefore astonished on turning over the tapestry to see only the blur of the Spanish girl's swirling skirt as she danced in a circle, and interpreted this as an accurate reflection of the feelings of greater vitality, energy and aliveness she had experienced by combining imagework with shiatsu. Another person was delighted by his tapestry which depicted an aerial view of a circular maze surrounded by cameos depicting scenes from his life. Initially he thought these were complete but then realised that some were still being worked on and others remained to be completed. He felt that the maze represented his path in life and was intrigued to discover what the complete picture would look like.

The woman described previously, who realised that her tapestry was free-standing and not a carpet as she had initially thought, was delighted by its colour, patterns and completeness, and reported that it has resolved a number of important issues for her. However, most tapestries are incomplete and they invariably highlight areas of a person's life that need attention. One woman imagined a garden in shades of yellows, golds and browns, which although 'absolutely gorgeous' needed balancing with something blue. She therefore added a clump of lupins, which she really liked. However, the border remained incomplete and she didn't know how to finish it. Nevertheless, although she didn't know how these parts 'would work out' she described feeling 'good' about them. Having completed the previous exercises on colour she realised that the blue lupins represented her need to allow her self-expression to flower. Another woman realised that her huge and powerful Chinese tiger lacked a foot, and was therefore insufficiently grounded, unbalanced and insecure.

Various sections of the tapestry may be incomplete rather than individual features. One woman's tapestry appeared as a country landscape in three sections which she equated with the past, present and future. The first section representing her past was worked in thick carpet wools which appeared like silks when viewed from the front. The middle section was worked in silks, indicating a better quality to her present life than her past; and she was able to see the incomplete third section, her future, being completed to her satisfaction as a rolling green landscape. Another woman's tapestry was partly incomplete on one side both front and back. The left side when viewed from the front appeared older, duller and incompatible with the right, although their theme was broadly the same. She associated a hayrick on the left side with her past and upon realising that she couldn't reconcile it with a large tree in the foreground on the right of the picture, she shrank both and moved them into the background where they became features of a much larger picture, giving her more un-worked area in the foreground, and a great deal of scope and possibilities in the newly created space. This tapestry seems to epitomise her creative and positive approach to life since her recent divorce.

Less positive but just as accurate is the imagery of a young woman whose enormous tapestry hung in a church so dark that none of its brighter colours were visible. From the front it showed her own face and neck in dull but normal skin and hair colours, but it was of such poor quality, with many holes and unfinished areas, that it made the portrait unpleasant. It was, she claimed, an accurate reflection of her very unhappy recent life and the numerous problems she faces. However, because the tapestry accurately reflects areas needing attention in a person's life it can provide insight into possibilities for change and the ways in which this can be achieved. Thus a woman whose tapestry portrayed a rather more brightly coloured garden that she had imagined herself working on but with a corner of 'mixed green and dark messy patches', realised that this related to her mixed feelings and confusion following the death of her husband, and that she wanted to bring more colour to her emotional life and achieve greater vitality. She was able to do this by imaginatively reworking the tapestry, and this helped her to 'work out' and through her feelings during a 'bad patch' in her life.

By working on her tapestry another woman was able to work out and resolve some of the long-standing difficulties of her life. Attempting the exercise for the first time she was unable to fathom the significance of imagery which provoked considerable anxiety: that of two inexpressive women in the sea although not swimming, facing towards but looking past each other, one to distant mountains in the background and the other to the ocean in the foreground. Although unaware of its significance she felt that she needed to rework the sea in what she described as a 'calm' green. Somewhat unsettled by the experience she was even more perturbed when later that day she began flicking through a magazine bought by a friend that afternoon and came upon the very picture she had imagined. This picture, a copy of which she included in her account of this exercise, depicts two Asian women in profile, one dressed in a red sari and staring past the other at some apparently snow-capped mountains in the distance, and the other dressed in gold looking into the blue sea in the foreground. Somewhat incongruously there is a thin crescent moon overhead in a pale blue sky.

When reviewing this picture in relation to imagery she had produced in previous exercises she realised that much of it evoked an overwhelming sense of floating in the sea, as if it was part of her. She realised that in a recently recurring dream she had a similar experience of being pushed to and from the shoreline as her breath became the tidal movements of the ocean. In an attempt to elucidate the meaning of these images which were being impressed so forcefully upon her she began to identify with every feature of the tapestry, and by so doing she became aware of intense and unfulfilled needs. While she felt that she wanted to hold on to the security of her past, represented by the safe and solid mountains, she recognised that these concealed painful memories which needed to be faced and resolved. She also craved new and exciting 'oceanic' experiences, although she regarded these as risky and terrifying, fearing that if she let go of the mountains she would be 'completely at sea' and might drown. Thus she was pulled in both directions, in exactly the manner of the tides in her dreams, between the painful but familiar past, and the unknown and disturbing future. In the process the present was totally overlooked. She realised that she lacked the positive qualities associated with the heart chakra and needed to develop her capacity for acceptance, forgiveness and unconditional love, to acquire understanding, openness, awareness and balance, hence her feeling that she needed to work green into the sea depicted in her tapestry.

Commenting some time later on her experiences she wrote, 'Relaxation and visualisation exercises have changed my life and continue to do so. By recognising my ties to the past and the need for change I have become aware of what I should address within myself. On a completely practical level my . . . plans have been abandoned . . . As a result of the exercises I have become much more aware of what is un/important in life'. She had come to realise that security and independence can be compatible and reconciled within herself, and that her preoccupation with the events of her past could be transformed into positive aids to self-discovery and self-healing in the here and now; 'a place where', she admitted 'until recently, I have spent little time'.

The transformative possibilities of the tapestry exercise are also highlighted in the account of a man who claimed that it had proved highly meaningful and enabled him to 'restructure' himself. On viewing the front of the tapestry initially he saw a carefree child dressed in red, playing with a red ball. He then noticed an ominous building on a hill in the background, and that a river running through the valley below remained incomplete. Suddenly a huge, black, menacing wolf appeared directly behind the child. This appeared to be out of place as though a panel had been superimposed on the front of the picture and not woven into the fabric underneath. He reported that following the exercise he felt 'slightly disturbed' by the presence of the wolf for the rest of the day and the thought that he had brought it into the world with him. It quickly disappeared, however, but over the next few weeks he continued to think about the tapestry and to work on it, imagining how it could change, and slowly transforming it into a more positive and meaningful pattern. This transformation is clear in the drawings which illustrate his personal account. Figure I depicts the original tapestry, which he interprets as follows.

> The child is me. It is gentle, carefree and happy; a very
> positive image – but vulnerable – hence the threat from the
> wolf. Red is a very vibrant colour, suggesting life and vitality.
> The ominous building is a place of great danger like the *Cave
> of Fear* or Theseus' labyrinth, holding great dangers to be
> overcome.

In Figure 2 there is a path leading up the hill to the doorway of the building, and on either side of it there are pieces of armour and weaponry. The river is complete and flows across the picture, separating the child from the wolf who no longer threatens the child, having gone back into the forest in the distance. The meaning of these features is quite clear to him.

> As the child moves up the hill he becomes stronger and better
> armed and protected against the dangers of the labyrinth. By
> the time he stands at the door he is a hardened fighter. From
> the child up to the building are all the aspects of him from soft
> to hard. Both are necessary: the hard protects the soft and the
> soft gives life to the hard.

A few weeks later he went for a walk and sat in some woods at the top of a hill watching people go by. As he did so he realised that he felt like a wild animal – shy rather than predatory, 'like a

Figure 1

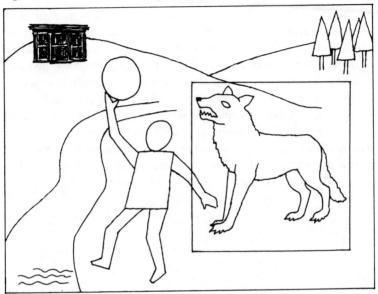

Figure 2

real wolf', and that the wolf from the tapestry was a 'wild' part of himself and not a monster. This awareness reminded him of Hesse's novel *Steppenwolf* in which the soul of the main character is divided between that of a man and a wolf. Thus by 'owning' his wolf he was put in touch with his soul, a connection which completed the tapestry, making it whole, and also healed the division within him. Fitting the wolf into place therefore solved the healing puzzle, enabling the 'wolf-man' to appreciate, as so many other people have done, that this is not a final solution but a new beginning; and realise – to paraphrase Carl Rogers – that when you accept yourself as you are, then you change.

Progressive Relaxation Augmented by Imagery

Find somewhere you can sit or lie with a reasonable degree of comfort. If too comfortable you are likely to drift into sleep, whereas if too uncomfortable or cold you are unlikely to sustain the motivation to achieve relaxation. Having done this, simply become aware of how your body is located in relation to its surroundings. Then close your eyes or, if this is not possible because of organic impairment or surgery, or difficult because of contact lenses, focus on a fixed point or object within your line of vision, such as a mark on a wall, ceiling or floor.

Then gradually draw your attention from your surroundings, and bring it to the boundary between your body and adjacent surfaces. As you do so, notice whether the contact is uncomfortable or painful, and adjust your position so as to maximise comfort and minimise pain. You may find that you need to remove restrictive clothing, shoes, jewellery or spectacles. At any point during the exercise when you feel the need to adjust your position to reduce discomfort or pain, do so.

When you are positioned as comfortably as possible turn your attention to your feelings. How *do* you feel? Do you feel silly or guilty about taking time to do the exercise?

How self-conscious are you? Are you worried about being seen by others or, if doing the exercise in company, by their proximity, and your body smells or sounds? Are you worried about falling off to sleep or snoring, or because you may not be able to 'do' the exercise? Your reactions may reflect some of the basic anxieties of your life and relate to some of the tensions you encounter as you proceed with the exercise. If during any part of the exercise thoughts, feelings, memories or impressions come to mind, make a mental note of them as they may have similar significance.

Now bring your attention to your toes. Without moving the overall position of your feet, push your toes down and away from you, as far as they will go, noticing as you do so the effect of this movement on the rest of your feet and legs. Sustain this action until you can identify the extent of its effects throughout your body and then let go. Repeat this movement two or three times, or as many times as is necessary for you to become aware of its full implications for the rest of your body. When you have done this, flex your toes upwards and towards you as far as you can, and sustain this action until you can feel its effects not only locally in your feet and legs, but also in more distant areas of your body. Then simply let go. Repeat the action three times.

Now rotate each foot through 360 degrees, first in one direction, then the other, noticing any grinds, clicks or other noises and accompanying sensations. Then let go, and for a few moments simply experience the sensations in your feet and legs.

It is important to recognise the sensation of 'letting go' in contrast to that of tightening and how both are achieved. The actions are sustained in order to enhance awareness of how muscle tension is achieved in a given muscle group and the effects it has on other parts of the body. This may highlight habitual tensions and pain, and prompt awareness of the situations in which these typically occur. The movements therefore have implications for the mind/body system as a whole and have particular relevance to the phenomenon of 'referred' pain, so through these exercises it may be possible to understand how the big toe, for example, can effect pain elsewhere in the body.

Now, bring your attention to your thighs, and press them firmly downwards against the chair or floor, noting the effect of this action throughout your body. When you have identified the furthest point of influence, let go. Then repeat the action three times.

Then, without moving the overall position of your legs, draw your inner thighs together and hold them thus, once again noticing the effect of this movement on the rest of your body before letting go. Repeat this three times.

Now bring your attention to your buttocks and press them down as hard as you can against the adjacent surface. As you are doing so ask yourself what in life you tend to bear down on or in what situations this action seems familiar. Then let go. Repeat the action three times, noting its effects throughout the body. Then draw in or 'dimple' the sides of your buttocks and sustain this action until you are aware of its implications for the remainder of your body, before letting go. Repeat this three times.

When you have done this, allow your legs and feet to 'flop' and take a few seconds to become aware of the sensations within them. If you encounter any residual tension work on it by tightening and letting go of the relevant muscles, and allow the latter sensation to generalise or spread throughout your lower limbs.

Having done this, bring your attention to your lower back. Without shifting your overall position push it against the adjacent surface and hold it there, noting its implications for the rest of the body. This is particularly important given that the lower back is a major stress point where bodily tensions typically manifest. Then let go and repeat three times. As you do so, ask yourself whether you generally feel that you have your back to the wall or feel 'up against it'.

Now push your lower back forward as far as you can, arching it, and holding this action until you can feel its effects throughout your body. Before you let go, ask yourself whether you have ever been described as 'arch' in manner or whether you frequently get your back up and, if so, about what. Now alternate the two movements, so that you are squirming like a belly-dancer. Continue for some moments before letting go.

Bring your attention to your stomach. Pull it in as far as you can and hold it so you can identify the effect of this action throughout your body. As you do so, ask yourself what you may be holding in and then let go. Repeat three times, and then allow your stomach and back to flop. Take a few moments to experience this sensation and allow it to spread throughout your lower body.

When you have done this, bring your attention to your chest. Notice your heartbeat. Is it quiet and regular or loud and irregular; pounding or racing? Pay attention to your breathing. Is it shallow, deep, regular, irregular, difficult or easy?

Now imagine that tattooed on your chest you have a large, exotic and colourful butterfly which has just emerged from its cocoon. Breathe in deeply and as you do so imagine the butterfly spreading its wings to their full extent. At the point where the butterfly seems about to fly off, breathe out and watch how this affects it. Repeat this five times.

Still paying attention to your breathing, raise your shoulders and observe the effect on the butterfly. Then drop them, observing the effect. Push your shoulders back and observe the effect on the butterfly. Then, doing likewise, draw your shoulders forward and hold in this position before allowing them to return to their former position.

Still attending to your shoulders, raise them to your ears and hold them in that position, noting the effects on the upper parts of the body, before letting them drop. Repeat three times. Raise each shoulder independently and as you do so ask yourself whether you have ever been described as having a chip on the shoulder. If so, which shoulder seems to be the likely candidate? Rotate each shoulder through 360 degrees, and then both shoulders together, observing the effect on the neck, chest, back and elsewhere.

Having done this, bring your attention down the right arm to your hand. Imagine that you are holding in that hand an ancient gold coin, the only one of its kind in existence and therefore priceless. Grip it so tightly that there is no danger whatever of it slipping from your hand, and as you do so observe the effects of this action, not only in your hand, lower arm, upper arm and shoulder, but also on your neck, head, jaw and elsewhere in your body. Follow the effects of the actions as far as they extend and, having reached the furthest point of influence, ask yourself what in life you are holding on to; what you have a firm grip on. Then, when the action is becoming too painful to sustain further, carefully transfer the coin to your left hand, once again gripping it so that there is no danger of it being lost. Tighten the grip and as you follow the effect to its furthest extremity, ask yourself which hand has the stronger grip. Then ask yourself whether you tend to hold on to different things with this side of yourself than the other and what they are.

When you have answered the questions, toss the coin from the left hand to the right and then throw it away, allowing the fingers of both hands to fall loosely as you so do and your arms to fall by your sides. Ask yourself what you have let go of in life, and what you need to let go of, and allow yourself to let go of them and the accompanying tensions.

Now imagine that the floor beneath you is beginning to rise. Resist this as forcefully as you can, spreading the fingers and the palms of your hands flat and pushing downwards. The floor continues to rise, forcing your hands upwards and obliging you to brace your arms against it. If the floor continues to rise you will be sandwiched against the ceiling, so press downwards with all your strength. The floor continues to rise nevertheless until, just as it seems that you cannot resist further, the floor falls away, and your hands and arms with it. Allow your arms to 'flop' at your sides, and take a few seconds to experience this sensation and allow it to spread.

Having done so, bring your attention to your neck. Shift your head 180 degrees to the right, holding this position for a few seconds; then 180 degrees to the left, doing likewise. Then rotate your head through 360 degrees, taking note of aches, pains and any other sensations. Be aware of the sheer weight of your head and the effort involved in keeping it upright. Then let it flop forward.

Bring your attention up the back of your neck and across your scalp. Try to wiggle your scalp and your ears if you can.

Raise your eyebrows and hold the action, observing the effects on the rest of your head and face. Then drop your brows. Now pull your brows down towards your chin and hold the action. Feel the effects of these movements on your head and neck. Now let go.

Bringing your attention to your nose, flare the nostrils as widely as possible. Do things 'get up your nose'? Tighten the nostrils and, as you do so, ask yourself whether you tend to sniff or turn your nose up at things. Stretch your upper lip downwards and hold this action. Do you usually try to keep a stiff upper lip?

Press your lips tightly together. As you hold this action notice its effects on the remainder of your face and ask yourself whether you are tight-lipped about anything.

Now clench your teeth as tightly as possible. Do you feel you grit your teeth against life? Or do you tend to bite off more than you can chew? Do you bite back what you want to say or snap at people? Notice the effects of this action on the muscles of the face, head, neck and chest. Do you tend to suffer pain in any of these areas?

Now shift your jaw from side to side. Notice the effects on the temples and elsewhere. Ask yourself whether your life is a grind.

Let your mouth hang open. It is impossible to be fully relaxed while the mouth is shut because it is necessary to tighten the jaw muscles to effect this. How do you feel when open-mouthed?

Now breathe in though your nose and out through your open mouth, observing how this feels and its effects on the body. Continue to breathe in this way for a few moments, then bring your attention back to your feet. Scan your body upwards noting any tightness, discomfort or pain in any region, and let go of it by alternately tightening and releasing the muscles there. If the tightness, discomfort or pain persists, make a mental note of it. This is significant because it needs to be dealt with before full relaxation can be achieved.

To the count of 1 – let go of the tightness in your feet and legs; 2 – let go of the tightness in your lower back and stomach; 3 – let go of the tightness in your arms, shoulders and chest; 4 – let go of your head; and 5 – let go of the tightness in your jaw.

Spend a few moments becoming aware of the sensations throughout your body. If relaxed your limbs should feel heavy and warm.

Now imagine yourself in a pleasant situation where you can feel relaxed, at ease, comfortable and secure. Notice whether you are alone, with other people or animals, and whether these are known to you or not. Pay attention to the sights, sounds, smells and sensations of this place, and how you feel in it. Notice all the details of the scene as vividly as possible and allow yourself to enjoy being there.

Spend some time exploring the situation and becoming fully

acquainted with it. Having done so ask yourself the following questions.

- How easy or otherwise do you find this imaginary exercise?
- What aspects of this imaginary situation do you find particularly restful or relaxing?
- What features of everyday life are you getting away from in this situation? If it isn't clear to you, compare the imaginary situation with the usual situations of your everyday life.
- What might this imaginary exercise tell you about the stressors in your life?

When you have answered these questions remember that this imaginary place is always there for you to go to. You carry it around inside yourself and can go there whenever you wish.

Prepare to open your eyes and return your awareness to your surroundings. Now do so and take a few moments to orientate yourself before recording the significant features of your experience, including your answers to the questions.

Gold-prospecting

Take some time to relax in whatever way best suits you. Now imagine that you are in open countryside on a fine day and that you have come across a shallow stream, and lying beside it, apparently discarded, gold-prospecting equipment; a large pan, sieve, waders, shovel, leather pouch, glass phial, small set of scales, polishing cloth, diary and pencil.

Equipping yourself in whatever way seems appropriate, you step into the middle of the stream and begin to pan for gold, observing what you get in the pan and sifting it carefully. When you think you have found gold, take it from the pan, wash it, dry it carefully and save it, putting large pieces in the leather pouch, and smaller specks and bits of gold dust in the phial. Continue panning for gold until you are sure that there is no more to be found. Then return to the side of the stream, and carefully weigh the gold and record the total amount in your diary.

Having done so take some time to relate these specks and pieces of gold to your present life, and record your observations.

It is recommended that this exercise is repeated on a daily basis, preferably at night before going to sleep, when the day's events can be reviewed in this way and that you keep a record of your discoveries. With practice you should find an improvement in your ability to find, recognise, appreciate and extract gold from your everyday life.

Bibliography

Abse, D.W., van der Castle, R.L., Buxton, R.L., Demars, W.D., Brown, J. P. & Kirschner, L.G. (1974) 'Personality and, behavioural characteristics of lung cancer patients'. *Journal of Psychosomatic Research*, 18, pp. 101–13.

Achterberg, J., Simonton, S.M. & Simonton, O.C. (1977) 'Psychology of the exceptional cancer patient: A description of patients who outlive predicted life expectancies'. *Psychotherapy: theory research and practice*, 14, 4 Winter, pp. 416–22.

Adams, C. & Laurikietis, R. (1976) *The Gender Trap. Book I. Education and Work*. London: Virago.

Argyle, M. & Henderson, M. (1985) *The Anatomy of Relationships*. Harmondsworth: Penguin.

Asistent, N.M. with Duffy, P. (1991) *Why I Survive AIDS*. New York: Simon & Schuster.

Assagioli, R. 'Psychosynthesis'. In *The New Age: an anthology of essential writings*, ed. W. Bloom, pp. 124–34. London: Rider.

Bach, E. (1931) *Heal Thyself: an explanation of the real cause and cure of disease*. Saffron Walden: C.W. Daniel & Co. Ltd.

Bahnson, C.B. & Bahnson, M.B. (1966) 'Role of the Ego defences: denial and repression in the etiology of malignant neoplasm'. *Annals of the New York Academy of Science*, pp. 827–45, 145(3).

Bahnson, C.B. (1975) 'Emotional personality characteristics of cancer patients'. In *Oncological Medicine* ed. A. Sutnick. University Park Press.

Bahnson, C.B. (1980) 'Stress and cancer'. *Psychosomatics*, 21, pp. 75–81.

Bancom, D. & Danker-Brown, P. (1979) 'Influence of sex roles in the development of learned helplessness'. *Journal of Consulting and Clinical Psychology*, 4 47, pp. 928–36.

Bandura, A. (1977) 'Self-efficiency: towards a unifying theory of behavioural change'. *Psychological Review*, 84, pp. 191–215.

Beattie, G. (1979) 'That's no way to treat a lady'. *Bulletin of the British Psychological Society*, 32, 97–9.

Beattie, G. (1980) 'Separating the men from the boys'. *Bulletin of the British Psychological Society*, 33, 51–3.

Bek, L. & Holden, R. (1989) 'Colour consciousness'. *Caduceus*, Spring, pp. 12–13.

Berke, J.H. (1979) *I Haven't Had To Go Mad Here: the psychotic's journey from dependence to autonomy*. Harmondsworth: Penguin.

Berne, E. (1974) *What Do You Do After You Say Hello? The psychology of human destiny*. Great Britain: André Deutsch Ltd.

Bowlby, J. (1951) *Maternal Care and Mental Health*. Geneva: World Health Organisation.

Brace, A. (1993) 'Experts hail cure for child dyslexia'. *The Mail On Sunday*, June 27, p. 10.

Branson, L. (1988) 'Chromotherapy: Nature's healing rainbow'. *Attitudes*, No. 9, Spring, pp. 4–7.

Broverman, J.K., Broverman, D.M., Clarkson, F.E., Rosenkrantz, P.S. & Vogel, S.R. (1970) 'Sex role stereotypes and clinical judgments of mental health'. *Journal of Consulting and Clinical Psychology*, No. 34, pp. 1–7.

Brown, G. & Harris, T. (1978) *The Social Origins of Depression*. London: Tavistock.

Buchan, N. (1991) 'Standing on their own roots'. *Observer*, Sunday 3 March.

Calhoun, L.G., Cheney, T. & Dawes, A.S. (1974) 'Locus of control, self-reported depression and perceived causes of depression'. *Journal of Consulting and Clinical Psychology*, 4, 42, p. 735.

Capra, F. (1988) *Uncommon Wisdom: conversations with remarkable people*. London: Rider.

Chesler, P. (1974) *Women and Madness*. London: Allen Lane.

Cohen, J. (1982) 'Psychological androgyny – stressful life events'. *Journal of Personality and Social Psychology*, 43, pp. 145–53.

Collee, J. (1990) 'A doctor writes'. *Observer*, Sunday 30 December, p. 50.

Collee, J. (1991) 'A doctor writes'. *Observer*, Sunday 20 January, p. 58.

Coopersmith, S. (1967) *The Antecedents of Self-Esteem*. San Francisco and London: W.H. Freeman Co.

Cousins, N. (1981) *Anatomy of an illness as perceived by the patient: Reflections on healing and regeneration*. New York and London: Bantam.

Coward, R. (1992) 'Are you really going mental?' *Observer*, Sunday 22 November, p. 56.

Crumbaugh, J. & Maholick, L. (1964) 'An experimental study in existentialism: The approach to Frankl's concept of noogenic neurosis'. *Journal of Clinical Psychology*, 20, pp. 200–7.

Davidson, J.D. (1972) Religious belief as an independent variable. *Journal for the Scientific Study of Religion*, 11, pp. 67–75.

De Bono, E. (1990) *Six Thinking Hats*. Harmondsworth: Penguin.

De Fleur, M.L. (1964) 'Occupational roles as portrayed on television'. *Public Opinion Quarterly*, 28, 57–74.

Derogatis, L., Abeloff, M. & Melistratos, N. (1979) 'Psychological coping, mechanisms and survival time in metastatic breast cancer'. *Journal of the American Medical Association*, 242, pp. 1504–8.

Deutsch, F. (1975) 'Effects of sex of subject and story characters on pre-schoolers' perceptions of affective responses and intrapersonal behaviour in story sequences'. *Developmental Psychology*, 114, pp. 112–15.

Dohrmann, A. (1975) 'A gender profile of children's education TV'. *Journal of Communication*, 24, p. 4.

Donaldson, M. (1992) *Human Minds: an exploration*. Harmondsworth: Penguin.

Dossey, L. (1982) *Space, Time and Medicine*. Boulder and London: Shambhala.

Dougherty, T.J. (1980) 'Photosensitization of malignant tumours'. *Adjuncts To Cancer Therapy*, ed. S. Economon, Philadelphia: Lea & Febiger.

Dougherty, T.J. (1989) 'Photoradiation therapy – new approaches'. *Seminars in Surgical Oncology*, 6–16.

Drury, N. (1991) *The Elements of Shamanism*. Shaftesbury, Dorset: Element Books.

Duck, S. (ed. with Silver, R.C.) (1990) *Personal Relationships and Social Support*. London: Sage.

Dwyer, J.W., Clarke, L.L. & Miller, M.K. (1990) 'The effect of religious concentration and affiliation on county cancer mortality rates'. *Journal of Health and Social Behaviour*, Vol. 31, June, pp. 185–202.

Ellison, C.W. & Firestone, I.J. (1974) 'Development of interpersonal trust as a function of self-esteem, target status and target style'. *Journal of Personality and Social Psychology*, 29, pp. 655–63.

Ellison, C.W. (1983) 'Spiritual well-being: conceptualization and measurement'. *Journal of Psychology and Theology*, 11(4) pp. 330–40.

Enstrom, J.E. (1975) 'Cancer mortality among Mormons'. *Cancer*, 36, pp. 825–41.

Enstrom, J.E. (1978) 'Cancer and total mortality among active Mormons'. *Cancer*, 42, pp. 1943–51.

Erikson, E. (1950) 'Growth and crises of the "healthy personality"'. In *Symposium on the Healthy Personality Vol 2: Problems of Infancy and Childhood*, ed. M.J.E. Senn, New York: Josiah Macy Jnr. Foundation.

Evans, C. (1974) *Cults of Unreason*. London: Routledge & Kegan Paul.

Eysenck, H.J. (1985) 'Personality, cancer and cardiovascular disease: a causal analysis'. *Personality and Individual Differences*, 5, pp. 535–57.

Eysenck, H.J. (1988) 'Personality, stress and cancer: prediction and prophylaxis'. *British Journal of Medical Psychology*, 61, pp. 57–75.

Frankl, V.E. (1969) *The Will to Meaning: foundations and applications of Logotherapy*. London: Souvenir Press.

Frankl, V.E. (1969a) *The Doctor and the Soul*. London: Souvenir Press.

Freud, S. (1915) *Repression*. Penguin Freud Library Vol. 2. Harmondsworth: Penguin.

Freud, S. (1933) *New Introductory Lectures on Psychoanalysis*. Penguin Freud Library Vol. 2. Harmondsworth: Penguin.

Fromm, E. (1941) *Escape From Freedom*. New York: Rhinehart.

Fromm, E. (1947) *Man For Himself*. New York: Rhinehart.

Fromm, E. (1951) *Psychoanalysis and Religion*. London: Gollancz.

Fromm, E. (1980) *Greatness and Limitations of Freud's Thought*. London: Cape.

Gallegos, E.S. (1983) 'Animal imagery, the chakra system and psychotherapy'. *The Journal of Transpersonal Psychology*, Vol. 15, No. 2, pp. 125–36.

Bibliography

Gallegos, E.S. (1990) *The Personal Totem Pole: Animal imagery the chakras, and psychotherapy*, 2nd edn. Santa Fe: Moon Bear Press.

Ganster, D.C. & Victor, B. (1988) 'The impact of social support on mental and physical health'. *British Journal of Medical Psychology*, 61, pp. 17–36.

Gibbs, H.W. & Achterberg-Lawlis, J. (1978) 'Spiritual values and death anxiety: implications for counselling with terminal cancer patients'. *Journal of Counselling Psychology*, 25, No. 6, pp. 563–9.

Gillman, P. & Gillman, L. (1993) 'Heart attack'. *The Sunday Times Review*, 30 May, pp. 1–2.

Goldberg, J.G. (1989) 'Psychosis of the body, cancer of the mind: the isomorphic relation between cancer and schizophrenia'. *Psychological Abstracts*, Vol. 14, Part 1, pp. 21–36.

Gove, W.K. & Tudor, J. (1972) 'The relationship between sex roles, marital status and mental illness'. *Social Forces*, 51, p. 34.

Graham, H. (1990) *Time, Energy and The Psychology of Healing*. London: Jessica Kingsley.

Graham, H. (1992) *The Magic Shop: an imaginative guide to self healing*. London: Rider.

Greer, S. & Morris, T. (1975) 'Psychological attributes of women who develop breast cancer: a controlled study'. *Journal of Psychosomatic Research*, 19, pp. 147–53.

Greer, S. & Watson, M. (1987) 'Mental adjustment to cancer, its measurement and prognostic significance'. *Cancer Surveys*, 6, pp. 439–53.

Grossarth-Maticek, Bastiaans, J. & Kanazir, D.T. (1985) 'Psychosocial factors as strong predictors of mortality from cancer, ischaemic heart disease and stroke: The Yugoslav prospective study'. *Journal of Psychosomatic Research*, 29, pp. 167–76.

Hamachek, D.E. (1982) *Encounters With Others: interpersonal relationships and you*. New York CBS College Publishing: Holt Rhinehart Winston.

Hancock, C.R. (1963) 'Lady and woman'. *American Speech*, 38, pp. 234–5.

Harlow, H.F. (1961) 'The development of affectional patterns in infant monkeys'. In *Determinants of Infant behaviour*, Vol. 2, ed. B.F. Foss. London: Methuen.

Hewitt, L. (1986) Women and drugs. Paper presented at the annual *Standing Conference on Drug Abuse*, York University.

Hochheimer, W. (1969) *The Psychotherapy of C.G. Jung*. Trans. Hildegard Nagel, New York: G.P. Putnam's Sons for the C.G. Jung Foundation for Analytical Psychology.

Hucklebridge, F. (1993) *Psychoneuroimmunology*. Seminar presented to The Biology Society, Keele University, 3 February.

Jackson, R. (1992) 'Psychotherapy: Beyond a phoney love'. *Leading Edge* 6, pp. 14–15.

Jarvis, G.K. & Northcott, H.C. (1987) 'Religion and differences in morbidity and mortality'. *Social Science and Medicine*, 25, pp. 813–24.

Jourard, S. (1971) *The Transparent Self*. New York: Van Nostrand & Co.

Jung, C.G. (1953) *Two Essays on Analytical Psychology*, Vol. 7, The Collected Works of C.G. Jung, Princeton: Princetown University Press (Bollingen Series XX), London: Routledge & Kegan Paul.

Jung, C.G. (1954) *The Archetypes and the Collective Unconscious*, Collected Works of C.G. Jung, Vol. 9 as above.

Jung, C.G. (1955) *Mysterium Coniunctionis*, Vol. 14, Collected Works of C.G. Jung (as above).

Jung, C.G. (1960) *The Structure and Dynamics of the Unconscious*. The Collected Works of C.G. Jung, Vol 8 (as above).

Jung, C.G. (1972) *Memories, Dreams, Reflections*. Trans. by R. & C. Winston, Glasgow Collins: Fontana.

Jung, C.G. (1978) *Psychology and The East*. London: Routledge & Kegan Paul.

Kaczorowski, J.M. (1989) 'Spiritual, well-being and anxiety in adults diagnosed with cancer'. *Hospice Journal*, Vol. 5, part 3–4, pp. 105–16.

Kalweit, H. (1988) *Dreamtime and Inner Space: The world of the shaman*. Trans. W. Wunsche London and Boston: Shambhala.

Karagulla, S. (1967) *Breakthrough to Creativity*. Santa Monica, Los Angeles, California: C.A. De Vorss.

Keenan, B. (1993) *An Evil Cradling*. London: Arrow.

Kempe, R.S. & Kempe, H. (1978) *Child Abuse*. London: Fontana.

Klaus, M.H., Jerauld, R., Kreger, N., McAlpine, W., Steffa, M. & Kennell, J.H. (1972) 'Maternal attachment – importance of the first post-partum days'. *New England Journal of Medicine*, 286, pp. 460–63.

Krishnamurti, J. (1971) *You are the World*. New York: Harper & Row.

Laing, R.D. (1960) *The Divided Self*. London: Tavistock.

Laing, R.D. (1972) *Self and Others*. Harmondsworth: Penguin.

Laing, R.D. (1976) *The Facts of Life*. Harmondsworth: Penguin.

Laing, R.D. (1978) *The Politics of the Family*. Harmondsworth: Penguin.

Lakoff, R. (1975) *Language and Woman's Place*. New York: Harper Colophon Books.

LeShan, L. (1959) 'Psychological states as factors in the development of malignant disease: a critical review'. *Journal of National Cancer Institute*, 22, pp. 1–18.

LeShan, L. (1966) 'An emotional life-history pattern associated with neoplastic disease'. *Annals of the New York Academy of Science*, 125, 780–93.

LeShan, L. (1989) *Cancer As A Turning Point: A handbook for people with cancer, their families and health professionals*. Bath: Gateway Books.

Levin, J.S. & Markides, K.S. (1986) 'Religious attendance and subjective health'. *Journal for the Scientific Study of Religion*, 25, pp. 31–40.

Levin, J.S. & Schiller, P.L. (1987) 'Is there a religious factor in health?' *Journal of Religion and Health*, 26, pp. 9–36.

Levine, B.H. (1991) *Your Body Believes Every Word You Say: The language of body/mind connection*. Boulder Creek, CA: Aslan Publishing.

Levy, S.M. (1984) 'The expression of affect and its biological correlates: mediating mechanisms of behaviour and disease'. In *Emotions in Health and Illness: applications to, clinical practice*, eds C. Van Dyke, L. Temoshok & L.S. Zegans. New York: Grune and Stratton.

Liberman, J. (1991) *Light: Medicine of the Future*. Santa Fe: Bear & Co.

Liberman, J. (1992) 'Light medicine of the future'. *Caduceus*, Summer, pp. 22–5.

Lidz, T. (1975) *The Origin and Treatment of Schizophrenic Disorders*. London: Hutchinson & Co. Ltd.

Llewelyn, S. (1981) 'Psychology and women: an examination of mental health problems'. *Bulletin of The British Psychological Society*, 34, pp. 60–3.

Maddi, S. (1967) 'The existential neurosis'. *Journal of Abnormal Psychology*, 72, pp. 311–25.

Mahler, M. (1968) *On Human Symbiosis and the Vicissitudes of Individuation, Vol. 1. Infantile Psychosis*. New York: International Universities Press.

Maslow, A.H. (1968) *Towards a Psychology of Being*, 2nd edn. New York: Van Nostrand.

Meares, A. (1977) 'Atavistic regression as a factor in the remission of cancer.' *Medical Journal of Australia*, 2, pp. 132–3.

Meyer, J. & Sobieszek, B. (1972) 'Effects of child's sex on adult interpretations of its behaviour'. *Developmental Psychology*, 6, Vol. 208 pp. 42–8.

Moberg, D.O. & Brusik, P.M. (1978) 'Spiritual well-being: a neglected subject in quality of life research'. *Social Indicators Research*, 5, pp. 303–23.

Moos, R.H. (1964) 'Personality factors associated with rheumatoid arthritis: review'. *Journal of Chronic Disorders*, 17, p. 41.

Moos, R.H. & Solomon, G.F. (1965) 'Psychological comparisons between women with rheumatoid arthritis and their non-arthritic sisters I: Personality test and interview rating data'. *Psychosomatic Medicine*, 27, 135.

Myss, C.M. (1991a) 'Business and intuition'. *Leading Edge*, Autumn, 5, pp. 7–8.

Myss, C.M. (1991b) 'Intuition as a pre-requisite for 21st century medicine: integrating subtle energy and consciousness'. Presentation to *Energy and Medicine: the first networking conference*, London: Nov–Dec.

Myss, C.M. (1991c) 'Redefining the healing process'. In W. Bloom, (ed.) *The New Age: an anthology of essential writings*. London: Rider.

Myss, C.M. (1992) 'The intimate language of wounds: why people don't heal'. *Energy and Medicine Networking Journal*, pp. 7–11. Collated London: S.K. McNeill.

McDonald, S.F. (1982) 'Effect of visible light waves on arthritis pain: a controlled study'. *International Journal of Biosocial Research*, 3, No. 2, pp. 49–54.

Newton, B.W. (1980) 'The use of hypnosis in the treatment of cancer patients: A five year report'. Presented at the Annual Science Programme of the American Society of Clinical Hypnosis, Minneapolis.

Oren, D.A. & Brainard, G.C. (1991) 'Treatment of Seasonal Affective Disorder with green and red light'. *American Journal of Psychiatry*, 148: 4 April.

Ott, J. (1991) Foreword to Liberman, J. *Light: Medicine of the Future*, pp. vv–xvii. Santa Fe: Bear & Co.

Palontzian, R.F. & Ellison, C.W. (1982) 'Loneliness, spiritual well-being and quality of life'. In L.A. Peplan & D. Perlman (eds) *Loneliness: a sourcebook of current theory, research and therapy*, pp. 224–37. New York: Wiley Interscience.

Perls, F.S. (1972) *In and Out the Garbage Pail*. New York: Bantam.

Perls, F.S. (1973) Preface to Perls, F.S., Hefferline, R.F. & Goodman, P. *Gestalt Therapy: Excitement and Growth in the Human Personality*. Harmondsworth: Penguin.

Bibliography

Perls, F.S. (1976a) *Gestalt Therapy Verbatim*. New York: Real People Press, Bantam.
Perls, F.S. (1976) *The Gestalt Approach and Eye Witness to Therapy*. New York: Bantam.
Perls, F.S. (1977) 'Theory and technique of personality integration'. In *Gestalt Is*, ed. J.O. Stevens. New York, Bantam, pp. 44–69.
Pervin, L.A. (1993) *Personality: Theory and Research*, 6th edn. New York: John Wiley & Sons.
Piaget, J. (1930) *The Child's Concept of Physical Causality*. London: Kegan Paul.
Popay, J. (1992) *Women's Health Matters*, ed. H. Roberts, London: Routledge, reported in A. Karpf, 'Sick and tired of being tired', *The Guardian*, Friday 29 May.
Putney, S. & Putney, G.J. (1974) *The Adjusted American: Normal Neuroses in the Individual and Society*. New York: Harper & Row.
Rheingold, H.L. & Cook, K.V (1975) 'The content of boys' and girls' rooms as an index of parents' behaviour'. *Child Development*, 46, pp. 459–63.
Roet, B. (1986) *Hypnosis: A gateway to better health*. London: J.M. Dent & Co.
Roet, B. (1988) Address given at the World Health Day, Holistic Health Centre, Farnham, April.
Roos, P.E. & Cohen, L.H. (1987) 'Sex roles and support as moderators of life stress adjustment'. *Journal of Personality and Social Psychology*, 52, pp. 576–85.
Roney-Dougal, S.M. (1989) 'The psychophysiology of the yogic chakra system'. *Caduceus*, No. 8, pp. 8–11.
Rogers, C.M. (1961) *On Becoming a Person: a therapist's view of psychotherapy*. London: Constable.
Rogers, C.R. (1980) *A Way of Being*. Boston: Houghton Mifflin.
Rogers, C.R. & Sanford, R.C (1989) 'Client-centred psychotherapy'. In H.I. Kaplan and B.J. Saddock (eds) *Comprehensive Textbook of Psychiatry*, Baltimore: Williams & Wilkins, pp. 1842–51.
Roos, P.E. & Cohen, L.H. (1987) 'Sex roles and social support as moderators of life stress adjustment'. *Journal of Personality and Social Research*, 52, pp. 576–85.
Roos, P.E. & Cohen, L.H. (1987) 'Sex roles and stressful life events'. *Journal of Personality and Social Psychology*, 32, 145–53.
Rutter, M. (1981) *Maternal Deprivation Reassessed*. Harmondsworth: Penguin.
Sarason, I.G., Sarason, B.R. & Pierce, G.R. (1988) 'Social support, personality and health': In *Topics in Health Psychology*, eds. S. Maes, C.D. Spielberger, P.B. Defares & I.G. Sarason. New York: Wiley & Sons, pp. 245–55.
Sarason, B.R., Sarason, I.G. & Pierce, G.R (1990) *Social Support: a transactional view*. New York: Wiley.
Scarlett, C. (1987) 'Helping poets help the aged'. *Pedigree Digest*, Vol. 14, No. 1, pp. 5, 11.
Schofield, W. (1964) *Psychotherapy: the purchase of friendship*, Englewood Cliffs, New Jersey: Prentiss Hall.
Schmale, A. & Iker, S.H. (1966) 'The effect of hopelessness and the development of cancer: 1. Identification of uterine cervical cancer in women with atypical cytology'. *Psychosomatic Medicine*, 28, pp. 714–21.
Schmale, A. & Iker, S.H. (1971) 'Hopelessness as a predictor of cervical cancer'. *Social Science and Medicine*, 5, pp. 95–100.
Schwarz, J. (1978) *Voluntary Controls: exercises for creative meditation and for activating the potential of the chakras*. New York: E.P. Dutton.
Schwarz, J. (1980) *Human Energy Systems*. Hillsdale New Jersey: Erlbaum.
Seavey, C.A., Katz, P.A. & Zalk, S.R. (1975) 'Baby X: the effect of gender labels on adult responses to infants'. *Sex Roles*, 1, pp. 103–9.
Shah, I. (1969) *The Book of the Book*. London: The Octagon Press.
Shaw, J. (1982) 'Psychological androgyny and stressful life events'. *Journal of Personality and Social Psychology*, 4, 43, pp. 145–53.
Shealy, C.N & Myss, C.M. (1988) *The Creation of Health: merging traditional medicine with intuitive diagnosis*. USA: Still Point.
Shrauger, J.S. (1972) 'Self-esteem and reactions to being observed by others'. *Journal of Personality and Social Psychology*, 23, pp. 192–200.
Shotter, J. (1975) *Images of Man in Psychological Research*. London: Methuen.
Shuvall, J.T., Antonovsky, A. & Davies, A.M. (1973) 'Illness: a mechanism for coping with failure'. *Social Science and Medicine*, 7, pp. 259–65.
Siegel, B.S. (1988) Foreword to C.N. Shealy and C.M. Myss, *The Creation of Health: merging traditional medicine with intuitive diagnosis*, p. xvii. USA: Still Point.
Siegel, B.S. (1990) *Peace, Love and Healing: Bodymind communication and the path to self-healing*. London: Rider.

Sigall, H. & Gould, R. (1977) 'The effects of self-esteem and evaluation demandingness on effort expenditure'. *Journal of Personality and Social Psychology*, 35, pp. 12–20.

Simonton, O.C. & Simonton, S.S. (1975) 'Belief systems and the management of the emotional aspects of malignancy'. *Journal of Transpersonal Psychology*, Vol. 8, pp. 29–47.

Simonton, O.C., Matthews-Simonton, S. & Creighton, J. (1978) *Getting Well Again*. New York: Bantam.

Simonton, O.C. (1983) 'On the suffering of patients, families and care givers'. Presentation at *Meet The Pioneers: Understanding, preventing and controlling the effects of cancer*, Conference of the Association for New Approaches to Cancer. London 14 June.

Simonton, O.C. (1988) in conversation with F. Capra, as reported in Capra, F., *Uncommon Wisdom: conversations with remarkable people*. London: Rider.

Sluckin, W., Herbert, M & Sluckin, A. (1983) *Maternal Bonding*. Oxford: Blackwell.

Snyder, C.R. & Smith, T.W. (1982) Symptoms of self-handicapping strategies (unpublished manuscript), cited S. Duck *Human Relationships*, 2nd edn. London and New York: Sage.

Solomon, G.F. (1969) 'Emotions, stress, the CNS and immunity'. Second Conference on psychophysiological aspects of cancer, *Annals of the New York Academy of Science*, pp. 335–42.

Solomon, G. & Temoshok, L. (1987) 'An intensive psychoimmunologic study of long surviving persons with AIDS'. *Annals of The New York Academy of Sciences*, Vol. 498, pp. 647–55.

Spiritual Care Work Group of the International Work Group on Death, Dying and Bereavement (1990) 'Assumptions and principles of spiritual care'. *Death Studies*, 14, pp. 75–81. Hemisphere Publishing Co.

Stussy, S. (1992) *The Look*, BBC2, 11 October.

Szasz, T.S. (1979) *The Myth of Psychotherapy: mental healing as religion, rhetoric and repression*. Oxford: Oxford University Press.

Temoshok, L. (1985) 'Biopsychosocial studies on cutaneous malignant melanoma: psychosocial factors associated with prognostic indicators, progression, psychophysiology and tumor-host response'. *Social Science Medicine*, Vol. 20, pp. 833–40.

Temoshok, L. & Heller, B.W. (1985) 'Stress and Type C versus epidemiological risk factors in melanoma', reported in the above.

Tillich, P. (1952) *The Courage To Be*. London: Fontana.

Toffler, A. (1984) 'Science and change', Foreword to Prigogine, I. and Stengers, I. *Order Out Of Chaos: man's new dialogue with Nature*. Britain: Fontana.

Tuormaa, T.E. (1992) 'Psycho-Neuro-Immunology: A review'. *Holistic Health Research Network Newsletter*, 7 Feb., pp. 8–9.

Vaux, K. (1976) 'Religion and health', *Preventitive Medicine*, 5, pp. 522–36.

Vaux, K. (1984) *Health and Medicine in the Reformed Tradition*. New York: Crossroad.

Wallston, K.A. & Wallston, B.S. (1982) 'Who is responsible for your health?: the construct of health locus of control'. In G. Sanders & J. Suls (eds) *Social Psychology of Health and Illness*. Hillsdale, New Jersey: Erlbaum, pp. 160–70.

Watson, M., Greer, S., Pruyn, J. & Van den Borne, B. (1990) 'Locus of control and adjustment to cancer'. *Psychological Reports*, 66, pp. 39–48.

Watson, M. (1988) 'Vital force and electricity'. *Caduceus*, Autumn, pp. 24–6.

Weinstock, C. (1984) 'Psychophysiological aspects of cancer'. *Medical Hypotheses*, 15, pp. 369–83.

White, R. (1989) 'Rainbows of health'. *Caduceus*, Spring, p. 14.

Whyte, A.M., (1987) 'Pets in prisons'. *Pedigree Digest*, Vol. 13, No. 4, pp. 10–11.

Will, J.A., Self, P.A. & Datan, N. (1976) 'Maternal behaviour and perceived sex of infant'. *American Journal of Orthopsychiatry*, 49, pp. 135–9.

Wilson, A. & Bek, L. (1981) *What Colour Are You? The way to health through colour*. Wellingborough, Northants: Aquarian Press.

Wilson-Ross, N. (1973) *Hinduism, Buddhism, Zen*. London: Faber & Faber.

Yalom, I.D. (1980) *Existential Psychotherapy*. New York: Basic Books.

Young, J. (1990) 'Meridians, chakras and psychic abilities: The work of Dr. Hiroshi Motoyama'. *Caduceus*, 10, pp. 9–13.

Zajonc, R.B. (1968) 'Attitudinal effects of mere exposure'. *Journal of Personality and Social Psychology* (Monograph Supplements 1–29).

Index

acting 6, 34–65
AIDS 47, 80, 214
alienation 40, 58, 111, 160, 172
alter-ego 84–91, 198
attitude(s) 4, 46, 80, 83, 93, 103, 114,
    149, 150, 164, 187, 192, 224, 233
anger 47, 51, 109, 110, 129, 224
anxiety 5, 19, 29, 31, 46, 50, 68, 70,
    83, 103, 112, 124, 130, 136, 205
Asistent, Niro 214, 215, 221, 237
Assagioli, Roberto 281–3
audience effects 67–74, 198–9
aura, the 239–245, 265

Bach, Edward, Dr 117, 190, 243–4
belief(s) 46, 47, 48, 80, 89, 98, 136,
    155, 163, 169, 221
Berne, Eric 100, 117–8, 192
Bowlby, John 120–25
Brennan, Barbara 98, 244, 253, 266

cancer(s) 2, 4, 14, 46, 70, 74, 200, 213,
    216
  cells 74
  mortality 163
  patients 100, 215
  regression 187
chakras 238–248, 268, 270
character 41–3, 64, 79, 127, 145
  analysis 258–9
  structure 259
childhood 28, 31, 42, 54, 83, 110, 269
children 25, 34–9, 42, 55, 121, 122, 129
colour(s) 9, 31, 33, 35, 55, 188, 193,
    202, 204, 238–48, 252–6, 261–4,
    272–4
  consciousness 265–6
  therapy 264–5

communication 8, 9, 25, 69, 91, 123,
    125
control(s) 45, 68, 70, 78, 80–81, 99,
    100, 105, 107, 183
Coopersmith, S. 69, 70, 128, 129, 130

death 13, 89, 149, 166, 187, 213, 219,
    223
depression 2, 14, 68, 70, 92, 101, 124,
    129, 130, 169, 173, 184, 187, 193
dis-ease 93–151, 120, 153, 155, 214,
    258
divorce 2, 13, 109, 110, 215
dream(s) 6, 8, 9, 89, 90, 108
dress 26, 27, 39–40, 48, 199–200

emotion(s) 46, 50, 110, 149, 187, 202
energy 41, 78, 85, 90, 101, 118, 188,
    189, 190, 235–48

fantasy 6, 8, 9, 47, 82, 225
fatigue 45, 98, 236
Freud, Sigmund 6, 44, 45, 126, 127,
    154, 162, 187, 256, 283
friends 92–4

gender 35–40, 43, 44, 79, 165
gestalt 20, 66, 72
  gestalten 18, 154
  psychologists 154
  studies 154
  therapy 17–19, 230, 284

healing 5, 22, 158, 174, 187, 189, 214,
    219, 226
health 4, 11, 20, 47, 119, 131, 132,
    159–62, 163

hypnosis 80–81, 82, 187, 289

identity 13, 23, 38, 40, 72, 96, 97, 127,
    135, 158, 162, 181, 219
illness 4, 10, 13, 19, 29, 45, 46, 68, 71,
    78, 100, 118, 121, 181
imagination 3, 5, 10, 23, 47, 89, 103
intuition(s) 47, 100, 117, 189, 191, 193,
    214
intuitive diagnosis 190–91
    medicine 190–93

Jourard, Sidney 94, 98, 99, 152, 181–7,
    189, 193, 216
juggling 193–7
Jung, Carl Gustav 21, 43, 47, 94, 153,
    154, 157, 158, 160, 166, 188, 192,
    213, 214
Jungian psychotherapy 95

Laing, R.D. 22, 73, 95, 96–9, 154,
    280, 281, 288
listening 97, 100, 117, 131, 189, 214
loss 2, 13, 14, 70, 89, 90, 110, 111, 219

marriage 42, 45, 94, 189, 217
Maslow, Abraham 71, 72, 78, 119, 121,
    122, 125, 152, 159–60, 161, 162,
    165, 188
meaning 155–6, 166, 173, 181
Maddi, Salvador 169, 170, 171, 178
medicine 153, 157, 182, 184, 187, 188,
    189, 190
meditation 48, 197, 223, 289
mother(s) 120–25
Myss, Caroline 100–101, 189, 190, 192,
    193, 216, 217, 220, 235, 246, 247,
    268, 279

needs 5, 19, 71, 73, 89, 117, 119–32,
    157, 194, 222
    emergent 142–7, 154, 162

pain(s) 3, 10, 11, 23, 30, 43, 193
parents 36, 118, 129–30
Perls, Frederick (Fritz) 17, 18, 19, 20,
    40, 42, 43, 47, 66–7, 71–8, 174,
    212, 217, 230, 277–86
personality 41, 46, 76, 77, 89, 94, 127,
    222, 277
psychopathology 122, 152, 157, 166, 214

psychotherapy 2, 4, 71, 153, 157, 158,
    187, 245, 279

Reich, Wilhelm 187, 257–60
relaxation 11, 30, 48, 81, 289, 297,
    320–8
religion(s) 152, 154, 156, 158, 160, 163,
    164
resentment(s) 51, 101, 114, 118, 138,
    148, 219, 220, 235
Rogers, Carl 19, 20, 51, 131, 161, 188,
    301
sadness 32, 47, 89, 90, 91, 111, 130, 224
script(s) 36–8, 40, 79, 82, 101, 110,
    192, 193
    indicators 117, 118
security 41, 55, 110, 112, 125, 129,
    138, 141, 185, 219
self 24, 25, 28, 43, 47, 48, 73, 75, 80,
    96, 100, 126, 131, 152, 219
self-actualisation 20, 43, 81, 119, 131,
    156, 159, 161, 162
self-actualisation 20, 43, 81, 119, 131,
    156, 159, 161, 162
self-alienation 46, 77, 96
self-awareness 4, 10, 31, 106, 199, 219
self-concept 3, 20, 34, 35, 46, 67, 80,
    83, 286
self-control 83, 92, 99–101, 120, 281
self-denial 5, 18, 46, 71
self-esteem 3, 57, 60, 67, 68, 69, 70, 71,
    73, 80, 94, 100, 103, 106, 107, 191
self-identity 34, 127, 199, 280
self-healing 132, 279–89
self-image 43, 51, 60, 63, 107
self-transcendence 156, 162, 165
Siegel, Bernie 13, 47, 125, 187, 189,
    214, 223
Simonton, Carl 43, 100, 111, 187, 200,
    213, 214, 215
    Stephanie 187
soul(s) 94, 153, 157–9, 239
spirit 152–97
spirituality 161–5
suicide 68, 89, 181, 182

tension(s) 11, 30, 48, 126, 205, 236
theatre 35, 41, 42, 153
therapist(s) 45, 131, 161

values 153, 159, 161, 163, 166